中国商务文化读本　BUSINESS CULTURE IN CHINA

Insights into Finance in China

透视中国金融

蒋先玲　编

中国出版集团
中译出版社

图书在版编目(CIP)数据

透视中国金融：汉英对照/蒋先玲编．—北京：中译出版社，2019.7
（中国商务文化读本）
ISBN 978-7-5001-5995-7

Ⅰ.①透… Ⅱ.①蒋… Ⅲ.①金融体系－研究－中国－汉、英 Ⅳ.①F832.1

中国版本图书馆CIP数据核字（2019）第129241号

出版发行／中译出版社
地　　址／北京市西城区车公庄大街甲4号物华大厦6层
电　　话／(010) 68359827，68359376（发行部）；53601537（编辑部）
邮　　编／100044
传　　真／(010) 68357870
电子邮箱／book@ctph.com.cn
网　　址／http://www.ctph.com.cn

出 版 人／张高里
总 策 划／贾兵伟
出版统筹／胡晓凯
责任编辑／范祥镇　王馨敏
封面设计／潘　峰

排　　版／北京竹页文化传媒有限公司
印　　刷／北京玺诚印务有限公司
经　　销／新华书店

规　　格／787毫米×1092毫米　1/16
印　　张／17.25
字　　数／280千字
版　　次／2019年7月第一版
印　　次／2019年7月第一次

ISBN 978-7-5001-5995-7　　定价：58.00元

版权所有　侵权必究
中译出版社

序

  金融业是指经营金融商品的特殊行业，它包括银行业、非银行金融机构及金融市场。银行是以吸收存款作为主要资金来源，以发放贷款为主要资金运用的信用机构，银行的基本职能是充当信用中介，进行信用创造和调节经济。因此，商业银行和中央银行是真正的银行。非银行金融机构主要包括保险公司、信托公司、证券公司、期货公司等。

  新中国银行业体系始于1948年中国人民银行的建立，当时的中国人民银行接管并改造了新中国成立前遗留下的不同性质的金融机构，全国所有的信贷业务与储蓄业务集中于中国人民银行。这期间一直到1979年，中国人民银行是我国唯一的银行，既作为管理机构，也是具体经营银行业务的经济实体。1979年至1994年，是中国银行业发展的第二个阶段。中国农业银行、中国工商银行、中国人民建设银行（现为中国建设银行）、中国银行分别作为专业银行经营具体银行业务，中国人民银行开始专门行使中央银行的职能。同时，一大批综合性商业银行亦开始出现，如交通银行、招商银行、深圳发展银行等。1994年之后，中国开始剥离上述四家专业银行的政策性业务，并在2004年完成股份制改革，成功上市。到2015年，中国的银行业在完成一系列改革之后，保持了较强的盈利能力和发展速度，目前依然在中国金融体系中起到了中流砥柱的作用。

  除此之外，中国银行业也对外放开，存在大量的外资银行。外资银行是指在本国境内由外国独资创办的银行。2007年中国银监会发布《中国银行业对外开放报告》，明确表示促进外资银行全面发展，鼓励外国银行设立或者将现有分行转制为中国注册的法人银行。众多外资银行来华设立法人银行，或通过持股中资银行参与中国银行业的发展。

为了及时防范和化解金融风险，维护金融稳定。中国于2015年1月正式实施存款保险制度，目前单个账户最高赔付限额为50万元人民币。从数量上来看，99.7%的存款人可以享受存款保险基金管理机构的"全额赔付"，绝大部分存款人的资金安全可直接通过存款保险得到全额保障。

金融市场是市场经济国家的一个非常重要的子市场，也是一国金融体系的重要组成部分。随着社会主义市场经济的发展和金融改革的不断深入，中国的金融市场有了长足的发展，逐渐形成了由货币市场、资本市场、外汇市场、黄金市场和期货市场等构成的，具有交易场所多层次、交易品种多样化和交易机制多元化等特征的金融市场体系，为推动国民经济发展、支持国家宏观调控实施、推进国有企业和金融改革、稳步推进利率市场化和完善人民币汇率形成机制、防范系统性金融风险和维护金融稳定发挥了重要作用。

蒋先玲

2015年于中国北京

PREFACE

The financial sector is a special industry that deals with financial products, including banking, non-bank financial institutions, and financial markets. By absorbing money deposits, banks serve as the principal source of capital, and loans are the primary mechanism of credit that puts capital to use. The fundamental function of a bank is to serve as an intermediary for providing credit, producing credit, and regulating the economy. As a result, commercial and central banks are true banks while non-bank financial institutions include insurance, bonds, securities, and futures.

The new Chinese banking system began in 1948 when the People's Bank of China (PBC) was established. At that time, the People's Bank of China took control over and reformed the various forms of financial institutions left over from before new China had been established. All of the credit services and savings services were centralized into the People's Bank of China, and the period when this bank was the only bank in China lasted up to 1979. During that time, China's sole bank was a management structure and also acted as an entity that ran the specifics of the banking industry.

The period from 1979 to 1994 is the second phase in the development of China's banking industry. The Agricultural Bank of China, Industrial and Commercial Bank of China, China Construction Bank, and Bank of China became specialized banks that provided banking for specific industries while the People's Bank of China began providing to function exclusively as a central bank. At the same time, a large number of integrated commercial banks began to appear, such as the Bank of Communications, China Merchants Bank, and Shenzhen Development Bank. After 1994, China began to divest from policy driven operations managed by the four specialized banks, and after they were reformed into a joint-stock structures, the banks were successfully listed in 2004. By 2015, after the Chinese banking industry had completed a series of reforms, they were able to maintain a relatively strong degree of profit and speed of development that has to this day played a cornerstone role in maintaining the Chinese financial system.

In addition to this, the Chinese banking industry has also opened itself up to foreign markets, and a large number of foreign investment banks exist. Foreign investment banks are banks that exist within the nation's border but are wholly owned by foreign banks. In 2007, the China Banking Regulatory Commission issued the "Chinese Banking Industry Opening up Report" which clearly promoted the comprehensive development of foreign investment banks. It also encouraged foreign banks to set up as, or restructure their subsidiary banks already in China, corporate banks. Numerous foreign investment banks have come into China as corporate bank or began holding shares in Chinese banks into to join in the development of the Chinese banking industry.

In order to stay on guard and defuse financial risks that could threatened the stability of the sector, China formally implemented the bank deposit insurance system in January of 2015. Currently, the largest payment that an individual account can make is 500,000 RMB. Looking at this in terms of quantity, currently 99.7% of depositor can enjoy the "full deposit reimbursement" debiting insurance fund management system, and the vast majority of depositor funds can securely and directly use deposit insurance to guarantee the entirety of their account.

The financial market of a market economy country is an extremely important sub-market and an important component of a nation's economic system. As the socialist market economy developed and financial reform has constantly penetrated deeper into the country, Chinese financial markets have undergone remarkable development. They have gradually developed into a financial market structure composed of a money market, capital market, foreign exchange market, gold market, and futures market that possess a multi-level marketplace, diversified market varieties, and a variety of transaction mechanisms. Such a system plays an important role in propelling forward the development of the people's market, supports the implementation of national macro-control, advances state owned enterprises and financial reform, steadily drives forward market-based reform of interest rates, refines the mechanisms for RMB exchange rates, and provides a system for preventing financial risks and safeguards financial stability.

Jiang Xianling
Beijing, China PRC
2015

目录

第一章　中国银行业概览　/ 001
　　一、中国银行业的历史沿革　/ 001
　　二、中国银行业的地位与发展水平　/ 003
　　三、中国境内银行的主要类型　/ 005
　　四、中国银行业发展趋势及展望　/ 011
　　五、Q&A　/ 013

第二章　中国非银行金融业概览　/ 015
　　一、证券业　/ 016
　　二、期货业　/ 017
　　三、基金业　/ 022
　　四、保险业　/ 026
　　五、信托业　/ 026
　　六、Q&A　/ 028

第三章　中国货币市场简介　/ 029
　　一、中国货币市场概况　/ 029
　　二、同业拆借市场　/ 030
　　三、债券回购市场　/ 033

四、票据市场 / 035

　　五、货币市场与货币政策传导机制 / 039

　　六、Q&A / 042

第四章　中国资本市场简介 / 043

　　一、股票市场 / 043

　　二、债券市场 / 049

　　三、金融衍生品市场 / 051

　　四、Q&A / 058

第五章　中国金融调控和金融监管体系 / 059

　　一、中国金融监管历史 / 059

　　二、中国金融监管现状 / 060

　　三、Q&A / 075

第六章　中国外汇管理体制 / 077

　　一、中国外汇管理体制历史沿革 / 077

　　二、中国外汇管理体制发展现状 / 081

　　三、Q&A / 087

第七章　新兴的互联网金融 / 089

　　一、互联网金融——中国金融业的新兴力量 / 089

　　二、互联网金融的主要业态 / 090

　　三、中国代表性的互联网金融机构 / 093

　　四、Q&A / 094

CONTENTS

Chapter 1　Overview of China's Banking Industry　/ 095
1.1　History of China's Banking Industry　/ 095
1.2　Status and Development Level of China's Banking Industry　/ 097
1.3　Major Types of Banks in Chinese Mainland　/ 100
1.4　Development Trend and Prospect of China's Banking Industry　/ 109
1.5　Q&A　/ 113

Chapter 2　Overview of China's Non-bank Financial Industry　/ 115
2.1　Securities Industry　/ 116
2.2　Bulk Trading System　/ 121
2.3　Futures Industry　/ 126
2.4　Fund Industry　/ 136
2.5　Insurance　/ 142
2.6　Trust Industry　/ 143
2.7　Q&A　/ 145

Chapter 3　Money Market in China　/ 147
3.1　An Overview of Money Market in China　/ 147
3.2　Inter-Bank Borrowing Market　/ 148
3.3　Bond Repo Market　/ 156
3.4　Paper Market　/ 161
3.5　Treasury Bond Market　/ 167
3.6　Central Bank's Innovative Financial Instrument　/ 168
3.7　Q&A　/ 170

Chapter 4　An Introduction to Capital Market in China　/ 172

4.1　Stock Market　/ 172

4.2　Bond Market　/ 182

4.3　Financial Derivatives Market　/ 186

4.4　Q&A　/ 194

Chapter 5　China's Financial Regulation and Financial Supervision System　/ 196

5.1　Overview of China's Financial Supervision　/ 196

5.2　The People's Bank of China　/ 204

5.3　China Banking Regulatory Commission　/ 206

5.4　China Securities Regulatory Commission　/ 215

5.5　The China Insurance Regulatory Commission　/ 222

5.6　Q&A　/ 228

Chapter 6　China's Foreign Exchange Administration System　/ 231

6.1　The Historical Development of China's Foreign Exchange Administration System　/ 231

6.2　The Development Status of China's Foreign Exchange Administration System　/ 239

6.3　Q&A　/ 252

Chapter 7　Emerging Internet Finance　/ 256

7.1　Internet Finance: An Emerging Power of China's Financial Industry　/ 256

7.2　The Main Types of Internet Finance　/ 257

7.3　China's Representative Internet Financial Institutions　/ 261

7.4　Q&A　/ 263

第一章
中国银行业概览

一、中国银行业的历史沿革

作为本书的开篇第一章,本章用整整一章的篇幅,来介绍中国的银行业,这是因为,就当前中国的金融体系而言,银行业不论从资产规模、从业人数还是在金融系统中的地位来看,都处于中国金融体系的核心地位。值得一提的是,本章所提到的银行业,是指中国人民银行[1]所颁布的《金融机构编码规范》所称的银行业存款类金融机构,该规范对"银行"的定义是:依法设立的吸收存款,发放贷款,办理结算等业务的企业法人,事实上,众多的教科书已经对银行这一特殊企业的业务范围有了诸多介绍,这里便不再赘述。

新中国银行业体系始于1948年中国人民银行的建立,当时的中国人民银行接管并改造了新中国成立前遗留下的不同性质的金融机构,全国所有的信贷业务与储蓄业务集中于中国人民银行。一直到1979年,中国人民银行是我国唯一的银行,既作为管理机构,也是具体经营银行业务的经济实体。

1979年至1994年,是中国银行业发展的第二个阶段。中国农业银行、中国工商银行、中国人民建设银行(现为中国建设银行)、中国银行分别作为专业银行经营具体银行业务,中国人民银行则专门行使中央银行的职能。同时,一大批综合性商业银行亦开始出现,如交通银行、招商银行、深圳发展银行等。

1994年之后,我国开始剥离前文提到的四家专业银行的政策性业务,并在2004年完成股份制改革,成功上市。到2015年,中国的银行业在完成一系列

---

[1] 中国人民银行(The People's Bank of China)是中国的中央银行,《金融机构编码规范》由中国人民银行调查统计司于2010年5月25日颁布。

改革之后，保持了较强的盈利能力和发展速度，目前依然在中国金融体系中起到中流砥柱的作用。

【案例】中国银行业发展缩影——中国银行的百年浮沉[1]

1912年2月，中国银行正式成立。从1912年至1949年，中国银行先后行使中央银行、国际汇兑银行和国际贸易专业银行职能，在民族金融业中长期处于领先地位，并在国际金融界占有一席之地。1949年以后，中国银行长期作为新中国的外汇外贸专业银行，统一经营管理国家外汇，开展国际贸易结算、侨汇和其他非贸易外汇业务。1994年，中国银行改为国有独资商业银行。2004年8月，中国银行股份有限公司挂牌成立。2006年6月、7月，中国银行先后在香港联交所和上海证券交易所成功挂牌上市，成为国内首家"A+H"发行上市的中国商业银行。2013年，中国银行再次入选全球系统重要性银行，成为新兴市场经济体中唯一连续3年入选的金融机构。

中国银行是中国国际化和多元化程度最高的银行，在中国内地、香港、澳门、台湾及37个国家为客户提供全面的金融服务。主要经营商业银行业务，包括公司金融业务、个人金融业务和金融市场业务，并通过全资子公司中银国际控股有限公司开展投资银行业务，通过全资子公司中银集团保险有限公司及中银保险有限公司经营保险业务，通过全资子公司中银集团投资有限公司经营直接投资和投资管理业务，通过控股中银基金管理有限公司经营基金管理业务，通过全资子公司中银航空租赁私人有限公司经营飞机租赁业务。事实上，中国银行已经初步实现了混业经营。

中国银行的发展历程，基本浓缩了新中国银行业的发展历史。从1949年之后，它的角色从专业银行发展为国有独资商业银行，再通过引进战略投资者并上市公开募资称为股份制商业银行，并在发展的过程中通过全资子公司控股的模式发展投资银行、保险、基金管理、金融租赁等业务，它的发展史在中国银行业极具代表性。

---

[1] 整理自中国银行官方网站.

二、中国银行业的地位与发展水平

正如前文所述，银行业居于中国金融体系的核心地位。如图 1-1 所示，我们发现，人民币贷款始终是中国最为主流的融资方式，虽然它的占比，从 2003 年的 80% 下降到 2014 年的 60%，但是依然处于一个绝对领先的地位。同时，委托贷款的占比亦不断扩大，委托贷款指的是由委托人提供合法来源的资金，委托业务银行根据委托人确定的贷款对象、用途、金额、期限、利率等代为发放、监督、使用并协助收回的贷款业务。这里所指的委托人包括政府部门、企事业单位及个人等。这一业务实质上借道了银行的信贷渠道，亦属于由银行参与的融资方式之一。

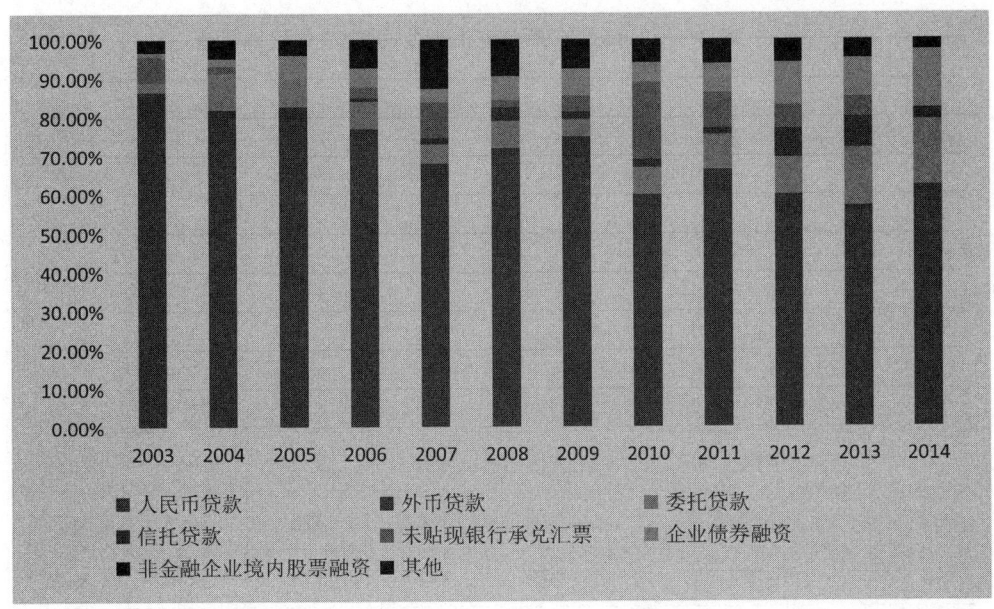

资料来源：中国人民银行、发展改革委、证监会、保监会、中央国债登记结算有限责任公司、中国银行间市场交易商协会

图 1-1 不同融资方式在中国社会融资规模中占比的变化趋势（2003-2014）

当然，从 2003 年到 2014 年，企业债券融资规模和股票融资规模的占比也在稳步提升之中，其中，企业债券融资规模从 2003 年的占比不到 2% 到 2014 年的占比接近 15%，增长幅度巨大。而股票融资的占比则在这 12 年间有增有减，这很大程度是由于中国的证券发行监管机构不时实行的暂停 IPO 政策。

总的来说，银行业所代表的间接融资规模从 2003 年的占比接近 90% 下降到 2014 年的占比 80% 左右，虽然略有下降，但依然占据了中国社会融资的绝对主导地位。

那么，在国内占据重要地位的中国银行业在世界范围内水平如何呢？

表 1-1 是 2015《福布斯》"全球上市公司 2000 强"榜单的节选，可以看到，中国的四家银行分别位列前四名，著名投资家巴菲特的伯克希尔哈撒韦公司紧随其后，位列第 5。不论是从销售额、利润、资产还是市值上来看，中国的银行都已经达到了比较高的水平。

表 1-1　2015 福布斯全球上市公司 2000 强榜单节选

排名	公司	国家	销售额	利润	资产	市值
1	中国工商银行	中国	1668	448	33220	2783
2	中国建设银行	中国	1305	370	26989	2129
3	中国农业银行	中国	1292	291	25748	1899
4	中国银行	中国	1203	275	24583	1991
5	伯克希尔哈撒韦	美国	1947	199	5346	3548
6	摩根大通	美国	978	212	25936	2255
7	埃克森美孚	美国	3762	325	3495	3571
8	中国石油	中国	3334	174	3877	3346
9	通用电气	美国	1485	152	6483	2535
10	富国银行	美国	904	231	17014	2783

资料来源：福布斯官网　　单位：亿美元

我们知道，对于银行业来说，不光是盈利能力和资产规模，不良贷款率、拨备覆盖率、资产充足率等反映银行抗风险能力的指标也十分重要，为了更为全面地对比中国主流银行与国际知名银行的各项指标，在这里我们列出了中国的大型商业银行之一——中国银行与美国著名商业银行——花旗银行的风险指标对比，之所以做这个选择，是考虑到中国银行作为中国最为国际化的银行，连续两次入选世界系统性重要银行，在中国的大型银行中，其业务结构和资产状况也较具代表性，具体如表1–2。

表1–2 中国银行与花旗银行主要风险指标对比

	中国银行	花旗银行
总资产（亿美元）	24583	18830
不良贷款率（%）	1.18	1.5
不良贷款拨备率（%）	187.6	168
一级资本充足率（%）	11.35	13

数据来源：中国银行、花旗集团年报，经作者整理计算

从表1–2可以看出，中国银行在资产规模上领先于花旗银行，此外，在不良贷款率和拨备覆盖率上也较花旗银行状况更好一些，但一级资本充足率落后于花旗银行。总的来看，中国银行与花旗银行在各项风险指标上水平相差不大，这表明，中国的银行业不仅盈利能力与资产总额冠绝全球，在风险控制上亦达到了合意的水平。

三、中国境内银行的主要类型

按照中国银行业监管当局的分类，中国境内经营的银行（银行业存款类金融机构）可分为以下9类，如表1–3：

表 1-3 中国境内银行业机构分类

类别	性质	数量	代表性机构
政策性银行	由政府发起、出资成立，为贯彻和配合政府特定经济政策和意图而进行融资和信用活动的机构。	3	国家开发银行／中国进出口银行／中国农业发展银行
国有商业银行	历史上是国有独资的商业银行，目前经过股份制改造引进了多元化的股东，控股股东是中国财政部所属的中央汇金投资有限责任公司。	5	中国工商银行／中国银行／中国建设银行／中国农业银行／交通银行
全国性股份制商业银行	股东背景更为多元化，由中国地方政府、大型国有企业、私有制企业等构成，分支机构遍布全国。	12	兴业银行／中信银行／华夏银行／招商银行等
城市商业银行	多由中国地方政府控制，经营范围和分支机构局限在银行所在地的小范围行政区域内，主要分布在市区。	140左右	日照银行／九江银行／宁波银行等
农村商业银行、农村信用合作（联）社、农村资金互助社	主要分布在中国的县域及农村地区，是中国县域地区的主流金融机构。	农村商业银行300家左右，尚未改制的农村信用合作社1400家左右	厦门农村商业银行／北京农村商业银行等
村镇银行	中国的新型农村金融机构，由较大型的商业银行作为发起机构设立的独立法人商业银行，区别于农村商业银行的是，决策链条更短，机构规模更小，直接面向农民。	1500家左右	宁夏中宁青银村镇银行／澳洲联邦银行（兰考）村镇银行等
外资银行	外国银行在华分支或子公司。	46	汇丰中国／渣打中国等

（续表）

邮政储蓄银行	由中国邮政公司分出部分业务形成，其特殊性在于之前作为国家行政机构经营汇款业务，是中国分支机构数量最大的银行，分支遍布中国几乎所有城市与乡村。	1	中国邮政储蓄银行
财务公司[1]	按照中国人民银行分类属于存款类银行业金融机构，大部分隶属于大型企业集团，以加强企业集团资金集中管理和提高企业集团资金使用效率为目的，为企业集团成员单位提供财务管理服务的金融机构。	186	五粮液财务/中海油财务等

资料来源：作者整理

下面，本书将一一介绍中国境内的9类金融机构。

（一）政策性银行

中国的政策性银行不以营利为目的，专门为贯彻、配合政府社会经济政策或意图，在特定的业务领域内，直接或间接地从事政策性融资活动，充当政府发展经济、促进社会进步、进行宏观经济管理的工具。

1994年，我国设立了国家开发银行、中国进出口银行、中国农业发展银行三大政策性银行，均直属国务院领导，三家银行各有分工。

中国进出口银行主要职责是为扩大我国机电产品、成套设备和高新技术产品进出口，推动有比较优势的企业开展对外承包工程和境外投资，促进对外关系发展和国际经贸合作，提供金融服务。2010年至2014年，进出口银行累计发放贷款3.2万亿元，支持了1.46万亿美元的产品进出口。

中国农业发展银行主要职责是以国家信用为基础，筹集资金，承担国家规定的农业政策性金融业务，代理财政支农资金的拨付，为农业和农村经济发展服务。2004年至2014年末，农发行累计发放粮棉油收储贷款4.78万亿元，每年支持粮食收购占当年商品粮总量的60%左右。

国家开发银行主要通过开展中长期信贷与投资等金融业务，为国民经济重大中长期发展战略服务，向我国基础设施建设、棚户区改造、新型城镇化建设、支持企业走出去等经济建设重点领域和薄弱环节提供了大量资金支持。截至去年年底，国开行累计发放铁路、公路、电力贷款超过5.2万亿元，支持铁路、公路里程分别占全国总里程的60%和30%，累计发放城镇化贷款超过8万亿元。

政策性银行在发展的过程中，许多原有的政策性业务逐步演化为商业竞争，政策性银行也因为商业性业务和政策性业务边界不清而受到了一些争议。2015年，中国政府在政策层面和功能层面上对政策性银行进行了重新定位，重新强调政策性职能定位，让政策性银行回归本职，并在酝酿政策性银行法的制定。

（二）国有商业银行

国有商业银行也称国有控股大型商业银行，是指由国家（财政部、中央汇金公司）直接控股的商业银行，现在有：中国工商银行、中国农业银行、中国银行、中国建设银行、交通银行共5家。

中国工商银行成立于1984年。作为中国资产规模最大的商业银行之一，数年来一直位列世界五百强企业。2010年英国《银行家》杂志按一级资本排序，中国工商银行名列"全球银行1000强"第16位，数年来一直入围美国《财富》全球500强，并被美国《远东经济评论》评为中国高质量产品（服务）十强。2013年4月18日《福布斯》2013"全球上市公司2000强"榜单出炉，中国工商银行超越埃克森美孚，成为全球最大企业。

中国农业银行是中国金融资本最雄厚的商业银行之一，最初成立于1951年，是新中国成立的第一家国有商业银行，也是中国金融体系的重要组成部分，总行设在北京，"全球银行1000强"第8位，穆迪信用评级为A1。

中国银行为中国历史最悠久的商业银行之一，中国银行全称中国银行股份有限公司，是中国大陆地区（不包括香港、澳门、台湾）四大国有商业银行之一，规模排列位列第三。中国银行于 1912 年 1 月 24 日由孙中山总统下令批准成立。1912 年 2 月 5 日正式开业，由 1905 年清政府成立的户部银行［1908 年起改称大清银行（Ta Ching Government Bank），负责整顿币制、发行货币、整理国库，行使中央银行权利］改组而来。中国银行先后是当时的国家中央银行、国际汇兑银行和外贸专业银行。其业务范围涵盖商业银行、投资银行和保险领域，旗下有中银香港、中银国际、中银保险等控股金融机构，在全球范围内为个人和公司客户提供全面和优质的金融服务。按核心资本计算，2008 年中国银行在英国《银行家》杂志"全球 1000 家大银行"排名中列第 10 位，位列世界 500 强企业。

中国建设银行是一家以中长期信贷业务为特色的国有商业银行，总部设在北京，在中国境内及各主要国际金融中心开展业务。建设银行在《银行家》杂志"全球 1000 家大银行"排名中位居第 29 位（按一级资本排名）。

交通银行始建于 1908 年，是中国近代以来历史最悠久的银行，也是近代中国的发钞行之一。现为中国五大国有银行之一。交通银行是中国境内主要综合金融服务提供商之一，并正在成为一家以商业银行为主体，跨市场、国际化的大型银行集团，业务范围涵盖商业银行、投资银行、证券、信托、金融租赁、基金管理、保险、离岸金融服务等诸多领域。

（三）全国性股份制商业银行

目前中国共有代表性的全国股份制商业银行 12 家，与国有商业银行相比，股份制商业银行有着更强的制度竞争力，更完备的员工激励机制，以及更高的公司治理水平。

具体来说，有着如下几个差异。

组织架构上，国有商业银行由于历史较长，员工众多，分支机构设立层次多，一般包括总行——一级分行——二级分行——支行——二级支行这样五个层次，而股份制商业银行设立之初即着眼于效率的提升，往往在总行下直接设置地市级别的分行，直接管理某个大区域的业务，在组织架构上比国有商业银行更为直接有效。

市场反应机制上，国有商业银行脱胎于专业银行，行长往往还兼备行政级别，因此在决策机制上，更类似于行政机构，也有着大机构普遍具有的反应慢、倾向于保守决策的特点。而股份制商业银行则更为市场化，一线的业务人员有着更为灵活的决策权力，同时决策链条也比国有银行短。

薪酬激励体系上，国有商业银行员工的工资较之股份制商业银行，表现出较为平均化的水平，同时，在绝对数上也比股份制商业银行低。

因此，在中国，股份制商业银行和国有银行扮演的角色稍有不同。国有银行体量巨大，信誉卓著，但是也存在着适应市场较慢的问题，股份制商业银行则船小好调头，在市场上有着更强的鲶鱼效应。

（四）城市商业银行

城市商业银行是中国银行业的重要组成和特殊群体，其前身是20世纪80年代设立的城市信用社，当时的业务定位是：为中小企业提供金融支持，为地方经济搭桥铺路。从20世纪80年代初到20世纪90年代，全国各地的城市信用社蓬勃发展。然而，随着中国金融事业的发展，城市信用社在发展过程中逐渐暴露出许多风险管理方面的问题。很多城市信用社也逐步转变为城市商业银行，为地方经济及地方居民提供金融服务。

20世纪90年代中期，中国以城市信用社为基础，组建城市商业银行。城市商业银行是在中国特殊历史条件下形成的，是中央金融主管部门整肃城市信用社、化解地方金融风险的产物。截至2012年5月，全国共有城市商业银行137家，营业网点近万个，遍及全国各省（市、自治区）。截至2004年底，从业人员16.9万，生产总额约14552亿元，占全国银行业金融机构总资产的6.27%，占全国股份制商业银行总资产的27.7%。

经过十几年的发展，城市商业银行已经逐渐发展成熟，尽管其发展程度良莠不齐，但有相当多的城市商业银行已经完成了股份制改革，并通过各种途径逐步消化历史上的不良资产，降低不良贷款率，转变经营模式，在当地占有相当大的市场份额。其中，更是出现了上海银行这样发展迅速，已经跻身于"全球银行500强"行列的优秀银行。城市商业银行，在中国正逐步发展为一个具有相当数量和规模的银行阶层，与五大国有股份制商业银行、邮政储蓄银行和12家股份制商业银行一起，形成中国银行业的多层次格局。

（五）农村商业银行、农村信用合作（联）社、农村资金互助社

农村商业银行是由辖内农民、农村工商户、企业法人和其他经济组织共同入股组成的股份制地方性金融机构。

目前，中国已组建农村商业银行约 303 家、农村合作银行约 210 家，农村银行机构资产总额占全国农村合作金融机构的 41.4%。另外，还有 1424 家农村信用社已经达到或基本达到农村商业银行组建条件。通过改革，农村信用社治理模式已经发生了根本性变化，长期存在的内部人控制问题得到有效解决，机构自身已经形成了深入推进深层次体制机制改革的内生动力。

（六）村镇银行

村镇银行是指经中国银行业监督管理委员会依据有关法律、法规批准，由境内外金融机构、境内非金融机构企业法人、境内自然人出资，在农村地区设立的主要为当地农民、农业和农村经济发展提供金融服务的银行业金融机构。村镇银行不同于银行的分支机构，属一级法人机构。截至 2014 年 12 月，全国共有村镇银行 1547 家。

四、中国银行业发展趋势及展望

随着中国金融业对内对外开放不断深化，中国银行业也在积极地采取应对措施，监管机构层面上，存款保险制度的推出、混业经营的逐步放开，有望进一步提升中国银行业的风险控制水平和竞争力，而作为市场主体，各家商业银行亦在不断探索混业经营的模式，近几年更是出现了中国平安、中国光大集团等横跨银行、保险、证券、信托等多金融业态的金控集团。最新的趋势是，保险公司乃至私募基金、电商企业亦开始寻求进军银行领域，混业经营出现了新的模式，典型的，如控股民生银行、成都农商行的安邦保险，发起设立浙江网商银行的阿里巴巴等。

（一）存款保险制度

存款保险制度是一种金融保障制度，是指由符合条件的各类存款性金融机构集中起来建立一个保险机构，各存款机构作为投保人按一定存款比例向其缴纳保险费，建立存款保险准备金，当成员机构发生经营危机或面临破产倒闭时，存款保险机构向其提供财务救助或直接向存款人支付部分或全部存款，从而保护存款人利益，维护银行信用，稳定金融秩序的一种制度。

中国于2015年1月正式实施存款保险制度，目前单个账户最高赔付限额为50万元人民币。事实上，长期以来，中国一直存在着隐形的存款保险制度，而显性存款保险制度的设立，可以更好地管理公众对自身存款安全的预期，也有利于中国的国有银行与其他银行在更公平的基础上进行竞争。

（二）混业经营趋势

至少到目前为止，中国的金融业监管依然采取分业监管的模式，中国人民银行负责货币政策的制定与实施，银行业监督管理委员会、证券监督管理委员会、保险监督管理委员会则分别负责银行业、证券业和保险业的监管。

不过在业务层面上，中国的金融业事实上正在不断地向混业方向发展，众所周知的美国《金融服务现代化法》通过后，美国金融机构主要以金融控股公司的子公司形式经营银行、证券和保险业务；或者说，金融控股公司模式是美国金融"混业经营"的主要路径。事实上，被1999年《金融服务现代化法》明确废止的只是1933年《银行法》的第20条、32条，即不再禁止商业银行和证券机构以连属关系间接从事对方的业务，但并未废止第16条、21条，也就是说，商业银行和证券机构仍不得直接从事对方的业务。

反观中国，银行业实际上已经通过独资子公司的方式涉足了金融业的其他业务，通过设立基金管理公司、直接从事资产管理或代销各种理财产品，银行深度介入资产管理业务；通过在香港设立类似美国的"第20款公司"的投资银行（如"中银国际"）方式回到内地，间接从事各类投资银行业务。

从金融实践上看，混业经营必将推动监管的混业化，事实上学术界对此也有颇多讨论，但同样有声音认为，中国目前的一行三会监管格局形成了所谓的"监管竞争"模式，在监管实践上有利于形成互相制约的局面，未来如何我们将依然拭目以待。

（三）金控平台的逐步形成

在银行业轰轰烈烈的跑马圈地过程中，中国国内也涌现出一批逐步壮大的金融控股公司，最为著名的有中国平安、中国光大集团以及中信集团，中国的五大国有银行和12家全国性股份制商业银行亦在近几年通过收购券商、信托公司以及自建的方式布局了金融控股公司。同时，安邦保险、九鼎投资等公司也异军突起，在几年间快速发展，称为横跨数种金融业态的公司，形成了事实上的金控平台。甚至，中国著名的电商企业阿里巴巴集团、京东集团，以及腾讯、百度等IT企业，也在不同程度上拥有了银行、基金、保险等子公司。

如阿里巴巴集团，其关联公司蚂蚁金服拥有基金公司天弘基金，拥有在线保险公司众安保险，同时拥有线上银行浙江网商银行，阿里巴巴的金融事业几乎在一夜之间平地起高楼。

竞争的不断加剧，表明中国的银行业已经进入了群雄割据的战国时代。

五、Q&A

（一）在中国，如何寻找银行网点，网点覆盖率如何？

答：中国的大中城市，包括北上广深，以及各省省会，金融机构的分支分布非常密集，国有商业银行和主要的全国性股份制商业银行网点都比较好找，当地的城商行网点亦较多。

中国的普通地市，建议选择国有商业银行办理业务，东部地区的普通地市，股份制银行的网点也基本能够覆盖，但中西部地区的普通地市，网点还是以国有商业银行为主。

中国的县城及乡镇地区，建议选择中国农业银行或中国邮政储蓄银行办理业务，这两家银行的网点基本能够覆盖中国所有县城。此外，当地的农商行亦有覆盖。

（二）在中国，有多少可以刷卡消费的地方，需要携带大量现金吗？

答：在中国的城市，在较大的餐饮、超市等地点，基本都可以实现刷卡消费，小型零售店则建议在消费之前询问店主是否可以刷卡消费。中国的城市地区，自助银行设备也分布较广，但需要注意的是，如果跨行取款，会出现一定费用。

若前往中国的县城乡镇地区，建议携带一定量的现金，一般县城的自助银行设备较少，集中分布在国有银行网点。

（三）中国刷卡消费是否需要密码，支票使用是否普遍？

答：在中国刷卡消费，不论是信用卡还是借记卡，均需要输入密码，现在部分地区可以使用"闪付"付款，这一支付方式不需密码，但这种支付方式普及程度仍很低。中国的消费者基本不使用支票进行消费，支票的开具在中国也较为复杂。

（四）中国的银行服务是否支持英语？

答：中国的银行服务基本不支持英语，大部分沟通使用中文，建议学习该语境下基本的中文单词，如"存钱""取钱""换人民币"等。

第二章
中国非银行金融业概览

截至 2014 年末,中国共有证券公司 121 家,其中上市证券公司 22 家,期货公司 153 家,基金管理公司 95 家。如图 2-1,展示了 2004 年到 2014 年中国证券期货行业经营机构数量的变化情况。

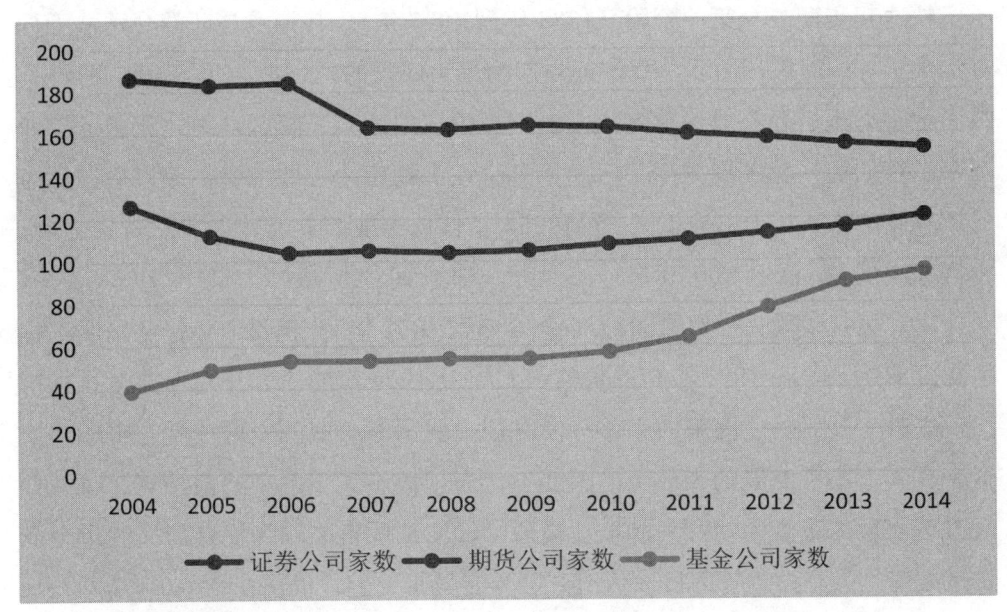

数据来源:中国证监会

图 2-1　2004—2014 年证券期货经营机构数量

从图中可以看出,在过去 11 年间,中国的基金行业发展较为平稳,基金公司的数目稳步上升,期货公司数量略有下降,而证券公司数量则没有太大变化,这主要是由于券商之间的内部整合在不断发生，行业的发展不断催生出抗风险能力更强，资本更多的券商，如2015年申银万国证券和宏源证券的合并，就是一次强强联手。

一、证券业

20世纪80年代，我国在境外设立的商业银行就已经做起了最早的证券业务。而1988年所建立的"深圳经济特区证券公司"，则是我国首家专业的券商。回顾证券业发展的历史，不难发现，归结起来我们可以将国内证券业的发展划分为三个阶段，分别是：起步时期、黄金时期和调整时期。具体而言可以分为如下三个阶段。

快速起步期——第一阶段（1988年到1995年）。其特点是证券公司从无到有实现了零的突破，而后，我国证券市场逐步成长的同时，券商飞速扩张规模，券商数目如雨后春笋般快速增加，资产规模成倍地高速膨胀，由此我国证券业迎来了它的第一轮发展高潮。一大批券商在大规模地进行增资扩股以后，其注册资本几倍甚至几十倍地扩大。到1995年，国内专业的券商就达到了97家之多，总资产规模多达8320000万元。

发展黄金阶段——第二阶段（1996年到2001年）。我国证券行业发展过程中拐点的到来是在1996年初的价值回归以及1999年的"五一九"井喷式行情出现之时。此后随之而来的牛市持续时期，我国证券业的发展在整个市场繁荣这个有利于股市发展的大环境的改变下，表现出了如下的一些新特征：（1）券商普遍出现大幅度的营业利润增加现象；（2）那些资产较为优良而又注重企业发展战略且具有先进管理技术的地方性券商异军突起，很快在竞争中脱颖而出，不少券商甚至通过兼并重组信托公司的证券营业部来达到规模扩张、业务拓展的目的。从法律上规定我国金融业分业经营的模式是以1999年7月1日正式开始实施《证券法》为标志；（3）截至2001年，发展了参股或控股券商四十多家，而参与发展参股控股的上市公司则多达上百家，由此参股证券公司成为时下的一股热潮。

调整阶段——第三阶段（2001 年 7 月至 2015 年）。一来经历了两年多的牛市之后，国内证券市场的泡沫越吹越大，并在 2001 年 7 月开始转入熊市，我国股市面临一轮强劲的跌势；另一方面，中国于 2001 年 2 月正式加入 WTO，在经济全球化的浪潮下，整个行业发生了一轮根本性的转变，与国际接轨的大趋势渗透到证券业的每个角落。此时期券商的发展则表现出以下的一些特点：业务大幅萎缩，利润大幅下滑，全行业整体亏损等；证券业务风险逐渐增大。

从 2001 年以来，国内各大券商的传统承销、经纪以及自营等三大主流业务风险不断加大，除此之外，诸如资产管理之类的创新业务也承受着风险增加的重重压力；2002 年 5 月中国证券业监督管理委员会统计的数据显示：当时全国 118 家券商的不良资产总额达到了 4600000 万元，达到逾 50% 的不良资产率。

我国证券业自发展以来，走过了一段令世人瞩目的辉煌发展征途。自《国务院关于推进资本市场改革开放和稳定发展的若干意见》发布至今，我国资本市场进行了一系列的改革和制度创新建设，特别是通过实施股权分置改革，有效改善了证券市场乃至整个资本市场的运行机制和外部运行宏观经济环境，解决了一些约束我国证券市场发展的一系列制度性问题。我国证券行业的未来发展正随着中国证监会推出以净资本为核心的风险控制指标管理办法的贯彻执行而迎来了一轮持续健康发展的高潮。证券业的未来发展必将沿着盈利模式多元化、经营管理规范化、发展逐步规模化和行业竞争国际化的方向迈进。

二、期货业

我国期货业的发展经历了一个从无到有，从简单到繁荣的漫长而曲折的过程。具体可以归纳为以下几个阶段：即初始创立、整顿治理以及规范发展阶段。具体分述如下。

初创时期： 二十世纪八十年代，农产品的价格波动幅度逐渐增大，同时生产资料价格的双轨制逐步向市场归一；因为经济体制改革的不断深入，所以市场机制发挥着愈来愈重要的作用。1988 年 3 月，国务院明确要求积极发展各类批发市场，探索期货交易。从那时起，全中国开始了漫长的期货交易实践探索。

在 1990 年的 10 月中旬，经最高国家行政机关国务院的批准，中国郑州粮食批发市场正式推出期货交易机制，奠定了中国期货市场的基础。然而由于受行业利益的示范效应驱动，地下期货交易四处泛滥，从业人员鱼龙混杂，加之相关法规不配套等多种原因，导致中国各种各样的期货交易所大量涌现，造成了我国期货市场表面经济繁荣的局面。

整顿规范期： 由于中国期货市场盲从扩充，国务院在 1993 年对期货市场进行了第一次整改，又在五年后对期货市场进行了第二次整改。首次整改的结果是把 15 家交易所定为试点交易所。在 1998 年的第二次整顿中，期货交易所的数量精简为 3 家，期货交易品种保留了 12 个。期货公司在次年（1999 年）的准入标准提高，注册资本需要大于或者是等于人民币 3000 万元。在 20 世纪的最后一年，也就是 2000 年，我国期货行业自律组织诞生了。

因此，这两次整改促进了期货市场自我管理能力的提高，维系了期货市场的生存，我国期货市场开始步入了规范有序的轨道，一个相对独立的期货业基本形成。

21 世纪初的恢复与持续发展期： 20 世纪 90 年代的清理整顿为依法治市构筑了外在条件和基础，但也凸显了市场萎缩且期货交易量和成交额双双触底的颓势；2003 年才开始恢复活力并驶入了良性发展的轨道。通过调查得出，2000 年期货市场总成交量为 5361.08 万手，还不到 1995 年的十分之一；而从 2003 年伊始，成交量和成交额均开始逐步攀升。我国期货业又迎来了第二个春天！

目前，国内有郑州商品交易所（简称郑商所）、大连商品交易所（简称大商所）、上海期货交易所（简称上期所）和中国金融期货交易所（简称中金所）这四家期货交易所。截至 2013 年底，上市交易的期货品种已由 2012 年的 24 个增长到 25 个（其中铁矿石期货于 2013 年 10 月 18 日正式在大连商品交易所上市交易，这也是一个可喜可贺的日子）。已经上市的商品期货品种覆盖了诸多产业或领域，形成了商品期货的一个比较完整的体系。国内四家商品交易所的成立时间及主要品种如表 2-1 所示。

表 2-1 中国期货交易所代表性交易品种

交易所名称	成立时间	期货品种
郑州商品交易所	1990年10月12日	硬麦、棉花、白糖、精对苯二甲酸、菜籽油、早籼稻、甲醇等
大连商品交易所	1993年2月28日	黄大豆、玉米、豆粕、豆油、棕榈油、线型低密度聚乙烯、聚氯乙烯等
上海期货交易所	1998年8月1日	铜、铝、锌、黄金、线材、天然橡胶、螺纹钢、燃料油等
中国金融期货交易所	2006年9月8日	国债期货、股指期货（沪深300、上证50等）、股指期权

资料来源：各交易所官网，经作者整理

下面分别介绍四家期货交易所的概况。

郑州商品交易所。到2012年末，郑州商品交易所（郑商所）共有会员209家，其中包括非期货公司会员42个和期货公司会员167个。2012年郑州商品交易所累计成交期货合约3.47亿手，同比下降14.61%，累计成交金额17.36万亿元，同比下降48.04%，全年累计成交量占全国市场份额的23.93%，全年累计的成交总额占全国份额的10.15%。

2012年，郑州商品交易所为了使会员服务功能逐步提高，所以持续加紧体系的创建。首先是交易结算系统改造升级，满足业务要求，完备了会员的服务功能。其次是在信息体系基本创建模块方面，逐步加快推动期货大厦和异地灾备系统建设、技术中心的机房基本设施建设和两地三中心数据保护项目建设。为了进一步提高未来的终端建设和托管机房上网服务成员合作，为成员提供安全和可靠的品质，推出会员端互联网服务网络升级项目。

在自律管理方面，郑州商品交易所贴近现货市场实际，逐步完善业务规则，加强日常监控，严格地查处日常违规交易行为，在2012年处理异常的交易为80多起。

大连商品交易所。截至2012年末，大连商品交易所拥有178家会员，包括期货公司会员163家，非期货公司会员15家。2012年是大连商品交易所交易规模实现历史性新高的一年,交易量、持仓量屡创新高。2012年大商所成交量为6.33亿手,同比增长119%;成交额同比增长97%,达到了33万亿元;在2012年度全球衍生品交易所成交量排名中,大连商品交易所列第11名。投资者开户数较以往增长13%,达1568000户。

在业务创新方面,大连商品交易所正式启动多层次商品市场建设工作。一是启动多层次商品交易服务平台建设。大商所成立了专门工作组,派出人员到印度、我国的重庆和天津等地进行了实地的考察和调研,形成了可操作性强的多层次市场建设方案,已进入呈批阶段。二是把期权上市准备工作提上日程。三是面向国际,着眼未来,对延长交易时间、多币种结算、现金结算、合约外挂等多个业务创新项目加强了研究,形成了初步报告。

在市场服务方面,2012年大连商品交易所按照改进工作作风、更加贴近社会、贴近市场的要求,深入基层调研,广泛深入听取会员、企业和投资者的意见建议,在此基础上积极完善业务规则,深化开展为"三农"和产业企业的服务活动,积极探索创新服务手段,使交易所的市场面貌和市场形象发生了很大的改变。首先是适应市场变化,积极完善业务规则制度。其次是深入开展服务"三农"和服务产业活动。大连商品交易所继续坚持"产业大会""千村万户""千厂万企"等市场服务品牌,积极开展各类培训和市场推广活动,引导更多产业企业科学利用期货市场。第三是积极地培育机构投资者和期货行业人才。2012年10月,大商所自主研发的金融实验室一期成功上线,这一新工具集研发策略、实验模拟、远程辅导等功能于一体,适应了期货公司研投一体化的发展方向,是市场服务方式的一个重要创新。

上海期货交易所。截至2012年末,上海期货交易所会员数208家,其中期货公司会员161家,占比77.4%,非期货公司会员47家,占比22.6%。2012年上海期货交易所交易规模整体平稳,主要得益于国家货币政策微调;反复下调交易手续费,大大降低了投资者的交易成本等因素。

在市场服务方面,上海期货交易所一是做深做精现有品种,进一步完善品种套期保值管理办法和降低手续费收入标准。二是优化交割运行机制,在国际期货市场交割仓库的设置和布局等课题的基础上,进行前瞻性探索。三是提升市场服务质量。由上海期货交易所领导带队,分片包干,与各片区会员和投资者代表面对面座谈，倾听意见和建议，并开展高级管理人员和分析师的培训。

在信息技术创新与发展方面，2012年上海期货交易所既保证了技术系统运行安全，又保持了行业技术系统的领先。一是完成信息安全等级保护年度测评，符合率比2011年提高了2个百分点。二是优化网络监测及应用性能分析系统，集设备管理、性能管理、故障管理、配置管理等功能模块于一体，明显提升保障速度。三是坚持常态化开展应急演练，顺利完成了中国证监会组织的行业信息安全联合应急演练。四是加快建设更新交易系统，建立了精确到微秒的时间测量机制，基本达到了国际一流的水平。五是启动网络规划咨询项目，对网络通信平台进行统一规划，目前已经完成系统评估及国外先进交易所网络现状调研工作。

中国金融期货交易所。2012年股指期货市场会员数量稳步增长。截至2012年底，中国金融期货交易所会员共计146家。这包括交易会员70个，全面结算会员15个以及交易结算会员61个。2012年股指期货平稳运行243个交易日，到年底累计开户12.7万户，累计参与交易客户11.3万个。

中国金融期货交易所高度重视技术安全工作，将其视为交易所安身立命之本。2012年通过不断提升安全运行保障水平，保持全年系统安全运行零事故。一是加强技术系统优化改造，顺利完成国债期货仿真及生产系统的改造。二是构建了技术系统分级保障体系。对全所19个信息系统进行分级，明确保障标准和流程，进一步提升运维管理水平。三是推动新一代体系建立。召开了70多场研讨会，完成系统建设组织与推进方案。

2012年也是中国金融期货交易所外事国际交流合作工作取得重要突破的一年，在拓展外事交往渠道、加强与境外机构交流合作等方面都取得了明显进展。一是通过外事来访、出访和参加国际会议，进一步拓展了对外交往渠道，与境外交易所和知名金融机构联系交流更加顺畅。二是顺利地加入世界交易所联合会，建立起中国金融期货交易所国际合作的基础平台。

在内部建设方面，该交易所坚持在发展的基础上进行党组织建设，精心谋划，有序推进，把中国金融期货交易所党建工作不断引向深入。一是坚持立足当前、着眼长远，从战略高度科学谋划党建工作。二是注重建章立制，制定相关制度，提高党委工作民主化、制度化水平。三是注重专职人员的配备。四是加强廉洁自律,确保党风廉政建设落实到位、责任分解到位。表 2-1 总结了中国期货交易所代表性交易品种。

三、基金业

我国基金行业大致上经历了三个发展阶段

2000—2007 年:初始高度集中度阶段。2000 年,国内基金行业仍处于发展初期的"老十家"阶段,基金公司数量较少,市场集中度较高,前 5 大基金公司的规模总和基本能占一半以上的市场份额。在随后的七年即 2000—2007 年期间,国内基金管理行业经历了飞速发展阶段,基金公司数量以平均每年 6 家的增速逐渐增多,基金公司数量由 2000 年的老十家增至 2007 年末的 57 家。在此过程中,后成立的基金公司不论在新发基金数量上还是在发行规模上,均和老基金公司不相上下,行业竞争格局加剧,导致老基金公司的规模占比逐年下降。前 5 大公司集中度由 2000 年的 58% 急速降至 2007 年的 32%,而前 10 大公司集中度由 2000 年的 100% 急速降至 2007 年的 50%。

2008—2012 年:停滞阶段。从 2008 年始,受金融危机的影响,监管部门对基金行业牌照的审批基本停滞。2008—2010 年期间,基本没有新基金公司成立,后在 2011 年逐渐放开,到 2012 年增加至 70 家,这期间由于行业管制依然较大,加之资本市场行情较差,行业竞争力相比银行理财、信托公司等有所下降,这期间行业集中度变化不大,基本维持在前 5 大公司占比 30% 左右,前 10 大公司占比 50% 左右的水平。

2013—2015 年:行业进入发展新阶段。2012 年金融创新尤其是新基金法颁布后,基金进入门滥降低、投资范围等大幅扩宽,新产品创新不断,基金行业格局发生较大变化,天弘基金因其推出的"余额宝"产品,广受市场青睐,其货币基金规模达 5700 亿元,占整个基金管理规模 15%,推动公司排名至第一位,使得前 5 大基金公司规模达到 40%,前 10 大达到了 57%。

从各类型基金净值历年变化情况看,基金市场发展初期,以封闭式基金和混合型为主,而随着牛市来临,主动股票型基金渐渐成为市场的主流,最高峰时占比达到50%。而近几年股票市场表现不佳,投资者转向低风险产品,以货币基金为代表的固定收益类产品规模和份额都经历了大幅增长。货币基金2012年达到了1/4的份额,2013年稍有下降,也有接近1/5。而股票型基金2013年则降低到1/3左右的水平,混合型基金目前保持1/5左右的占比。从未来趋势上看,结合发达国家的经验,风险收益特性比较明确的股票型基金(代表高风险高收益)和货币基金(代表低风险低收益)会受到不同风险偏好的投资者的青睐,而混合型基金由于定位比较特殊,加上投资特点不显著,从而渐渐边缘化。

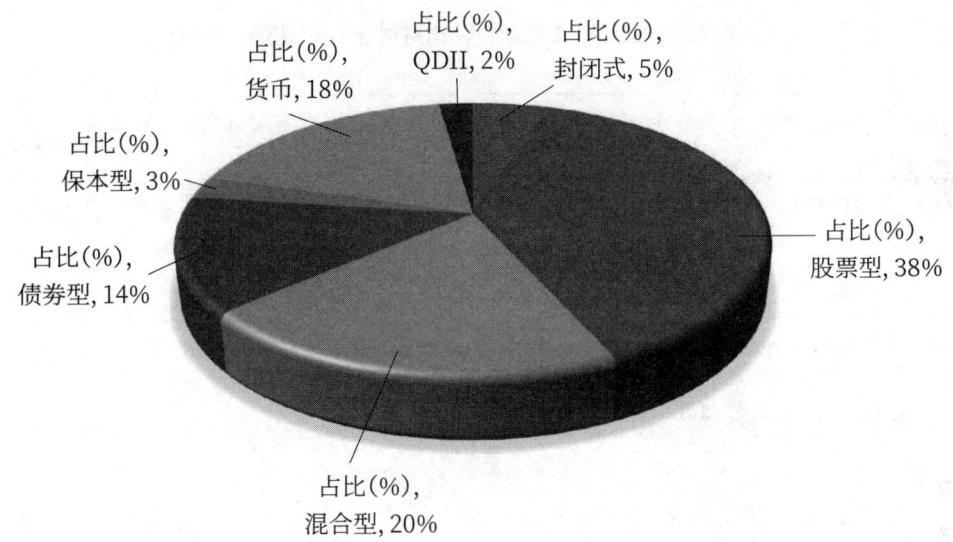

资料来源:中国基金业协会

图2-3 各类型基金资产规模占市场份额

近年来,中国基金行业亦不断进行创新。

投资范围创新。由于证监会已经对基金的投资范围有明确规定,因此基金在投资范围上的创新主要在于投资范围的细化和投资比例的限制。权益类基金经过范围细化出现了较多主题型基金和行业基金,债券型基金经过范围细化出现了诸如纯债基金、可转债基金的细分债券型基金。在对股票投资比例进行不同设定后,出现了全攻全守型基金、偏债配置型基金和仓位随日期变化的生命周期型基金等创新产品。QDII 基金进行投资范围细化后出现了主题型 QDII 和地域型 QDII。指数型基金在创新后出现了跟踪股债复合指数的基金。近期随着创新的加速，出现了投资黄金商品的基金，在投资范围创新上迈出了重要的一步。

表 2-2　基金投资范围创新汇总

创新点	主题类型	具体基金举例
主题型权益类基金	新兴产业主题、医药主题、消费主题等	上投新兴产业、汇添富医药保健等
细分债券型基金	纯债基金、可转债基金、理财债券型	中银纯债、博时可转债
股票投资比例创新	全攻全守型基金、偏债配置型基金	富国宏观策略等
QDII主题型基金	房地产信托基金、资源QDII	诺安全球受益不动产、信诚全球商品
商品型基金	黄金ETF	华安黄金ETF等
股债复合指数基金	股债复合指数基金	银华中证成长股债等

资料来源：各基金公司官网，经作者整理

投资范围的细化能带来风险—收益确定性更高的工具型产品供投资者选择。部分投资范围创新产品从短期来看并未给基金公司带来明显的规模扩张，但从长期来看，产品的个性化和产品线的完善能够为基金公司增强竞争力，有助于规模的发展。

运作模式创新。基金在运作模式上经历了由封闭到开放，再到封闭/定期开放/半封闭/ETF 等多种运作模式的发展历程。债券型基金封闭运作更能够避免申赎资金的冲击，从而获得更高确定性的收益，由此产生了封闭运作的债基、定期开放型债基和费率引导定期开放的债基。以富国强收益债为例，基金设立每季度一次的受限开放期和每年一次的自由开放期。在自由放期赎回基金不收赎回费，在受限开放期赎回基金需要收取 1% 的赎回费。且在受限开放期如果净赎回数量超过基金资产的一定比例（初始为 10%），则对当日赎回申请按一定比例进行部分确认，确保基金资金规模不会受到过大的影响。除了封闭及半封闭债基外，运作模式的重要创新还包括分级基金、ETF等。分级基金将基金收益进行分配，以适应不同风险偏好的投资者的需要。ETF基金则将指数基金与一揽子股票的价格直接挂钩，提升了指数型基金的跟踪效率，部分ETF成为融资融券标的，也为基金公司扩大规模奠定了基础。

表2-3 基金运作模式创新举例

创新点	主要类型	具体基金举例
定期开放型债基	定期开放型债基、定期半开放型债基、费率引导定期开放的债基	华夏一年定期开放、华安稳固收益
主动清算基金	达到条件主动清盘的绝对收益特征基金	融通通则一年
分级基金	指数分级,主动股票分级,债券分级	富国创业指数分级
封闭运作债基	封闭运作债基	工银四季收益、招商信用添利
跨市场ETF	跨市场ETF与跨境ETF	嘉实沪深300ETF
货币EFT	货币ETF	汇添富快钱

资料来源：中国基金业协会

服务创新。相对于产品创新而言，基金公司亦推出服务创新以加强竞争优势。

定制账户。基金公司提供的基金产品与投资者的投资需求无法对接是多年来该行业累积下的顽疾。基金产品多为标准化的，追求相对收益；而投资者需要的是绝对收益，且多数基金投资者不具有基金投资的专业知识，在时机选择和基金选择上缺乏专业指导。嘉实基金基于此成立了"投资者回报中心"，由专业人士为投资者提供"定制账户"服务。定制账户根据风险等级分为"锐意进取组合""从容稳进组合"和"安逸理财组合"。投资者使用"定制账户"服务，就直接将资金交给定制账户管理人打理。

货币型基金T+0。近年来兴起的另一项服务是货币型基金T+0服务。货币型基金在所有基金类型中是与投资者风险偏好和绝对收益需求对接较好的一个品种，但由于其流动性略差，且缺乏宣传，虽然收益率远高于银行活期存款，但不为广大投资者所熟知，规模也没有发展壮大。2012 年以来，货币型基金逐渐出现了多种形式的 T+0 服务，许多货币型基金在特定渠道——或是银行，或是网络直销渠道上能够实现赎回 T+0 到账。实现方式部分由银行垫资，部分由基金公司垫资。在该服务的基础上，货币型基金的流动性向银行活期存款靠拢，为货币型基金争夺银行活期存款市场提供了基础。

渠道创新。销售渠道一直是基金公司的竞争焦点。历史上，销售基金的主渠道一直是银行。近几年，第三方销售渠道逐渐崭露头角，伴随逐渐发放的第三方支付机构牌照，第三方销售表现出了其销售优势。最为典型的是天弘基金与支付宝的合作。支付宝用户可以通过支付宝直接购买天弘旗下的货币型基金——天弘增利宝。不仅可以提供良好的流动性（余额宝内资金可随时在淘宝上消费），而且购买起点低（1 元即可购买），且支付宝本身具有广大的客户基础和沉淀资金。据媒体报道，自 2013 年 6 月 13 日余额宝上线，至 9 月初规模已近 500 亿元。

四、保险业

30 年前，中国保险市场只有中国人民保险公司一家，保险业务都是清一色的计划指标。如今，保险市场主体已经突破 100 家，市场规模增长 1500 多倍。近 30 年，中国保险业有两个亮点最为突出，一是保险业 30 年中保持了年均 30% 左右的增长速度，堪称国民经济发展最快的行业之一；二是在我国金融业中，保险业无论是开放时间、开放力度，还是开放步伐，都是走在前列的。30 年的改革历程，保险业在促进经济社会的稳定和发展中发挥着越来越重要的作用。

由于本系列将专设一册介绍保险行业，故这里不再赘述。

五、信托业

信托与银行、证券、保险并称为金融业的四大支柱，其本来含义是"受人之托、代人理财"。按照《信托法》第一章第一节对信托的定义,信托"是指委托人基于对受托人的信任,将其财产权委托给受托人,由受托人按委托人的意愿以自己的名义,为受益人的利益或者特定目的,进行管理或者处分的行为。"

信托在世界上已有 3800 年的历史,因为它一头连着货币市场,一头连着资本市场,一头连着产业市场,既能融资又能投资,被誉为具有无穷的经济活化作用。用美国信托权威思考特的话说,"信托的应用范围,可以和人类的想象力相媲美。"

中国的信托业始于 20 世纪初的上海。1921 年 8 月,在上海成立了第一家专业信托投资机构——中国通商信托公司,1935 年在上海成立了中央信托总局。新中国建立至 1979 年以前,金融信托因为在高度集中的计划经济管理体制下,信托没有能得到发展。

1979 年 10 月,国内第一家信托机构——中国国际信托投资公司宣告成立,此后,从中央银行到各专业银行及行业主管部门、地方政府纷纷办起各种形式的信托投资公司,到 1988 年达到最高峰时共有 1000 多家,总资产达到 6000 多亿,占到当时金融总资产的 10%。

一开始,中国的信托投资公司主要从事与银行类似的业务,真正的信托投资业务也有开展,如金信信托投资股份有限公司于 1992 年发行的浙江省内第一只共同基金"金信基金",1995 年 8 月推出的"个人特约集合委托存款"业务。但是由于缺乏法律上的规范和信托投资公司的管理经验,在 1999 年人民银行对信托业进行第五次整顿前,信托投资公司仅剩下 239 家。

2015 年,中国的信托行业资产规模经历连续 7 个季度同比增长率逐季下滑的尴尬后,终于在这一年二季度实现了扭转。公开资料显示,截止到二季度末,全国信托资产规模突破 15 万亿元,同比大增 27.16%。

中国信托业协会发布的《2015 年 2 季度中国信托业发展评析》显示,截止到二季度末,全国 68 家信托公司管理的信托资产规模达到 15.87 万亿元,比 2015 年一季度末的 14.41 万亿元环比增长 10.13%,比 2014 年二季度末增长 27.16%。这也是自 2013 年三季度至 2015 年一季度,连续 7 个季度信托资产规模同比增长率逐季下滑后,首度迎来回暖态势,信托业迈入"15 万亿元时代"。

六、Q&A

（一）外国人或外国公司是否可以在内地设立纯外资，或外资控股的证券投资咨询公司？

答：外资证券投资咨询公司设立的相关规定。根据 CEPA 补充协议九、十的相关规定，"允许符合外资参股证券公司境外股东资质条件的香港证券公司与内地具备设立子公司条件的证券公司，在内地设立合资证券投资咨询公司。合资证券投资咨询公司作为内地证券公司的子公司，专门从事证券投资咨询业务，香港证券公司持股比例最高可达到 49%。在内地批准的'在金融改革方面先行先试'的若干改革试验区内，允许港、澳资证券公司在合资证券投资咨询公司中的持股比例达 50% 以上。"

（二）境外银行如何申请人民币合格境外机构投资者的资格？

答：若该银行（机构）希望申请 RQFII 资格，应满足：（1）注册地及主要经营地在新加坡的金融机构；（2）在新加坡证券监管部门取得资产管理业务资格，并已经开展资产管理业务。其余要求按照《人民币合格境外机构投资者境内证券投资试点办法》及相关法规执行。满足上述要求的新加坡商业银行可申请 RQFII 资格。根据规定，申请人应通过具有合格境外机构投资者托管人资格的境内商业银行向中国证监会递交材料，在申请过程中遇到的疑问可向托管人或相关监管机构咨询。

第三章
中国货币市场简介

一、中国货币市场概况

　　1998年以后,随着我国央行货币政策调控手段的变化和经济货币化、金融市场化程度的提高,中国货币市场的发展取得了长足进展,主要成效是包括银行间同业拆借市场、银行间债券市场和票据市场三大子市场在内的货币市场发展均呈加速趋势。目前,同业拆借市场已成为金融机构管理头寸的主要场所;银行间债券市场已成为中央银行公开市场操作的主要平台;票据市场已经成为企业短期融资和银行提高流动性管理、规避风险的重要途径。据统计,2014年,银行间市场拆借、现券和债券回购累计成交302.4万亿元,同比增加28.5%。其中,银行间市场同业拆借成交37.7万亿元,同比增加6.0%;债券回购成交224.4万亿元,同比增加41.9%;现券成交40.4万亿元,同比减少3.0%。至2003年末,同业拆借市场成员为616家,较年初增加80家,债券市场成员为2895家,较年初增加1994家。2003年度企业累计签发商业汇票2.77万亿元,同比增长72.7%,累计票据贴现和再贴现4.44万亿元,同比增长91%。2003年末,已签发的未到期的商业汇票余额为1.28万亿元,同比增长73.5%;票据和再贴现余额8934亿元,同比增长69.7%。

　　上述情况表明,中国货币市场发展的确处于加速成长阶段,每年的速度以几何级数递增,这在发达国家和发展中国家的货币市场中都是很少见的。但加速增长只能说明表面现象,要研究中国货币市场发展的实际状况,则需要从多方面加以考察,经过深入研究中国货币市场的形成背景、制定框架、操作模式、运行激励，可以得出一个初步结论：目前中国货币市场充其量还是处于一个开放程度不高、市场化手段、结构发展不均衡、技术设施尚落后的初级发展阶段。

二、同业拆借市场

同业拆借市场，是金融机构之间进行短期、临时性头寸调剂的市场，是货币市场的重要组成部分。它不仅是实施流通性管理的重要手段，也是中央银行制定和实行货币政策的重要依据。

同业拆借市场有以下几个特点：一是融通资金的期限比较短，我国同业拆借资金的最长期限为4个月，因为同业拆借资金主要用于金融机构短期、临时性资金需要；二是参与拆借的机构基本上在中央银行开立存款账户，在拆借市场交易的主要是金融机构存放该账户上的多余资金；三是同业拆借基本上是信用拆借，拆借活动在金融机构之间进行，市场准入条件较严格，金融机构主要以其信誉参与拆借活动。

我国的同业拆借市场作为金融改革的重点项目之一，起始于20世纪80年代，它经历了起步、快速发展和规范化统一三个阶段。

1986—1991年：起步阶段。 那时同业拆借市场迅速发展，但是也存在一系列问题：经营资金拆借业务的机构混乱，拆借资金用途不合理，利率过高，期限不断延长等。特别是1988年，由于部分地区金融机构违反有关资金拆借的规定，用拆借资金搞固定资产投资，拆借资金到期无法收回。中国人民银行根据国务院指示，对同业拆借市场的违规行为进行了一次整顿，撤销融资公司，严格限制非银行金融机构进入拆借市场，接着对拆借利率实行上限控制，并严格规定拆借主体、拆借期限及拆借资金的用途。但是这些措施效果并不明显，拆借市场的交易量并未显著下降，1989—1991年，交易量分别为2200多亿元、2370多亿元和2927多亿元。同期，中国人民银行还下发了《同业拆借管理试行办法》，第一次用专门的法规形式对同业拆借市场管理做了比较系统的规定，使得拆借市场有了一定的规范和发展。

1992—1995 年：发展与理清阶段。 1992 年开始，我国金融形势趋于好转，同业拆借市场也出现了高速增长，仅 1993 年一年的同业拆借交易量就达到了 4000 亿元左右，但如此迅速的发展使我国同业拆借市场出现了极度混乱的局面：拆借市场的准入资格形同虚设，市场交易主体的范围大大扩大，甚至一些个人也参与其中，拆借利率被肆意拉高，月利率有的高达 150%，在南方一些城市甚至高达 200%。拆借期限不断拉长，甚至达到 5 年，大量拆借资金被用于房地产投资、固定资产投资、开发区项目及炒买炒卖股票，这种混乱局面严重影响了我国拆借市场的健康发展，干扰了金融市场的正常运行。于是，1993 年人民银行出台了一系列规章制度，1994 年 2 月 15 日中央银行颁布的《借贷资金管理暂行办法》对拆借种类、数量、期限、用途及交易主体都进行了更严格的规定。经过这次整顿，同业拆借市场秩序有了明显好转，市场违规行为大大减少，拆借市场开始步入正轨。1994 年的同业拆借交易量就达到了 5000 亿元左右，1995 年则突破万亿。

1996—2015 年：规模发展阶段。 1996 年 1 月 4 日，中国人民银行发布了全国统一的同业拆借利率——中国银行同业拆借市场加权平均利率，并从 6 月 1 日起取消同业拆借利率上限，全面放开拆借利率，实现了由利率管制向利率市场化的转变。从货币市场交易期限结构看，1997 年 7 天以内（包括隔夜）的同业拆借的比重为 32.5%；而 2000 年同业拆借的期限结构发生了根本性的改变，7 天以内（包括隔夜）的同业拆借比重已上升为 71.4%。这一指标的变化表明，同业拆借市场已成为金融机构之间调节短期头寸的重要场所。2006 年底进入全国银行间同业拆借中心的金融机构总共 703 家，拆借市场迎来了历史性突破。与十年前相比，2006 年底机构规模已经增加 12.8 倍；1998 年全国拆借总量不足 2000 亿，2006 年已经突破 2 万亿。1996 年以来，我国同业拆借市场运行良好，没有再出现极度混乱无序的局面，市场拆借利率也有了很大提高。

表 3-1 2000 年—2008 年我国银行间同业拆借量

年份	2000年	2001年	2002年	2003年	2004年
同业拆借总额（亿元）	6728.07	8482.05	12107.26	22220.33	13616.56
年份	2005年	2006年	2007年	2008年	
同业拆借总额（亿元）	12303.93	21483.66	106284.5	150491.8	

数据来源：根据中国社会科学院金融研究所统计数据整理所得

但我国目前的同业拆借市场还存在不少明显的不规范之处以及缺陷。一是尽管在形式上我国同业拆借市场已初具规模，但从运行机制及管理体制诸方面看，还不是规范意义上的货币市场。截至 2015 年还只允许银行和非银行金融机构参与市场拆借，不允许非金融机构入市。并且 1 个月以上的短期拆借比重过大，在很大程度上具有短贷性质，对商业银行基层行短期资金尤其是头寸弥补需要重视不够，同业拆借经营目标出现明显偏离，短款长用现象严重。拆借市场业务以行政手段管理为主，还没有真正脱离计划性和行政性束缚。

二是同业拆借市场主体市场化程度不高，影响了拆借市场规范发展。特别是国有商业银行正处于经营机制转轨时期，信贷经营还未实现真正的市场化操作，因而其拆借业务往往并不是处于平衡头寸的需要，在很大程度上带有寻求信贷资金的性质，并且大多用于填补信贷缺口。不少不具有拆借资额的其他金融机构，由于市场缺乏必要的约束和监督，以拆借的名义从事其他如证券回购、投资股票等业务，影响了拆借市场的正常发展。

三是放开的同业拆借利率，并不反映真实的市场资金供求关系，很难为中央银行货币政策调控所利用。在其他借贷利率特别是银行借贷利率严格控制，而只有同业拆借利率放开的格局下，同业拆借利率大大高于银行贷款利率。据 1996 年 9 月 20 日同业拆借利率资料，日拆至 3 个月利率为 11.34%~11.768%，而同期中央银行 3 个月再贷款利率为 9.72%，商业银行半年期贷款利率为 9.18%，利差大于两个点以上。这为正处于经营机制调整的商业银行及其他金融机构躲避区域性风险转移资金提供可能，也为一些银行机构套取中央银行资金提供便利。

三、债券回购市场

债券回购是债券市场上进行的一种短期融资、融券交易。即债券持有者作为卖方与买方在所签订的债券交易协议中规定,卖方在卖出该笔债券后须在某个双方约定时间,以约定的价格再买回该债券,并付以约定的利率计算的利息。不难看出这份协议对卖方而言是一份回购协议,而对买方则是一份逆回购协议,故这笔债券交易实质是一笔卖方以债券为抵押获得买方短期借款的交易。回购协议中进行交易的对象一般以国库券为主,其他还有抵押或担保公司债券,银行承兑汇票和是商业票据等。目前上海证券交易所开设的回购业务则是用标准化的金融债券抵押方式,也就是说不分券种,统一按债券面值计算持券量进行融资、融券业务。

债券回购作为货币市场中的一种重要交易方式,为国债市场的发展,中央银行公开市场业务的开展和各类商业、金融机构根据需要调整金融资产结构,提供了一种十分有效的手段。

我国国债回购业起步较晚,始于 1989 年国家允许国库券在市场上流通转让之时,且发展较快,尤其是 1993 年起,随着证券市场的扩容,国债现货市场的活跃及金融机构盘活资金的需要,国债回购发展迅速,成为国债市场中不可缺少的交易品种之一。场内交易业务(在证券交易所或期货交易所内由交易所设计并经政府主管部门批准进行的标准化回购),由于简化债券回购品种的设置,场内交易自律机制健全,故发展迅速,包括上交所、深交所、STAQ 系统、天津证券交易中心,武汉交易中心以及其他证券交易中心在内的众多证券交易场所,均开设了此项业务。

随着机制完善和投资者投资意识的加强,回购市场交易日趋活跃。一方面回购业务成交量增长迅速,尤其是上交所债券回购业务实行全额券值抵押,坚持活跃与规范并重的原则,使回购市场发展得有条不紊,加上其回购业务具有高回报率、低手续费、强安全性等优点,对投资者吸引力较大。2014 年,债券市场现券和回购交易结算量为 352.55 万亿元,同比增长 30.03%,相比 2013 年增速提高了 28.98 个百分点。其中全市场现券结算量为 40.61 万亿元，同比下降 6%；全市场的回购交易结算量为 311.54 万亿元，同比增长 36.88%，比上年提高了 16.2 个百分点。另一方面，各证交所的国债回购交易额占证券市场国债交易额的份额都比较大。就 1995 年而言，天津证交中心的回购交易总额为 680 多亿元，占整个市场国债交易额的 90%；武汉证券中心的回购交易额为 15000 多亿元，占整个市场国债交易总额的 45%；而 STAQ 系统的回购交易额为 1047 亿元，占整个市场国债交易总额的 90%。

表 3-2　2010 年银行间质押式回购期限分布

回购品种	面值额（亿元）	占比	结算笔数（笔）	平均每笔交割量（万元/笔）
R001	578270	63.02%	90293	64044
R002	13954	1.52%	2184	63891
R003	132464	14.44%	21302	62184
R007	125405	13.67%	32649	38410
R014	44051	4.80%	11448	38479
R021	7379	0.80%	2521	29270
R1M	8812	0.96%	2985	29522
R2M	3666	0.40%	984	37260
R3M	2491	0.27%	655	38033
R4M	415	0.05%	91	45651
R6M	592	0.06%	182	32510
R9M	93	0.01%	25	37220
R1Y	54	0.01%	14	38645
全部	917647	100.00%	165333	55503

数据来源：中国债券信息网

债券回购是一种灵活的融资、融券方式；加上它在我国刚刚起步，管理层经验尚不丰富，相关法规还不健全，所以在交易所之外金融机构之间进行的场外回购业务还不规范,存在一些问题。

一是期限过长,制造风险。按照回购市场惯例,回购期限一般不宜超过一年,但时下一些交易商作的所谓债券回购业务期限多在一年以上。这种人为延长回购期限的做法,不仅不能很好地满足融资方根据需要作短期筹资,也给融券方的投资带来一定风险,不利于交易商根据利率期限结构调整交易类型,规范交易行为。二是假借回购,套取信用。按规定,融资者应将债券按即期价格卖给融资方,回购期满时再按合约价格购回,但目前一些证券就在未持有相应债券的情况下作债券回购。究其实,这种做法是证券交易商钻了国库券发行与买卖可以开具代保管债券业务的规定的空子,是假回购国债之名,行发行公司债券之实;它套取了国家信用,是一种国家禁止的卖空行为;这种行为既欺骗了融资方,又扰乱了金融市场的正常秩序。三是擅抬利率,加剧通胀。由于前一段时期约束机制的欠健全,有些公司便通过抬高利率的方法变债券回购为套取国家信用替本单位筹资的手段,然后再把所筹资金用作固定资产、股票、期货的投资和对企业的贷款。他们发行的国债回购券年利率不仅超过了企业债券条例中规定的企业债券利率的浮动幅度,而且远高于即期国债二级市场上的收益率,更高于新发行国债的票面利率。从筹资的角度来说,这种擅抬利率的做法严重违反了国家关于金融市场利率要求统一的规定,属不正当竞争行为,同时也严重影响了财政部在一级市场上发行国债,扰乱了正常的国家财政部署。从投资角度看,这种行为混淆了货币市场和资本市场,不仅增加了回购市场风险,还无形中膨胀了信贷规模,增加了通胀压力,加剧了股票市场和期货市场的投机程度。

四、票据市场

在现代市场经济中,票据是指企业或个人签发的体现债权人和债务人信用关系的书面债据,可以转让,作为支付和流通手段;也可通过贴现和再贴现作为融资工具,相当于变相的贷款而无须严格地评级审批,方便快捷,被称为是半直接融资。在西方发达国家,票据行为是市场经济中企业往来支付、融资的主要手段。票据市场作为货币市场的子市场，在一国金融市场中处于基础性地位，发挥着其他金融市场不可替代的作用。

（一）我国票据市场发展概况

我国曾长期明令禁止商业信用，因此不存在商业票据，未形成相应的票据承兑和贴现业务，自然不存在票据市场。改革开放后，商业信用活动逐渐得以恢复，票据市场逐步形成，但其发展却经历了颇为曲折的过程。

1982—1994 年：票据推广使用阶段。我国票据业务起步于 1981 年。该年上海等地开始试行商业汇票承兑与贴现业务。1984 年底，中国人民银行颁布了《商业银行承兑贴现暂行办法》，鼓励工商企业之间的商业信用实现票据化。1986 年又颁布了《中国人民银行再贴现试行办法》。但在 1994 年以前基本处于停止状态。1994 年底，中央银行会同有关部门提出在部分行业和品种的赊销环节推广使用商业汇票，开办票据承兑授信和贴现、再贴现，至此票据业务才真正开始。

1995—1999 年 9 月：票据市场的制度建设阶段。以 1995 年《中华人民共和国票据法》的颁布为标志，初步建立并逐步完善了有关票据业务的法规和制度，对再贴现政策做了比较大的调整。此间，大幅下调了再贴现利率，改进并完善了贴现利率的生成机制。

1999 年 10 月—2015 年：票据市场快速发展阶段。在这一时期，票据业务一直发展迅速，业务总量成倍增长。1999—2002 年，每年商业汇票的签发、承兑量不断刷新，2002 年全国商业票据签发量达到 16139 亿元；金融机构办理的票据贴现量由 2400 亿元增加到 21000 亿元（含部分转贴现），分别增长 3.1 倍和 7.7 倍。同期，商业汇票未到期金额由 1595 亿元增加到 7500 亿元；票据贴现余额由 547 亿元增加到 5743 亿元，分别增长 3.7 倍和 9.5 倍。

表 3-3 1995 年以来中国银行承兑汇票市场规模

年份	承兑余额（亿元）	贴现余额（亿元）	再贴现余额（亿元）
1995	865	150	322
1996	1285	505	416
1997	1335	581	337
1998	1595	547	331
1999	1873	552	502
2000	3676	1535	1256
2001	5110	2795	655
2002	7347	5200	68
2003	12776	8167	766
2004	15000	10000	33
2005	19600	13800	2
2006	22100	17200	18

数据来源：Wind 金融资讯

（二）我国票据市场存在的问题

票据市场的建立和发展，将企业、商业银行及中央银行有机联合起来，成为传导货币政策的有效载体，在规范和引导商业信用、发展票据市场融资、强化宏观调控、降低风险等方面发挥了重要作用。但是在充分肯定票据业务快速发展、票据市场作用明显的同时，我们也应看到当前票据市场在迅猛发展过程中存在一些问题。

1. 票据市场基础薄弱

（1）票据市场信用基础较差。信用制度的不健全和信用状况欠佳是我国票据市场发展的最大障碍。首先，企业信用观念淡薄，配套的社会信用评估制度、信息披露制度、市场信用风险的预防和控制机制等规范管理制度尚未出台，往往存在票据的"不真实"问题。其次，票据市场利率缺乏弹性。目前，我国票据利率从根本上来说仍属于官定利率，抑制了票据市场的发育，挫伤了商业银行票据贴现的积极性。而且，价格体系混乱，利率竞争无序。另外，票据市场缺乏准入和退出机制。由于缺乏专门的票据鉴定中介机构，商业票据的真实性查询也非常困难，特别是鉴别真假汇票和票据背后是否有真实的商品交易难度很大。

（2）票据法律体系不完善。1995年我国颁布了《中华人民共和国票据法》，这是调整票据法律关系的一部重要法律。但票据法自身存在理论误区，把早已过时的"真实票据原则"作为立法基础，阻碍了票据市场化进程；从世界其他国家票据市场发展进程看，融资性票据所占比重不断上升，甚至达到70%-80%，而我国则把融资票据排斥在商业票据之外，缩小了票据市场的发展空间；大量采用了银行结算的规则，使票据市场交易链条无法稳定和协调运转。

（3）票据市场的基础建设滞后。目前尚未建立全国统一的票据业务信息系统，票据的签发、承兑以及流通、转让和查询、查复等，都是采取实物券形式和手工操作。与股票市场、债券市场以及同业拆借市场相比，票据市场发行、交易的现代化程度很低。

2. 票据市场规模有限

经过近几年快速发展，我国票据市场已经初具规模，但是与西方发达国家相比，我国票据市场的规模仍然较小。从货币市场体系来看，1994年美国票据市场交易额为6250亿美元，而我国到2001年票据市场交易额仅为31169亿元，票据市场的交易额仅占货币市场总额的39%。与我国其他货币市场如国债回购市场及资本市场相比，我国票据市场发展也严重滞后。到2002年末，商业汇票未到期金额仅相当于金融机构人民币信贷资金总量的4%，票据贴现余额所占各项贷款的比重不足5%。尤其是我国企业习惯于银行贷款，对利用票据进行融资的积极性不高，目前我国商业汇票仅占GDP的13.39%。同时，我国票据市场目前集中分布于全国各大中心城市，没有形成一个固定的、统一的票据市场，容易导致地方保护、地域封锁局面，给票据市场带来诸多不便。我国票据市场规模还受制于票据市场工具单一，交易方式较少。虽然我国《票据法》规定了票据包括本票、汇票和支票三种，但实际交易的只有交易性票据，没有融资性票据。即使在有限的交易性票据中，也是银行承兑汇票一枝独秀。由于银行承兑汇票的承兑手续费虽然仅为票面金额的万分之五，承兑银行却需承担企业到期付款的信用风险，从收益和风险角度来衡量，二者不匹配，使其在票据市场中处于被排斥地位。从票据品种最多的上海票据市场来看，目前仅有银行承兑汇票、商业承兑汇票两种承兑汇票，而国际市场包括商业本票、承兑汇票、短期国债、大额可转让定期存单等丰富品种，而且其主流品种已是纯融资性票据——商业本票，承兑汇票市场则已萎缩。目前我国票据市场中，交易工具和品种与发达国家相差甚远，存单、保险单等纳入工具还属空白，影响了票据作用的发挥。同时，我国票据市场上，缺乏区域性经票据业务的票据公司或贴现银行等票据市场中介机构和市场专业主体，这也是我国票据市场发展滞后的一个重要原因。迄今，我国票据业务没有一家专门从事票据发行、管理、经营于一体的有法人资格的票据公司参与，导致票据流通不畅，变现性差，致使我国商业票据市场举步维艰。

五、货币市场与货币政策传导机制

货币市场的政策功能，是指货币市场为货币政策实施提供市场条件的功能。从货币政策的传导机制来看，如果没有完善的货币市场，货币政策工具的实施到货币政策目标的实现这一过程根本无法顺利进行。

存款准备金率的传导机制

中央银行提高或降低存款准备金率，就会造成商业银行的存款准备金减少或增加，进而引起货币供应量减少或增加；与此同时，由于商业银行的存款准备金减少或增加，将会导致银行同业拆借市场利率提高或降低，进而引起市场短期利率和长期利率提高或降低。

贴现政策传导机制

中央银行提高或降低贴现率，就会造成商业银行的存款准备金减少或增加，进而又会引起货币供应量减少或增加；与此同时，由于商业银行存款准备金减少或增加，将会导致银行同业拆借市场利率提高或降低，进而引起市场短期利率和长期利率提高或降低。

公开市场业务

中央银行买卖有价证券,将会对商业银行存款准备金产生影响,造成商业银行存款准备金增加或减少,进而又会引起货币供应量增加或减少;与此同时,由于商业银行存款准备金减少或增加,将会导致银行同业拆借市场利率提高或降低,进而引起市场短期利率和长期利率提高或降低。

(一)同业拆借市场对货币政策效果的影响

在西方发达国家,同业拆借市场的交易对象涉及同业拆借市场利率和商业银行的超额准备,而这两个指标都是中央银行进行货币政策操作的重要手段:首先,由于商业银行在中央银行账户上的多余资金是同业拆借市场的交易对象,中央银行就有可能通过调整存款准备金率来改变商业银行缴存存款准备金的数量,以实现对商业银行信贷扩张能力和规模的调控。其次,由于同业拆借市场利率代表了市场资金价格,反映了同业拆借市场资金供求状况的变化,实际上这一利率已成为确定其他资金价格的基本参照利率;因此,中央银行不但把同业拆借市场利率作为其制订利率政策的重要参数,而且就有可能通过调控同业拆借市场利率来影响其他利率,以实现货币政策目标。

1996年1月我国建立了全国统一的同业拆借市场,标志着我国银行间同业拆借市场的发展进入新阶段,为我国利率市场化改革和宏观金融调控向间接调控机制转变创造了条件,但目前我国银行间同业拆借市场的发展还远不能适应中央银行进行货币政策操作的需要,表现在第一,同业拆借市场交易主体偏少。目前进入同业拆借市场的仅仅是商业银行的总行和极少数省级分行,而数以万计的商业银行分支行被排斥在同业拆借市场之外。另外,目前我国的同业拆借市场只是全国银行间同业拆借市场,而不包括非银行金融机构。第二,同业拆借市场交易规模小,品种少。1996年以来,我国银行间同业拆借市场交易量持续下降,主要原因是受风险成本增大和交易不畅等因素的影响。毫无疑问,同业拆借市场日均几亿或十几亿元的这种"微量"交易额,根本不足以影响整个市场的资金流动。我国同业拆借市场交易品种少,交易主要集中于少数几个品种上。第三,同业拆借市场利率还不能完全反映货币市场真实的资金供求水平。这是因为我国货币市场其他子市场的发育程度都还很低,特别是票据市场发展滞后,影响了商业信用与银行信用的有效结合,难以将资金的供求信息准确传到给商业银行,从而使同业拆借市场利率失真;另外,同业拆借市场交易主体少、交易规模小、交易品种少也是影响同业拆借市场利率机制不健全的重要原因。

(二)票据贴现市场对货币政策效果的影响

央行运用再贴现政策这一货币政策的重要工具调节货币供应量、实现扩张或收缩信用的目的,是通过对商业银行和贴现机构再贴现,间接地实现对每个企业的贴现来完成的。无论是贴现还是再贴现,都必须依附于票据市场来进行。近年来我国票据市场得到了长足发展,商业汇票的使用范围和业务总量在逐渐扩大,承兑、贴现与再贴现的结构比例得到改善,但与西方发达市场经济国家的票据市场相比,尚处于初期发育阶段,存在的主要问题是:第一,票据市场业务量非常有限;第二,票据市场工具单一,主要是银行承兑汇票,商业汇票和本票都比较少;第三,票据市场各行为主体还很不规范。我国票据市场这种状况无法满足央行进行宏观调控需要,从而再贴现政策这一货币政策工具效果难以发挥。

(三)短期国债市场对货币政策效果的影响

在西方发达市场经济国家,国债市场尤其是短期国债市场是货币市场中最为活跃的子市场,它是中央银行进行公开市场操作的重要场所。央行根据货币政策需要,通过在国债二级市场买卖国债来进行公开市场操作,依靠国债市场吞吐基础货币,调节商业银行的资金头寸,进而导致货币供应量增减和利率升降变化,以实现货币政策的目标。国债市场上的国债运作有利于货币政策和财政政策的有机结合。

近年来,我国国债市场发展较快,特别是国债一级市场上的国债发行规模不断扩大,但总体仍处于初级阶段,还很不完善,无论是一级市场还是二级市场都存在许多问题:首先,国债一级市场还不规范,突出表现为国债期限结构缺乏均衡合理分布,国债大部分以中期国债为主,短期国债数量较少。其次,国债二级市场运行不畅,交易主体单一、债券不足。由此可见,我国短期国债市场要成为央行进行公开市场操作的市场依托,即建成具有一定广度深度,并富有弹性的短期国债市场还任重道远。

六、Q&A

（一）外国投资者能否投资中国债券？

答：中国政府已经批准在香港、伦敦和新加坡的外国投资者可以通过所谓的人民币合格境外机构投资者项目在股票和债券市场进行总量2746亿人民币（452亿美元）的投资。这个项目允许人民币基金在海外融资，然后在国内证券中进行投资。更早的一个从2002年开始的合格境外机构投资者项目总计向中国以外的机构基金批准了492.5亿美元的配额，并在2012年开始允许这些投资者购买债券，而不仅仅是股票。

（二）吸引外国投资者进入中国债券市场的力量是什么？

答：高收益率正在将投资者吸引到中国债券。在国内市场交易的十年期国债收益率是4.6%，离岸的人民币债券收益率大约是3.9%，而同期的十年期美国国债收益率虽然相比5月的低位有上扬，也仅仅是2.93%。

（三）外国投资者进入中国债券的风险是什么？

答：中国债券市场的这种高收益率中的一部分需要被多种风险所抵消，包括本地评级机构倾向于给几乎所有公司的担保都给出最高的评分，现代资本市场的常态以及违约的风险并未被计入等等。中国债券市场尚未经历完整的信用周期，这意味着债券市场将来可能会出现波动。尽管中国国债比其他国债具有更高的收益率，但中国国债流动性要大大低于其他主要国家的国债。部分投资者选择在离岸市场投资中国债券以取得比本土市场更高的收益率，美国加息预期也让部分投资者对中国债券望而却步。

第四章
中国资本市场简介

一般来说,投资期限在一年以上的资金融通活动的市场就被称为资本市场。它包括一年以上的证券市场和银行信贷市场。但在我国一般认为资本市场就是指证券市场,包含股票市场、债券市场和投资基金市场这三个部分。

成熟的多层次资本市场,应当能够同时为大、中、小型企业提供融资平台和股份交易服务,在市场规模上,则体现为"金字塔"结构。我国的资本市场从1990年沪、深两市开办至今,已经形成了主板、中小板、创业板、三板(含新三板)市场、产权交易市场、股权交易市场等多种股份交易平台,具备了发展多层次资本市场的雏形。

一、股票市场

(一)主板市场

主板市场也称为一板市场,指传统意义上的证券市场(通常指股票市场),是一个国家或地区证券发行、上市及交易的主要场所。主板市场先于创业板市场产生,二者既相互区别又相互联系,是多层次资本市场的重要组成部分。相对创业板市场而言,主板市场是资本市场中最重要的组成部分,很大程度上能够反映经济发展状况,有"国民经济晴雨表"之称。主板市场对发行人的营业期限、股本大小、盈利水平、最低市值等方面的要求标准较高,上市企业多为大型成熟企业，具有较大的资本规模以及稳定的盈利能力。中国大陆的主板市场包括上交所和深交所两个市场。

图 4-1　上海证券交易所

一般而言，各国主要的证券交易所代表着国内主板主场。例如，美国全美证券交易所（AMEX）即为美国主板市场；我国的上交所和深交所即为我国的主板市场。证券市场按证券进入市场的顺序可以分为发行市场和交易市场。发行市场又称一级市场，交易市场也称为二级市场。这同主板市场、二板市场，以及三板市场完全不是一个概念。

（二）中小板市场

中小企业板——是深圳证券交易所为了鼓励自主创新，而专门设置的中小型公司聚集板块。板块内公司普遍具有收入增长快、盈利能力强、科技含量高的特点，而且股票流动性好，交易活跃，被视为中国未来的"纳斯达克"（NASDAQ）。

中小板就是相对于主板市场而言的，中国的主板市场包括深交所和上交所。有些企业的条件达不到主板市场的要求，所以只能在中小板市场上市，中小板市场是创业板的一种过渡。

（三）创业板市场

创业板 GEM（Growth Enterprises Market）是地位次于主板市场的二板证券市场，以 NASDAQ 市场为代表，在中国特指深圳创业板。在上市门槛、监管制度、信息披露、交易者条件、投资风险等方面和主板市场有较大区别。其目的主要是扶持中小企业，尤其是高成长性企业，为风险投资和创投企业建立正常的退出机制，为自主创新国家战略提供融资平台，为多层次的资本市场体系建设添砖加瓦。

　　创业板又称二板市场，即第二股票交易市场。在我国，主板指的是沪、深股票市场。创业板是指专为暂时无法在主板上市的中小企业和新兴公司提供融资途径和成长空间的证券交易市场，是对主板市场的重要补充，在资本市场有着重要的位置。创业板出现于20世纪70年代的美国，兴起于90年代，曾孵化出微软等一批世界500强企业的美国纳斯达克市场就具有代表性。到目前为止，有6000多家企业在纳斯达克上市，同时也有2000多家企业先后退市。可以说，创业板是一个门槛低、风险大、监管严格的股票市场，也是一个孵化科技型、成长型企业的摇篮。

（四）新三板市场

1."新三板"市场的形成

　　2001年7月16日中国证券业协会为解决原STAQ、NET系统挂牌公司的股份流通问题，开展了代办股份转让系统（即"老三板"），指证券公司以其自有或租用的业务设施，为非上市公司提供的股份转让服务。代办股份转让系统规模很小，股票来源基本是原NET和STAQ系统挂牌的不具备上市条件的公司。2001年年底，"水仙"成为中国第一家从主板退市的上市公司。为解决退市公司股份转让问题，2002年8月29日起退市公司纳入代办股份转让试点范围。可见，解决历史遗留问题是三板市场创建之初所承担的重要任务。而三板开设的另一个目的是承接主板的退市股票，在特定时期起到化解退市风险的作用，并弥补证券市场的结构性缺陷。

　　为了改变场外交易的落后局面，同时为更多的高科技成长型企业提供股份转让场所，2006年1月，中关村科技园区非上市股份有限公司股份报价转让系统（即"新三板"）正式推出，成为国内主板、中小板及创业板市场的重要补充。2006年10月25日，中科软和北京时代正式公告定向增资，这标志着"新三板"融资大门正式打开。2010年，与创业板发行"三高"的火爆局面相呼应的是，"新三板"定向增发迎来井喷。到2013年，证监会宣布国务院批准"新三板"扩容，同时全国中小企业股份转让系统公司（即"新三板公司"）正式成立。2013年2月"新三板"公司出台了业务规则及配套文件，至此除了做市商制度以外，"新三板"的制度规则基本完备。

2. "新三板"的作用

"新三板"是经国务院批准，依据证券法设立的全国性证券交易场所，主要为创新型、创业型、成长型中小微企业发展服务。对非上市公司来说：一是成为企业融资的平台："新三板"的存在，使得高新技术企业的融资不再局限于银行贷款和政府补助，更多的股权投资基金将会因为有了"新三板"的制度保障而主动投资；二是提高公司治理水平：依照"新三板"规则，园区公司一旦准备登录"新三板"，就必须在专业机构的指导下先进行股权改革，明晰公司的股权结构和高层职责。同时，"新三板"对挂牌公司的信息披露要求比照上市公司进行设置，很好地促进了企业的规范管理和健康发展，增强了企业的发展后劲。

对投资者来说：一是为价值投资提供平台："新三板"的存在，使得价值投资成为可能。二是通过监管降低股权投资风险："新三板"制度的确立，使得挂牌公司的股权投融资行为被纳入交易系统，同时受到主办券商的督导和证券业协会的监管。三是成为私募股权基金退出的新方式：股份报价转让系统的搭建，对于投资"新三板"挂牌公司的私募股权基金来说，成为一种资本退出的新方式，挂牌企业也因此成为私募股权基金的另一投资热点。

（五）区域性股权交易市场、证券公司主导的柜台交易市场

1. 区域性股权交易市场

区域性股权交易市场是我国多层次资本市场的重要组成部分。究其本质而言，区域股权市场是金融市场中的私募市场，该市场的活动主要是股权、债券的转让和融资的资本行为，同时只为特定的区域服务。区域股权市场可以在中小型企业股权交易中起到促进作用，对企业中的资本进行创造，弥补了实体经济环节的薄弱，已成为资本市场发展的重要内容。

区域性股权交易市场的运作机制是主要通过"一个中心、两种资源、三类机构、四大板块"完成的。一个中心，指区域性股权交易中心是特定区域股权交易市场的重要平台。两种资源，指当前区域股权市场中未上市股份公司资源

及股权转托过程中具有需求的企业资源，这种资源可以在很大程度上提升企业的发展效益，是实现股权融资、债券融资、股权转让的前提。三类机构主要指区域股权市场中的会员机构，即推荐机构、战略合作机构、专业服务机构。上述三类机构相互促进、相互引导，形成了区域股权市场运作的基本核心。四大板块主要包括股权转让和融资、债券转让和融资、股权登记托管服务、金融创新业务。其中股权转让和融资为企业发展提供了基础，改善了企业的资本结构和股权组成；债权转让和融资通过对部分债券或债券产品的融资处理，为企业资本发展拓宽了渠道；股权登记托管服务依照非上市公司的股权状况对各项指标进行了托管、等级、变更、转让等控制，实现了企业管理内容的规范化；其他金融创新业务为企业带来了更多的发展机会，通过区域股权市场环境下的债券抵押及融资私募等完成了产品衍生。

2. 证券公司柜台交易市场

证券公司柜台交易，是指证券公司与特定交易对手方在集中交易场所之外进行的交易或为投资者在集中交易场所之外进行交易提供服务的行为；证券公司柜台交易的产品包括经国家有关部门或其授权机构批准、备案或认可的在集中交易场所之外发行或销售的基础金融产品和金融衍生产品。《证券公司柜台交易业务规范》所说的"柜台交易市场"与之前我们所提的"柜台交易市场"是有差别的。之前所说"柜台交易市场"主要是指做非上市公司股权的挂牌转让交易，而目前这个柜台交易市场主要是为券商自己或代销的金融产品提供流动性，柜台交易产品定位为私募产品，柜台交易市场建设初期配合资产管理业务创新，以销售和转让证券公司理财产品、代销金融产品为主。

在交易方式上，证券公司柜台交易业务主要是将以协议交易为主，同时未来会逐步尝试开展报价交易或做市商交易机制。所谓协议交易，指的是交易双方双边报价、点对点的交易；而报价交易，则是指在柜台上进行公开的意向报价；做市商交易，一般指的是发行产品的券商为投资者提供双边报价，比如券商资管发行的一款一年期的理财产品，不能赎回，在此期间，如果投资者急于用钱怎么办？券商通过按产品当时的净值进行双边报价，有意转让产品的投资者和接盘的投资者达成协议，前者获得资金，后者则继续持有存续期的产品，这些报价交易方式与银行间市场类似，都是场外市场的模式，只不过银行间市场目前主要以债券等固定收益类产品交易为主，而证券公司柜台交易市场现阶段以证券公司理财产品、代销金融产品为主。

证券公司柜台市场仅为非上市私募金融产品的报价转让平台，不同于交易所市场，具有以下特征：

第一，证券公司柜台交易市场明确定位于私募市场，是证券公司发行、转让、交易私募产品的平台。因此，柜台市场建设初期应高度重视风险控制，以风险相对较低的产品为主，采取非公开的转让模式。

第二，市场高度开放、转让方式灵活，可为投资者提供多样化甚至个性化的服务；转让功能与多样化投融资服务功能是柜台市场的主要功能定位，是以提供流动性为主要服务内容的平台，而非集多种功能于一体的交易所组织。

第三，柜台交易客户以机构客户为主，各证券公司制定了相应的柜台交易适当性管理制度，根据不同产品制定了不同的投资者准入标准，并通过建立客户分类和产品风险评级制度，实现不同风险偏好的客户和不同风险级别的产品之间的匹配。

第四，不采取会员制度，直接面向投资者提供转让服务，不设置经纪商，不建立会员制度；柜台交易业务将以协议交易为主，同时尝试开展报价交易或做市商交易机制，不进行竞价交易。

第五，在产品管理上只进行风险评估与控制，不设置其他准入条件。进入市场转让的产品由行业主管部门或其授权部门、单位进行审核批准，柜台市场只从风险上进行控制，凡适合柜台市场合格投资者认购的私募类金融产品均可进行柜台转让。

第六，对转让进行实时监控和管理，产品及发行主体、中介机构由监管部门及监管部门授权或要求的部门或单位进行监管，柜台市场根据监管部门要求进行配合和支持。柜台市场以提供转让服务为主，根据行业主管部门要求对转让行为进行监控，并定期向主管部门递交业务报告。

二、债券市场

目前的中国债券市场主要由银行间债券交易市场、沪深交易所债券市场及商业银行柜台债券交易市场组成。1997 年中国人民银行成立银行间债券交易市场,并要求全国的商业银行退出原来的交易所债券市场,因此中国银行间债券交易市场成了目前中国债券市场的最大组成部分,是当前中国债券市场的主体。从债券托管总量上来看,银行间市场的债券存量及债券交易量占了中国债券市场总量的百分之九十以上。沪深交易所债券市场是中国债券市场的重要构成部分,在沪深交易所债券市场有大量机构和个人投资者,活跃了我国债券市场。沪深交易所债券市场由两部分构成:一个是债券零售市场,在这个市场中实行集中撮合交易,二个是债券交易的批发市场,由大宗债券交易系统和固定收益交易平台构成。商业银行柜台债券交易市场属于场外债券交易市场,是债券零售市场,也可以说是银行间债券市场的衍生,不过参与债券交易的多是个人投资者和少部分机构客户。

经过几十年的发展,中国债券市场上目前已包含了十分丰富的金融产品种类,主要有国债、中国人民银行的票据、各地方政府债券、企业债券和短期融资券等债券品种。从债券期限上来讲,中国债券市场上不但有期限 3 个月的短期债券产品,也有期限长达 30 年、50 年的超长期债券产品。

(一) 境外机构参与银行间债券市场的最新状况

随着人民币国际化进程的加速,越来越多的海外地区争做人民币离岸中心。香港与境内的人民币流通渠道较为完善,凭借天然优势,成为境外人民币存量最大的城市和全球最大的人民币离岸市场。

随着 RQFII 试点范围的不断扩大以及离岸人民币市场的发展,更多不同类型的境外机构投资者有了进入我国债券市场的渠道。RQFII 的试点从香港延伸到新加坡、伦敦、德国、韩国,传统国际金融中心城市的离岸人民币市场建设也初具雏形,离岸人民币存款、离岸人民币债券发行以及基于人民币利率和汇率衍生的金融产品随之得到快速发展。境外机构投资者对于成为 QFII 以及

RQFII，或者以境外人民币参加行身份进入境内银行间债券市场，均表现出极大热情。尽管新增加的投资额度相对于庞大的债券市场存量依然微不足道，但却改变了市场中参与机构的交易行为预期，同时也增加了新的交易对手选项。未来，境外机构投资者数量的进一步增加和投资总额度的不断提高，将成为必然之势头。

截至 2014 年 9 月底，已有 125 家包括港澳清算行、境外参加行、境外保险机构、RQFII 和 QFII 等境外机构获准进入银行间债券市场，境外机构投资者数量较 2013 年底增长 23%。其中共有 87 家境外参加行以及清算行，投资者数量较去年年底增长近 9%；共有 30 家 RQFII 已经获得人民银行批复，比 2013 年底增加了 43%；8 家 QFII 成为首批参与到银行间债券市场的合格境外机构投资者。

（二）境外机构参与中国债券市场的特点

从境外机构投资债券的角度看，截止到 2014 年 9 月境外机构持有的债券总面额占全市场债券持有量比重仅为 1.74% 左右，即便是境外机构接受程度最高的国债，占比也仅为 2.42% 左右。虽然境外机构投资者所持有的各种债券占全部银行间债券市场的份额不断增大，但从存量看对整个债券市场影响较小，但由于诸如被限定只能参与二级市场交易、额度集中批复和开户时间较为一致导致建仓期重叠等因素，导致在一些境外机构集中建仓的月份，银行间债券市场深度不足的问题会被放大，境外机构的投资方向成为影响当时市场的重要标杆。

另一个显著的特点，就是境外机构的投资偏好较为一致，由于对中国信用市场缺乏足够的了解，境外机构普遍将国债和政策性金融债作为首选的投资工具。

不过，随着我国信用债市场的不断规范以及信用评级的不断发展，短期融资券和中期票据在内的银行间市场主流的信用产品已逐渐成为部分境外机构的投资标的。除境外央行出于自身投资指引的严格控制导致其对信用产品很少触及之外，其他境外机构对于信用类产品越发表现出了浓厚的兴趣。值得一提的是，由于 RQFII 率先在香港试点，包括新加坡在内的大中华圈内的投资者熟谙国内信用市场的发展。对于信用类债券,对短久期的短期融资券以及超短期融资券以及同时具有国际评级的高评级债券较为偏好。

第三个特点是增长潜力巨大。从境外机构在银行间债券市场的交易行为来看,近年来,境外机构的买入数量持续增长。2013年第三季度开始,得益于去年下半年以来持续走高的收益率以及监管当局审批速度的加快,买入数量呈现飞跃式的发展。2014年收益率震动较大,但境外机构参与银行间债券市场投资行为的活跃趋势并未改变。2014年更多境外机构的审批完成,境外机构投资银行间债券市场的增长潜力仍然非常巨大,并将持续保持高速的增长规模。

可以说,境外机构投资于境内银行间债券市场,是我国实体经济以及金融环境发展到一定程度的必然产物,也是我国不断推进人民币国际化的客观要求。我国实体经济发展规模不断增大,需要引入更多的资金投资于国内市场;我国跨境贸易的不断发展,跨境贸易人民币结算范围不断扩大,人民币跨境直接投资业务不断深化,海外投资者也迫切需要更多的人民币回流渠道。

三、金融衍生品市场

(一)金融衍生品

金融衍生品的概念和特征。金融衍生品至今没有一个统一的定义,从字面看,可以理解为,金融衍生品就是在如银行信贷、债券、股票等基础性金融产品的前提存下衍生出来的新的金融产品,主要包括远期外币或人民币外汇交易、期货交易和外币掉价交易等。无论哪一种金融衍生品,都具有以下特征:

虚拟性。金融衍生品的本身是没有价值的,它只是一种获得收益的凭证,它的价值由标的的资产价格决定,具有相对独立性。

杠杆性。保证金制度是金融衍生品交易共同采用的制度。金融衍生品市场在交易中,双方都要缴纳一定的保证金。交纳保证金后可以进行交易。所以这种交易具有杠杆效应。保证金的多少和杠杆效应成反比,而风险和杠杆效应成正比。

风险性。由于其高杠杆性因而风险集中。衍生品的虚拟性和未来的不可预知性使它的风险性增强。

契约性。金融衍生品是双方对未来交易的约定，该合约对交易者的未来权利和义务有明确性，并具有法律效力。

（二）我国金融衍生品市场现状

我国金融衍生产品的发展可以追溯到1992年6月认股权证交易第一次在沪深股市出现，之后相继出现了国债期货、外汇期货、股指期货等金融衍生品，但是这些产品在1996年前后因违规操作和需求不足等原因停止交易。经过了20世纪90年代的早期实践和之后的严肃整改，在中国加入WTO之后，随着中国金融市场逐渐开放，汇改的实施，以及利率市场化的逐步加深，中国金融衍生品市场的建设也重新回到正轨。

在人民币外汇类金融衍生产品方面，2005年8月15日银行间市场正式推出了远期人民币外汇交易业务，2006年4月人民币与外币掉期业务银行间外汇市场正式推出，并在2007年末将货币掉期业务扩大到5个币种。2011年3月，在银行对客户市场推出人民币外汇货币掉期业务，完善货币掉期市场结构。同年4月在银行对客户市场和银行间外汇市场推出人民币对外汇期权业务，进一步丰富外汇市场产品。此外，利率衍生品市场也逐渐形成。2005年6月，工商银行与兴业银行达成了首笔债券远期交易。2006年3月，人民币利率互换登上历史舞台。2007年10月，远期利率协议正式开始启动。期货市场从1990年10月12日在中国郑州粮食批发市场开始，经历了初期发展，清理整顿和逐步规范三个阶段已经发展初具规模，现在我国共有四个期货交易所，分别是大连商品交易所、郑州商品交易所、上海期货交易所和中国金融期货交易所。

截至2013年初，中国金融衍生工具在21世纪特别是2005年后有了快速发展，品种进一步得到丰富。从人民币金融衍生产品的种类来看，利率类衍生产品有债券远期、利率互换和远期利率协议；外汇类衍生产品有外汇远期、外汇和货币掉期以及外汇期权，股权类衍生产品有认股权证等；信用类衍生产品有银行间市场信用风险缓释工具（CRM）；期货四大交易所种类总计达到32种。

此外还有众多包含了挂钩于利率、汇率、股票或股指、信用、商品或商品指数的结构性衍生产品的理财产品。

从交易规模上看，虽然在2008年席卷全球的金融危机对我国金融衍生产品有一定影响，但是在2009年后还是表现出来一定的活力，人民币外汇和货币掉期和利率互换等金融衍生品交易规模一直在保持高速稳健增长。以人民币外汇类金融衍生工具为例，银行间外汇远期市场成交量为886亿美元；银行间外汇与货币掉期业务一枝独大，累计成交量为25000亿美元，比上一年增加42.5%，占人民币外汇类衍生产品市场的份额为96.4%；银行间外汇期权市场交易累计成交名义本金达到33亿美元，同比增长2.3倍。而在人民币利率类衍生产品市场，2012年，人民币利率互换交易名义本金总额为29021亿元，同比增长8.45%。

（三）国内金融衍生品市场的缺陷

1. 金融衍生品的品种少

国际金融市场上的金融衍生品包括期货、汇率、股票期权、利率远期合约等；而国内金融市场的衍生品品种和数量却不多，例如上海证券交易所只有可转换债券和权证两种金融衍生品。品种不足阻碍了我国金融衍生品的领域扩展和投资规模扩大。人民币衍生品市场不够活跃，衍生品的参与者不够广泛，也制约了我国金融衍生品市场的发展。

金融衍生品在设计方面存在缺陷。与国外金融衍生品市场相比，我国为客户定做的衍生品同质性较高，这就导致在实际应用中出现了多种产品共存，但没有转移风险反而使风险扩大的情况。

2. 金融衍生品的监管主体分散

理论上说，金融衍生品的监管应该是由政府、行业协会和交易所三者共同建立的三级监管系统。但由于我国刚开始设立衍生品市场时就没有明确监管部门的责任，所以直到现在也没有形成一个健全的监管体系。各金融机构都从自身角度出发对金融衍生品进行管理，监管主体的分散性导致了政策方法的不协调、不稳定，从而使监管效率低下。

3. 金融衍生品监管的法律法规体系不完备

目前，我国在金融衍生品方面的立法相对滞后。首先，从发展历史来看，当前与金融衍生品相关的法律法规都是各监管机构根据具体的金融衍生品制定的，缺乏统一的监管法规来完善。金融衍生品的跨领域性风险使得在出现具体问题时缺乏相应的法律保障。其次，在目前的法律法规中，限制性条文居多，鼓励性法律较少，虽然这些限制性法令对防止金融风险的扩大蔓延有积极作用，但同时也制约了衍生品市场的扩大和发展。

4. 市场均衡价格缺失

我国的金融衍生品市场目前还处于初级阶段，大多数金融衍生品的价格与市场均衡价格相差很大。金融衍生品的价格与基础性金融产品的价格有密切联系，再加上我国对金融价格和外汇管制很严，所以国家政策很大程度上主导了金融衍生品的价格。而且，人民币在目前资本项目下无法实现自由兑换，这就导致了衍生品的价格不是由市场控制的价格。两者之间的差价成为投机者争夺的关键，一定程度上增加了金融风险。

5. 信息披露的公开性和透明度不够

对于参与者来说，准确的信息是做出正确判断的前提，因此，金融市场必须具备一套完备的信息披露制度。我国现在的信息披露缺乏公开性和透明度，不能真实地反映金融衍生品的市场状况，所以无法使投资者对市场做出理性的判断和预期，对我国金融衍生品交易的发展产生了负面影响。而且，信息的透明和公开可以减少投资者的投资风险，但错误的信息将导致对预期的错误判断，从而产生严重的损失甚至危害国家金融体系。

6. 市场参与者的素质不高

金融市场的参与者是个人或机构。目前，我国金融衍生品市场的参与者素质普遍偏低，对金融衍生品的预期判断缺乏相应的理论知识和理性的判断，盲目的投资和跟风行为加剧了我国金融衍生品市场的不稳定和风险性。

【案例】中国股市"第一"回顾

第一家证券交易所——上海证券交易所

1990年12月19日,经国务院授权、中国人民银行批准,上海证券交易所正式成立。这是中华人民共和国成立以来在大陆开业的第一家证券交易所。

第一只公开发行股票——飞乐音响

1984年11月18日,飞乐音响向社会发行1万股,成为新中国第一只公开发行的股票。初始发行面值50元,社会法人股0.3万股,内部职工股0.7万股,总股份1万股,股份总额50万元。

第一个证券交易柜台——静安证券业务部

1986年9月26日,第一个证券柜台交易点在当时工行上海信托投资公司静安分公司成立。小小的柜台交易被评为"1986年全国十大经济新闻"之一。

第一个大户室——申银证券上海大户室

1990年12月19日,申银证券公司开设上海第一个大户室,出现了中国第一代个人证券投资大户。原上海申银证券公司和原上海万国证券公司于1996年7月16日合并成申银万国证券股份有限公司。

第一家亏损公司：一汽金杯

"金杯"是沪市除浙江凤凰外最早上市的异地股，但自1994年起，由于产品无法适销对路，国产化水平上不去，投入产出的效率不高，公司业绩不断大幅下滑，1995年净利润出现2.54亿元亏损。

第一只退市的股票——PT水仙

2001年4月23日中国证券发展史上写下了一件值得纪念的大事："PT水仙"股票终止上市，成为我国证券市场上第一只被摘牌的股票。

四、Q&A

（一）境外投资者进入中国资本市场可供参考的法规文件有哪些？

答：随着股权分置改革基本完成，《外国投资者对上市公司战略投资管理办法》《关于外国战略投资者开立 A 股证券账户等有关问题的通知》《关于外国投资者并购境内企业的规定》等相关法规的陆续出台，为通过资本市场引进境外投资者提供进一步法律支持。

（二）境外战略投资者进入中国资本市场的路径有哪些？

答：在股权分置改革之前，外资并购上市公司的方式主要为场外协议收购非流通股、间接收购（如控股上市公司大股东）等方式。随着股权分置改革的基本完成，境外战略投资者可通过定向增发、场内协议转让、要约收购、发行定向可转换债券进入中国资本市场。

（三）外国人如何在中国开立股票账户？

答：据现在的相关规定，外国人不可以在中国直接开户买 A 股，但他们可以买 B 股。不过外国人可以通过购买进入中国的 QFII 公司的基金，QFII 公司用募集的资金购买 A 股，这种曲线的方式购买 A 股。很多大的国际投行金融机构都有中国 QFII 的基金产品。

第五章
中国金融调控和金融监管体系

金融监管涉及的内容广泛而全面,它涵盖了丰富的理论知识和实践知识,并随着时间的推移而日益走向科学化和规范化,深入研究金融监管体制的理论知识,有助于为中国金融监管体制改革的发展方向提供理论依据。

一、中国金融监管历史

第一阶段,计划经济管理体制(1949—1978)

从 1949 年新中国成立到 1978 年开始实行改革开放政策之前,中国实行严格的计划经济管理体制,当时中国几乎没有金融市场,一切信用归银行。并且在相当长的时间里,中国只有一家银行即中国人民银行,它既从事信贷业务又有金融监管的职能,当时可谓是集中统一的金融监管体制。"大一统金融"虽然具有高度的计划性,但是它作为在特殊历史时期的存在,对当时的经济发展是发挥了极为重要的推动作用。

第二阶段,中国人民银行成为复合型央行(1978—1982)

这一阶段中国相继建立四大国有商业银行、中国人民保险公司、中国国际信托投资公司等金融机构,并为规范其经营行为出台了一些行政性规章制度。中国人民银行作为复合型央行,既承担制定货币政策的职能,也经营商业银行业务,同时还负责全国金融机构的监管工作。其金融监管的主要重点是:配合监督、检查金融机构执行国家金融政策、业务分工和规章制度情况,并打击金融投机和金融犯罪。在此期间，金融监管更多地采取行政监管，而专业性的监管手段相对弱化，严格来说，中国人民银行并没有真正履行金融监管职能。

第三阶段，中国人民银行金融监管体制（1982—1992）

1983年9月中国人民银行成为独立的中央银行，金融监管职责开始专门化，这标志着中国中央银行金融监管模式的确立。但是这一阶段，中国仍处于计划经济体制向市场经济体制转化的初期，对金融机构的市场化监管还不明显，中国人民银行的监管手段主要依托于行政体制和权力，依据行政性规章制度。而且由于中国金融监管机构的行政机关，对金融监管存在过多行政干预，金融监管权力弱化，使得这一时期的金融监管体制与市场经济发展的内在要求并不匹配。这种监管体制仍然带有行政管制特征，而不是由明确的法律授权确立的。

第四阶段，一行三会分业经营监管格局（1993—2015）

1993年之后，国务院公布的《关于金融体制改革的决定》为分业监管体制的形成呈奠定了基础，提出要转换央行的职能，强化金融监管，根据业务不同对金融机构进行分别管理，也即是分业监管。1998年，中国证券监督管理委员会和中国保险监督管理委员会相继从中国人民银行分离，分别负责证券、期货市场和保险业的监管，2003年，中国银行业监督管理委员会挂牌成立，负责对银行业金融机构的独立监管，不过中国人民银行仍然保持对货币市场、反洗钱、征信体系等方面的金融监管，与之前成立的中国证券监督管理委员会、中国保险监督管理委员会一起，标志着中国现行分业监管体制的正式形成，实际上金融监管由"大一统"转化为"四分天下"的局面。这一格局的形成，有利于加强对银行和新生的证券和保险行业的专业化管理，有利于防止在我国金融业管理水平不高的阶段因混业经营而产生金融风险[1]。

二、中国金融监管现状

（一）金融监管的必要性

对于金融监管的必要性理论，目前占主流的主要有两大体系：金融脆弱说

---

[1] 中国金融监管体制改革——邓明辉。

和公共利益说,也有学者称之为金融市场失灵论和金融社会崩溃市场论,但不论如何,它们都是建立在新古典微观经济学理论基础之上的。

1. 金融脆弱说

该理论主要从金融系统内部的不稳定性,说明了金融监管的必要性。由于银行业较高的杠杆率,资产又多配置给不透明的、非流动的、比较困难的市场,因而在存款人与银行之间信息严重不对称的情况下,加剧了公众预期的不确定性。并且,银行之间的拆借及其支付系统使它们的财务更紧密地缠绕在一起,使得银行的支付困难产生传染效应,即一家银行对另一家银行的违约会影响到该银行承担另一家银行的责任,从而使任何家银行的困难甚至破产都会很快传播到其他银行。另外,银行经营失败涉及的利益相关者众多,发生较快,所以银行业的确存在着较高的脆弱性和传染性,一旦金融恐慌引发挤兑,很容易出现连锁的"技术性破产"。

2. 公共利益说

公共利益说认为,金融市场同样存在失灵,从而导致金融资源的配置不能实现"帕累托最优",金融监管作为一种公共产品,是一种降低或消除市场失灵的手段。金融市场失灵主要表现在自然垄断、外部效应和信息不对称等方面。

(1) 自然垄断。规模经济可能存在于银行业,规模越大,则成本越低,收益越高。这意味着它具有一定的自然垄断倾向。金融部门的垄断可能造成价格歧视、寻租等有损资源配置效率和消费者利益的不良现象,对社会产生负面影响;会降低金融业的服务质量和有效产出,造成社会福利的损失。所以,应该通过监管消除垄断。

(2) 外部效应。外部效应是指提供一种产品或劳务的社会费用(或利益)和私人费用(或所得)之间的偏差。在金融中介过程中存在风险与收益的外部性,存在监督、选择信贷的外部性,存在金融混乱的外部性。尤其是银行业作为一个特殊行业,其破产的社会成本明显地高于银行自身的成本。并且,个别银行的破产因多米诺骨牌效应,有可能导致整个银行系统的崩溃而引发金融危机,从而需要政府监管来消除这些外部性,防止多米诺骨牌效应的发生。

（3）信息的不完全和不对称。银行等中介机构的存在，有效地解决了信用过程中授信主体之间信息严重不对称的问题，能够同时沟通两类人或企业（存款人和贷款人）的资产组合偏好。如果在金融市场上，信息是完全的，则资金盈余者可以判断潜在的借款人是否值得信任、他们将资金投入运作后是否能产生预期的效益、到期归还本息是否有保障等。但在现实运行中，金融市场的表现则是一个信息不对称、不完全的市场，形成了存款人与银行、银行与贷款人之间的信息不对称，由此产生了"柠檬问题"，即金融市场中的逆向选择与道德风险问题，进而造成金融市场失灵。信息不对称程度越大，逆向选择与道德风险问题就越严重，市场失灵也就越明显。不完全信息的第二个结果是，价格体系不再有效地传递有用信息，从而引起市场参与者较高的信息成本，无法实现信息效率市场的均衡，造成金融市场的低效率。不完全信息引起金融市场失灵的第三个重要方面是信息具有公共产品的性质。因此，为了解决对金融中介机构的"监视"，只能由没有私利的政府来提供金融监管这种公共产品，保证金融市场的健康与安全。

（二）中国金融监管体系（一行三会）

1. 金融监管定义

所谓金融监管，是政府通过特定的机构（如中央银行）对金融交易行为主体进行的某种制定或规定。金融监管的本质上是一种具有特定内涵和特征的政府规制行为。

金融监管也有狭义和广义之分。狭义上的金融监管是指央行或其他金融监管当局依据国家法律法规的授权对整个金融业，包括金融机构以及金融机构在金融市场上所有的业务活动，实施的监督管理；广义上的金融监管是在狭义的金融监管之外，另外包括了金融机构内部的控制与稽核，同业自律性组织的监管，还有社会中介组织的监管等。

2. 监管体系类型

从国际范围来看，由于各国经济、社会、历史与传统、文化等方面的不同，各国采取了不同的金融监管体制，它既没有统一的模式，也不可能是一成不变的，根据不同的划分标准，金融监管体制有着不同的分类。根据金融监管主体权力的集中程度以及分配机构和层次，金融监管体制大体可分为以下三类。

（1）单元单头体制

单线单头体制也就是中央集权体制，是指从中央到地方仅由单一的金融监管机构统一负责监管各类金融机构，机构集中进行监管。这类模式的代表性国家如英国。大部分发展中国家也采取这种金融监管体制。

（2）单元多头体制

这里的"单线"是指金融监管的权力集中于中央，即将全国的金融监管权集中于中央。中央一级监管机构的数目没有统一规定，但都是由两家或两家以上的机构共同负责，地方则没有独立的权力。德国、日本等国均属于这种体制。

（3）双线多头体制

"双线"是指金融监管的权力集中于中央和地方两级政府，它们都对金融机构有监管权（双线），同时，每一级又由若干机构共同类行使监管职能（多头）。美国和加拿大等联邦制国家多实行这种监管体制。

上述三种体制类型，越往后其中央的金融监管权力越小，而地方的金融监管权力越大。

在混业经营下，金融创新活动模糊了不同金融机构提供的产品和服务的界限，不同金融机构的业务互相交叉、功能趋于一致，机构监管体制面临着各金融机构的不公平竞争、监管套利、监管资源浪费以及存在监管漏洞等诸多问题，因而更适用功能监管。为适应金融业务综合化发展趋势，同时避免功能监管在整体监管方面的缺陷，综合监管应运而生，由于混业经营的发展，银行、证券和保险三大金融服务合并在单一的金融机构中经营的趋势明显，对这些金融集团的监管必须在合并的基础上进行，实现有效并表监管，从而有利于管理和控制整个金融体系的风险。金融危机的爆发使金融消费者保护与审慎监管目标间的内在冲突问题充分暴露，也使各国监管当局普遍意识到，只关注金融机构的利益诉求而忽视对消费者利益的切实保护，会破坏金融业赖以发展的基础，影响到金融体系的稳定性。

3. 目前中国监管的现状

我国目前的金融监管体系属于单元多头监管体制。监管权限高度集中于中央政府，但在中央一级成立多个监管机构对不同的金融机构实施监管，形成了我国分业监管的主要格局。在现行"一行三会"监管模式下，人民银行主要负责制定和实行货币政策，维护金融稳定；银监会负责监管银行、金融资产管理公司、信托投资公司和其他存款类金融机构；证监会负责监管证券期货经营机构、证券投资基金管理公司、证券登记清算公司、期货清算机构和证券期货投资咨询机构；保监会负责监管境内保险机构及非保险机构在境外设立的保险机构。

4. 中国金融监管体系

"一行三会"是我国金融调控与监管体系的主要组成部分。"一行三会"是对中国人民银行、中国银行业监督管理委员会、中国证券监督管理委员会、中国保险监督管理委员会这四家金融管理和监督部门的简称，它构成了中国金融业分业监管的格局。

中国人民银行（宏观调控）

中国人民银行为国务院组成部门，是中华人民共和国的中央银行，是在国务院领导下制定和执行货币政策、维护金融稳定、提供金融服务的宏观调控部门。

银监会、证监会和保监会（行业监管）

中国银行业监督管理委员会（简称银监会）为国务院直属正部级事业单位。根据国务院授权，统一监督管理银行、金融资产管理公司、信托投资公司及其他存款类金融机构，维护银行业的合法、稳健运行。

中国证券监督管理委员会（简称证监会）为国务院直属正部级事业单位，依照法律、法规和国务院授权，统一监督管理全国证券期货市场，维护证券期货市场秩序，保障其合法运行。

中国保险监督管理委员会（简称保监会）为国务院直属正部级事业单位。根据国务院授权，履行行政管理职能，依照法律、法规统一监督管理全国保险市场，维护保险业的合法、稳健运行[1]。

---

[1] 中国人民银行：《金融知识国民读本》，北京，中国金融出版社，2014

第五章
中国金融调控和金融监管体系

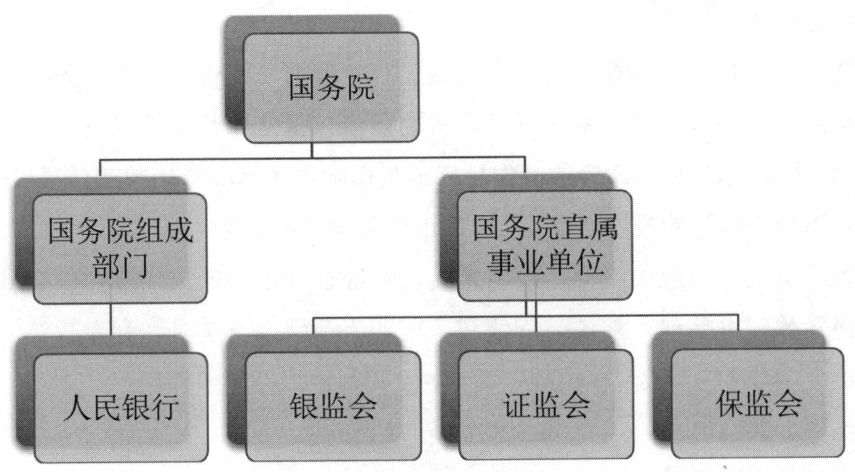

图 5-1　中国金融监管体系

（1）我国的中央银行——中国人民银行

中国人民银行是中华人民共和国的中央银行，主要职能为制定和执行货币政策、维护金融稳定、提供金融服务。

制定和执行货币政策

货币政策是人民银行运用货币政策工具，调节货币供求以实现宏观经济调控目标的策略和方针的总称。货币政策的要素包括货币政策的最终目标、货币政策的中间目标、货币政策的操作目标、货币政策工具和货币政策传导机制。

我国货币政策的最终目标是：维护币值稳定，并以此促进经济增长。

为了实现货币政策目标，中国人民银行综合使用公开市场操作、存款准备金、再贷款与再贴现、常备借贷便利、短期流动性调节工具、利率政策等多种工具组合，同时健全宏观审慎政策框架，发挥其逆周期调节作用。

维护金融稳定

金融是现代经济的核心，金融市场一旦出现动荡，整个经济和社会都会大受影响。历史上，股灾、银行倒闭、金融危机屡见不鲜，而金融危机的后果往往是经济发展停滞和社会动荡。

中国人民银行作为我国的中央银行，承担着防范和化解系统性金融风险、维护国家金融稳定的重要职责。中国人民银行通过监测和评估金融风险、处置金融领域风险隐患、推进金融业改革发展、强化金融安全网建设、承担最后贷款人职能，保持金融体系流动性，确保金融体系平稳运行。中国人民银行综合运用利率和汇率政策、公开市场操作、资本账户管理、再贷款和支付体系支持等工具，以及宏观审慎管理、监管协调机制、金融消费权益保护等制度安排，为金融机构和市场的稳健运行创造良好环境，维护金融体系的整体稳定。

提供金融服务

在许多人眼里，中国人民银行只是一个制定和实施货币政策、维护金融稳定的国家机关，似乎与人们的日常生活离得很远。事实却不是这样，中国人民银行也为全社会提供金融服务，而且这些服务与老百姓的生活息息相关。

人们平常普遍使用的人民币，就是中国人民银行印制和发行的。您在不同银行间进行的每一笔转账或汇款，都要通过中国人民银行建设的清算系统。您去商业银行申请贷款时，也需要借助中国人民银行建立的征信系统提供信用证明。

中国人民银行提供的金融服务还远不止这些，它还经理国库，管理国家外汇储备和黄金储备，统计金融数据，组织反洗钱工作……您能够享受方便快捷的金融服务,这背后就有中央银行的重大贡献。

(2)中国银行监管委员会

银行业金融机构主要包括银行、金融资产管理公司、信托投资公司及其他存款类金融机构。由于中国是间接融资为主的国家,加上居民储蓄率居高不下的特点,有效监督管理银行业金融机构对中国金融起到至关重要的作用。

中国银监会主要履行了一般性监管的职责,其主要目的就是统一监督管理银行、金融资产管理公司、信托投资公司及其他存款类金融机构,维护银行业的合法、稳健运行。(银行业监管的方式主要由三部分组成:监管当局的一般性监管、存款保险制度和最后贷款人制度。在中国最后贷款人制度由中国人民银行执行,存款保险制度尚未建立完善,而监管当局的一般性监管由银监会执行。)

市场准入监管

银行是一个高利润行业,因而人们投资办银行的积极性很高。但银行又是一个高风险行业,其负债经营的特性决定了银行必须将"安全性"放在首要位置。因为银行的破产倒闭将使存款人遭受损失,并导致"多米诺骨牌效应",引发一系列连锁反应。为了防范风险,各国和地区在加强对银行监管的同时,往往对银行的市场准入，尤其是对民间资本办银行加以严格限制。

市场准入，即对银行业金融机构的开业申请加以审查，将不合格的申请者挡在银行业大门之外的监管措施，它是保证银行业稳定的第一道防线。因此，银监会的主要职责包括依照法律、行政法规制定并发布对银行业金融机构及其业务活动监督管理的规章、规则；对银行业金融机构的董事和高级管理人员实行任职资格管理。

例如，2014年以来，银监会开展了首批民营银行试点工作，提出开展民营银行试点的框架性建议，获国务院同意，目前试点已取得阶段性成果。在市场准入实践中，民间资本主要通过发起设立、认购新股、受让股权、并购重组等方式进入银行业。2014年3月，银监会公布首批5家民营银行试点名单，正式启动民营银行试点工作，并遵循自主意愿、商业可持续原则，积极协同各发起主体完善筹建方案。

试点选择标准主要考虑五个因素：一是具有承担剩余风险的制度安排。二是具有办好银行的资质条件和抗风险能力。三是具有股东接受监管的协议条款。四是具有差异化的市场定位和特定战略。五是具有合法可行的恢复与处置计划。首批试点五家民营银行体现了服务中小微企业、"三农"和社区的经营特色。其中，天津金城银行坚持"公存公贷"，浙江网商银行坚持"小存小贷"，深圳前海微众银行坚持"个存小贷"，上海华瑞银行和温州民商银行则坚持"特定区域"经营模式。

2014年7月，银监会批准深圳前海微众银行、温州民商银行、天津金城银行筹建申请；9月，银监会批准上海华瑞银行、浙江网商银行筹建申请。其中，深圳前海微众银行、上海华瑞银行分别于2014年12月和2015年1月获批开业；温州民商银行和天津金城银行于2015年3月获批开业。

其意义在于改变银行业的市场竞争结构，强化银行业的市场化程度，培育具有现代管理体系的银行机构。民间资本发起设立中小型银行等金融机构，激发了民间资本参与金融服务也的积极性和创造性，是对金融资源的有力补充，有利于促进金融机构股权结构多元化，进一步提升金融机构的市场活力。

审定金融机构的业务范围

监管当局对银行业务活动范围的监管，是指金融机构一旦成立后，应按照许可的营业范围从事金融活动，不得越位。例如，《中华人民共和国商业银行法》规定商业银行可以经营下列部分或者全部业务：吸收公众存款；发放短期、中期和长期贷款；办理国内外结算；办理票据承兑与贴现；发行金融债券；代理发行、代理兑付、承销政府债券；买卖政府债券、金融债券；从事同业拆借；买卖、代理买卖外汇；从事银行卡业务；提供信用证服务及担保；代理收付款项及代理保险业务；提供保管箱服务；经国务院银行业监督管理机构批准的其他业务。经营范围由商业银行章程规定，报国务院银行业监督管理机构批准。商业银行经中国人民银行批准，可以经营结汇、售汇业务。

对金融机构经营过程中进行审计检查

对金融机构经营过程中的审计检查，主要包括现场监管和非现场监管。现场监管，是指监管当局对银行进行不事先通知的实地检查，以防银行因事先得知要检查而隐瞒真相。非现场监管，是指监管当局对银行业金融机构报送的各种经营管理和财务数据、报表和报告，运用一定的技术方法就银行的经营状况、风险管理状况等情况进行分析，以评价银行业金融机构的风险状况。两种监管有效结合，才能有效控制银行业风险。

对有问题金融机构的处理

由于金融风险的传染效应，单个金融机构的问题很可能引发系统性风险，对有问题金融机构的处理就特别重要。例如，中国银监会有权利对已经或者可能发生信用危机，严重影响存款人和其他客户合法权益的银行业金融机构实行接管或者促成机构重组；对有违法经营、经营管理不善等情形的银行业金融机构予以撤销。

（3）证监会

中国证监会为国务院直属正部级事业单位，依照法律、法规和国务院授权，统一监督管理全国证券期货市场，维护证券期货市场秩序，保障其合法运行。

从证券监管内容看，证监会对证券市场监管主要包括四个方面，包括对证券发行及上市的监管，对交易市场的监管，对上市公司的监管以及对证券经营机构的监管。

对证券发行及上市的监管

目前中国股票发行实行核准制，即证券的发行不仅要以真实状况的充分公开为条件，而且必须符合证券管理机构制定的若干适于发行的实质条件。符合条件的发行公司，经证券管理机关批准后方可取得发行资格，在证券市场上发行证券。核准制有利于新兴市场的健康发展，适合于证券市场不完善、投资服务机构的道德水准与业务水平不高、投资人缺乏经验与业务水平、缺少对信息的判断能力的地区。

核准制意味着监管方需要对新股发行公司进行辅导，建立严格信息披露制度并且符合发行条件，因此中国采用了保荐人制度，即由保荐人（券商）对发行人发行证券进行推荐和辅导，并核实公司发行文件中所载资料是否真实、准确、完整，协助发行人建立严格的信息披露制度，承担风险防范责任，并在公司上市后的规定时间内继续协助发行人建立规范的法人治理结构，督促公司遵守上市规定，完成招股计划书中的承诺，同时对上市公司的信息披露负有连带责任。

【案例】注册制改革

党的十八届三中全会《关于全面深化改革若干重大问题的决定》提出资本市场的改革任务之一，是推进股票发行注册制改革。2013年11月30日，证监会发布《关于进一步推进新股发行体制改革的意见》，标志着新股发行从核准制向注册制的过渡拉开序幕。

1998年《证券法》开始颁布实施，该法律明确宣布股票发行制度将实行核准制。在实行核准制的情况下出现以下弊端：第一，监管者代替投资者对股票进行价值判断并不准确。从监管的逻辑看，发行审批部门在新股发行过程中对拟上市公司递交的资料严格审核，其出发点是把不合格的公司拦在股票市场之外，把优秀的公司选拔出来并推荐给市场投资者。而市场实践表明，我国实施多年的发行核准制并没有把不好的公司拦在股票市场之外，相反，很多公司在发行股票之后经营业绩就每况愈下，也就是说，监管者无法替代投资者对股票进行价值判断。第二，滋生寻租行为，扭曲股票价格的形成机制。大量的垃圾股价值被严重高估，这些股票对新股的发行数量相当敏感，为了维护这些被高估的股价，就必然要控制新股发行的数量和节奏。结果是大量的公司无法通过股票市场来融资，而大量的储蓄没有合适的投资渠道，股市无法发挥它应有的配置资源功能。总之，这些弊端严重降低了资本市场效率。

注册制使得市场参与主体各自的责任归位，倒逼自我约束的加强，有利于完善资本市场投融资功能，降低企业融资成本，提高融资便利性，有利于促进直接融资市场的发展。

注册制是证券发行制度，是证券市场的一项基本规则，涉及市场各参与者，改革方案需循序渐进，政策的推出也尤为重要。第一，新股发行注册制同以往的和核准制相比主要是市场的作用更为重要，实际则是政府与市场的关系调整。注册制的核心是信息披露，发行人的依法与证券发行有关的各种信息的公开，保荐机构和中介机构同样承担更大的责任，而投资者也需要做出价值判断，自担风险。监管主体也需要从事前监管为重转为时候监管为重。第二，注册制的目的是更好地发挥市场的作用，然而本身的实现也要由市场来决定。一方面要以市场化程度较高、运作比较规范的市场和较完善的法律法规为保证；另一方面要求发行人和承销商等中介机构有较强的自律能力、投资者具备比较成熟的投资理念、管理层的市场化监管手段比较成熟等。然而，就目前的状况看，我国的资本市场距离这些标准还有不小的差距。第三，注册制改革需要立法先行，通过法律的约束形成更为诚信的市场运作环境，以及合理的投资者保护机制。

对交易市场的监管

对交易市场的监管包括证券交易所的信息公开制度、对操纵市场行为的监管、对欺诈客户行为的监管和对内幕交易行为的监管。

对上市公司的监管

对于上市公司的监管主要体现在信息披露监管。由于证券市场上信息不对称的天性，影响市场效率，因此信息披露显得尤为重要。信息披露是上市公司的法定义务，该制度有利于约束证券发行人的行为，促使其改善经营管理；有利于证券市场发行价格与交易价格的合理形成；有利于维护广大投资者的合法权益；有利于进行证券监督，提高证券市场效率。

信息披露监管即要求证券发行人对现实或潜在购买者提供有关交易证券的公开财务信息。包括：发行前披露，上市后的持续信息公开。例如，上市公司需要发布招股说明书与上市公告书、定期报告和临时报告。

对证券经营机构的监管

对证券经营机构的监管包括证券经营机构准入监管、对证券公司业务的核准和对证券公司日常监管。

（4）保监会

保险业是社会经济补偿制度的重要组成部分，为广泛的人民提供保障，对社会经济稳定负有很大的责任，然而其负债性的特性造成其有较高的经营风险，保险业的监管就显得极为重要。其次，保险业专业性要求对其进行专门监管。同时，中国保险业的发展相对滞后，监管保证其能与国际保险接轨，实现保险业的区域化、国际化经营发展。综上，保险业的监督管理显得尤为必要。

1998年11月18日，国务院批准设立中国保险监督管理委员会，专门负责保险监督管理职能。根据保险监管的内容，可以分为机构监管、业务监管、财务监管和偿付能力监管。

机构监管

机构监管一般包括保险市场的准入与退出以及保险公司的组织形式等。

保险企业在开业时不仅要有一般企业拥有的供经营用的资产,而且还必须拥有开业以后前期的应付巨灾或巨额风险的准备金,否则不能履行其合同义务。因此,没有一定的资本和准备金是不能经营保险业的。对资本金或准备金的要求,由于各个国家的国情不同,各国保险法对法定资本金最低数额的要求也不尽相同。

为了避免保险企业破产,以保障被保险人的合法权益,对经营不当、财务发生危机的保险企业,政府一般采取扶助政策,利用各种措施帮助其渡过难关,继续正常营业。但是,保险企业若违法经营或有重大失误,以致不得不破产时,政府便以监督者身份,令其停业或发布解散令,选派清算员,直接介入清算程序。其具体监管措施包括整顿、接管、解散与清算等。

保险人以何种组织形式进行经营，各个国家根据本国国情，有特别限定。例如美国规定的保险组织形式是股份有限公司和相互公司两种。英国除股份有限公司和相互保险社外，还允许劳合社采用个人保险组织形式。根据我国《保险法》和《公司法》的有关规定，保险公司应当采取股份有限公司和国有独资公司的形式。

业务监管

业务监管主要包括对业务范围、保险条款、保险费率和再保险等的监管。对业务范围的监管，是指政府通过法律或行政命令，规定保险企业所能经营的业务种类和范围。保单条款审定的内容，除了要求保单内容与形式统一，理论与实务并重，简单易行外，更重要的是要对保险合同当事人双方相互的权利和义务做出明确规定。保险费率的监管方式因保险业务的性质不同而不同。即使同一性质的保险业务，不同国家也有不同的做法。归纳起来，保险费率的监管方式大致可以分为强制费率、规章费率、事先核定费率、事先报批费率、事后报批费率和自由竞争费率等。我国关系社会公众利益的保险险种、依法实行强制保险的险种和新开发的人寿保险险种的保险费率，应当报保险监督管理机构审批，其他险种的费率由保险公司拟定，报主管机关备案。对再保险业务进行监督管理，有利于保险公司及时分散风险，保持经营稳定，有利于限制保险费外流，保护民族保险业的发展，在发展中国家和地区，一般都由政府出资成立官方专业再保险公司或开展半官方的政策性再保险业务。

财务监管

财务监管，主要是对保险公司资产负债情况进行监管，其中保险准备金的提取和资金运用成为财务监管中的重点。保险准备金是指保险人根据政府有关法律规定或业务特定需要，从保费收入或盈余中提存的一定数量的资金。政府对准备金的监管主要体现在提取准备金的种类和数额上，其内容因险种而异。一般地说，财产保险业务提存的准备金主要有未到期责任准备金、赔款准备金和特别准备金；人身保险业务提存的准备金主要有责任准备金、未到期保费准备金和特别准备金。资金运用是保险企业收入的一项重要来源，也是壮大和保证保险企业偿付能力的重要手段，保险资金运用应坚持投资的三原则——安全性、流动性和收益性，这是各国对保险企业资金运用进行监督管理的宗旨所在。

但由于各国经济体制和金融市场的发育状况的不同,对保险企业的资金运用的管制也就各有特点,一般监督管理的主要内容是资金运用的程度、范围,资金投向和比例限度等。

偿付能力监管

偿付能力监管,主要包括资本金要求、风险资本要求、保证金提取、信息指标体系建立、保险保障资金建立等一系列保证保险公司具有偿付能力的监管、是保险监管的核心内容。

保险企业的偿付能力一般是指保险企业对所承担的风险在发生超出正常年景的赔偿和给付数额时的经济补偿能力。偿付能力的监督管理是国家对保险市场监督管理的首要目标,也是其监督管理的核心内容。各国保险法对保险公司偿付能力标准的要求各有其特点。

三、Q&A

(一)沪港通的设计初衷是什么?

答:沪港通是党中央、国务院根据内地与香港资本市场发展战略需求作出的重大决策,是贯彻落实党的十八届三中全会决定和《国务院关于进一步促进资本市场健康发展的若干意见》的重大改革举措,是资本市场的一项重大制度创新。沪港通是充分发挥和尊重市场创新的结果。沪港通的构想来源于市场,根植于实践,是沪、港交易所敏锐把握两地资本市场需求、联合创新的成果,体现了两地资本市场合作的意愿,得到了两地市场各方的大力支持和积极响应。沪港通在制度设计上充分考虑了两地市场的实际,不改变两地市场现行规则,充分尊重对方市场的交易习惯,实行投资股票标的管理、额度控制和资金封闭运行,在我国资本项目尚未完全实现可兑换的情况下,开创了操作便利、风险可控、稳妥有序的跨境证券投资新模式。这种新的跨境投资模式,也推动两地监管机构完善跨境监管合作机制,加大跨境执法协查力度,共同构建适应开放型资本市场体系的监管制度。

沪港通是我国资本市场双向开放取得的重大突破。沪港通丰富了两地投资品种，优化了市场结构，拓展了市场的广度和深度，有利于巩固上海和香港两个金融中心的地位，增强我国资本市场的整体实力。沪港通为境外资金投资A股市场提供了便利，也为内地投资者投资香港股市提供了机会，有利于两地资本市场的共同繁荣发展。沪港通也为资本市场改革以及金融改革搭建了新的平台，用好这个平台，有利于推进资本市场全面深化改革，推动人民币国际化，便利跨境资本流动和金融交易可兑换程度。在各方的通力协作下，沪港通能够产生"一加一大于二"的效应。

（二）目前，中国银行业的存款保险制度一直未建立。市场最直观的感觉是，在一直存在的隐性全额担保制度中，银行存款并未出现较明显的风险损失。监管方推进存款保险制度对中国有哪些积极意义？

答：存款保险制度的建立将使我国金融体系更加完善，对整体的金融改革具有积极意义。第一，存款保险制度解决的了风险处置的问题，是利率市场化的前提条件。第二，存款保险促进银行业对内对外开放，增强了民间资本进入的信心，民营银行往往是中小型金融机构，在信用、规模和竞争中天然处于劣势地位，存款保险制度的建立有助于形成有效的竞争环境，为民营银行生存和发展创造有利条件。第三，存款保险制度的破题为银行业市场化退出机制的建立拉开了序幕，金融机构的市场化退出机制有赖于存款保险制度为问题银行的破产处置提供保障。第四，存款保险制度与银行监管机构和央行共同构成了金融安全网三大支柱，存款保险机构的存款可以防止银行挤兑和危机传染，减轻监管部门的工作压力和中央银行的救助压力，三者之间的协调配合将使我国金融安全网更加完善和牢固。

第六章
中国外汇管理体制

一、中国外汇管理体制历史沿革

中国在改革开放以前，实行高度集中的计划经济体制，由于外汇资源短缺，采取了严格的外汇管制。1978年实行改革开放后，中国对外汇管理体制进行改革，沿着逐步缩小指令性计划、培育市场机制的方向，稳步有序地由高度集中统一的外汇管理体制向与社会主义市场经济相适应的外汇管理体制转变。1996年12月中国实现了人民币经常项目可兑换，初步建立了适应社会主义市场经济的外汇管理体制。中华人民共和国成立以来，中国外汇管理体制大体经历了计划经济时期、经济转轨时期、社会主义市场经济体制初步建立时期和社会主义市场经济体制进一步完善时期四个阶段。

（一）计划经济体制下建立的高度集中统一的外汇管理体制（1949—1978年）

外汇集中计划管理。从中华人民共和国成立到改革开放之前，中国长期处于外汇短缺时代。在这一时期，由于较低的生产力水平和较弱的商品出口能力，致使中国外汇资金缺口很大，在组织进口物资及参与国际交往等方面都显得支付力量不足，更谈不上对外投资。

针对这种情况，中国对外汇实行高度集中的计划管理，统收统支，以应对外汇资源的短缺，确保有限的外汇资金的合理、恰当使用。经国务院授权，中国人民银行行使外汇管理职责，中国银行是中国唯一的外贸外汇专业银行。中国所有外汇收入都必须上缴国家,所有外汇支出都由计划分配。同时限制对外借款和外商来华直接投资,这一时期中国既无外债也无内债。国家每年制订外汇收支计划,"以收定支,以出定进",通过指令性计划和行政手段来保持外汇收支平衡,并且实行固定汇率制,人民币汇率只作为计划核算工具。

(二)经济转型时期的中国外汇管理体制(1979—1993年)

外汇管理体制改革起步。从1978年改革开放到1993年,为了适应经济改革发展和对外开放的需要,中国在外汇分配领域逐步引入市场机制,实行计划分配与市场调节并存的双轨制,在保留原有的计划收支制度的基础上,引入市场分配机制。

1979年中国成立国家外汇管理局,其主要职责是统一管理外汇,做好外汇收支的计划管理和检查监督。在汇率上,国家实行双重汇率制度,即官方汇率和外汇调剂市场汇率并存,为调节汇率逐步发挥作用奠定了基础。

同时,为鼓励企业出口创汇,并确保有限的外汇资源集中用于国民经济建设,国家实行外汇留成制度,即外汇由国家集中管理、统一平衡、保证重点的同时，适当留给创汇企业一定比例的外汇，以解决进口物资所需的资金。在此基础上，国家开始建立有形的外汇调剂市场。如果企业留成的外汇有多余，可通过这个市场卖给需要用汇的企业。至此，市场机制开始被引入外汇分配领域。

1985年11月，中国境内第一家外汇调剂中心在深圳经济特区成立。截至1993年底，总共121个外汇调剂中心在中国成立，其中18个为公开调剂市场。当时80%的中国进出口收付汇采用了外汇调剂市场价格结算。这反映出在外汇供求方面外汇调剂市场起到了重要的作用，也体现出当时中国外汇制度的改革适应了经济改革开放的需要。

为适应我国经济对外开放对金融服务的需要，国家及时地放松了银行外汇业务的准入，允许办理外汇结算业务的银行从原来中国银行一家扩大到工行、农行等其他商业银行。在引进外资方面，国家制定并且执行鼓励利用外资政策，放宽对外资使用的限制，鼓励外资进入中国，对进入中国的外资企业根据有关政策分别实行免税、低税、退税等一系列优惠政策。同时，允许境内居民个人持有外汇，允许其在银行开立外汇储蓄账户，并且发行了外汇兑换券。在资本管制方面，对资本对外输出给予限制。

总体而言，这一时期，中国外汇管理体制处于由计划体制开始向市场调节的转变过程，在原有的计划收支制度基础上，市场机制萌生并不断发育，对于促进吸引外资、鼓励出口创汇、支持国内经济建设发挥了积极作用。

（三）社会主义市场经济条件下的中国外汇管理体制初步建立（1994—2000年）

社会主义市场经济条件下的外汇管理体制框架初步确定。这一时期中国在抵御亚洲金融危机冲击的同时，进一步推进经常项目可兑换，初步构建与社会主义市场济相适应的外汇管理体制框架。

适应中国建设社会主义市场经济体制的要求，1994年中国对外汇管理体制进行了重大改革。主要是：取消外汇上缴和留成，实行银行结售汇制度；汇率并轨，实行以市场供求为基础的、单一的、有管理的浮动汇率；建立全国统一规范的银行间外汇市场；进一步放开人民币经常项目的限制条件，为实行人民币经常项目有条件可兑换奠定了基础；继续重申禁止境内外币计价、结算和流通，停止发行外汇兑换券并逐步退出流通。1996年12月，中国正式宣布接受《国际货币基金组织协定》第八条款，实现人民币经常项目完全可兑换，全部取消了所有经常性国际支付和转移的限制，初步确立了市场配置外汇资源的基础地位。这是中国融入世界市场经济进程的又一重要里程碑，在中国外汇管理体制改革历史上具有标志性意义。1997年，亚洲金融危机爆发，给中国经济社会持续健康发展和金融稳定带来巨大冲击。为防止危机进一步蔓延，保持国民经济持续健康发展，中国做出人民币不贬值的承诺，在保持人民币汇率稳定的同时，切实履行经常项目可兑换义务，把管理重点放在加强资本流出管制上，成功抵御了亚洲金融危机的冲击，赢得了国际社会的高度赞誉和肯定。

总体来看，这一阶段，中国初步确立了适合中国国情、与社会主义市场经济体制相适应的外汇管理体制框架，外汇供求的市场基础不断扩大，奠定了市场机制配置外汇资源的基础性地位。

（四）以市场调节为主的外汇管理体制进一步完善（2001—2015年）

市场调节为主的外汇管理体制进一步完善。这一阶段，顺应加入世贸组织和融入经济全球化的新形势，以简政放权和提高履职能力引领外汇管理转型。

2001年底，中国加入世界贸易组织，中国经济全球化加速，对外开放进一步推进，国际收支顺差继续增大，海外资金不断涌入，外汇形势发生根本性改变。同时，中国国内经济发展情况良好，综合国力进一步增强，国际影响力不断扩大，深化外汇管理体制改革的条件日渐成熟。适应改革开放和发展社会主义市场经济的要求，中国对外汇体制进一步改革。2005年7月21日，中国宣布进行人民币汇率形成机制改革，从单一盯住美元改为实行以市场供求为基础，参考一篮子货币进行调节、有管理的浮动汇率制度；货币兑换起始水平从8.2765元人民币/美元调整为8.11元人民币/美元。不断完善外汇市场建设，推出询价交易方式，人民币对外币远期、掉期、期权等避险工具，改进银行挂牌汇价等基础性制度安排，夯实汇率形成的微观基础。同时，实施一系列配套外汇管理政策，包括提高人民币资本项目可兑换程度，实现直接投资项下基本可兑换，推出合格境内机构投资者和合格境外机构投资者制度，取消所有跨境担保事前审批，允许跨国公司在集团内部开展外汇资金集中运营试点；扩大银行为客户办理远期结售汇业务和开办人民币与外币掉期交易；提高个人因私购汇指导性限额和简化手续凭证；调整银行挂牌汇率管理；并加强外汇政策的宣传和培训等。这些举措为改革开放新时期的企业、银行逐步适应市场汇率波动的变化创造了条件。

2009年以来，针对跨境资金流向复杂和规模增大、市场主体便利化需求不断增长的情况，中国加快外汇管理理念和方式的转变，重点从审批向监测分析转变，从事前监管向事后管理转变，从行为管理向主体管理转变，从"正面清单"向"负面清单"转变等，在守住风险底线的前提下，尽可能为市场主体对外贸易投资活动提供便利。

总体来看，这一阶段，外汇管理体制改革进一步深化，外汇管理的理念和方式加快转变，市场配置外汇资源的作用不断增强，对于促进外贸持续快速发展、引导资本有序双向流动、充分利用两个市场两种资源、服务实体经济发展等发挥了积极的作用。2010年6月19日汇改重启。2012年11月，为进一步深化直接投资外汇管理改革，简化行政审批程序，外汇局在全面梳理直接投资项下外汇管理法规的基础上，发布了《关于进一步改进和调整直接投资外汇管理政策的通知》，对直接投资外汇管理政策进行了重大调整，进一步促进投资贸易便利化，放松资本项目的外汇管制。

二、中国外汇管理体制发展现状

随着经济的发展和对外开放的扩大，中国的国际收支发生了巨大的变化，新中国成立初期到改革开放前，中国国际收支规模很小，外汇储备一直维持在较低水平。1978年，中国外汇储备仅有1.67亿美元。改革开放后，中国的外汇储备有了较大幅度的增加，外汇储备规模不断扩大，2014年中国外汇储备达38430亿美元。但是近年来外汇储备增幅放缓。2014年，剔除汇率、价格等非交易价值变动的影响，中国国际储备资产增加1178亿美元，同比少增73%。其中，外汇储备资产净增加 1188 亿美元，同比少增 73%；特别提款权和在国际货币基金组织的储备头寸净减少 10 亿美元。

从经常项目看，在过去的五年间，2010 年的经常账户差额最大，达到 16043 亿元人民币，2011 年的经常账户差额最小，为 8736 亿元人民币。人民币经常账户差额在 2014 年相较 2013 年有所提升，但是小于 2010 年的人民币经常账户差额。2014 年，经常项目顺差 2197 亿美元，同比增长 48%，与 GDP 之比为 2.1%，仍保持在国际公认合理水平之内。2014 年，中国经常项目收入 27992 亿美元，同比增长 5%；支出 25795 亿美元，同比增长 3%；顺差 2197 亿美元，同比增长 48%。货物贸易继续稳定增长，2014 年，按照国际收支统计口径，中国货物贸易顺差为 4760 亿美元，同比增长 32%。中国服务贸易逆差 1920 亿美元，同比增长 54%。收益逆差大幅收窄，经常转移逆差扩大。

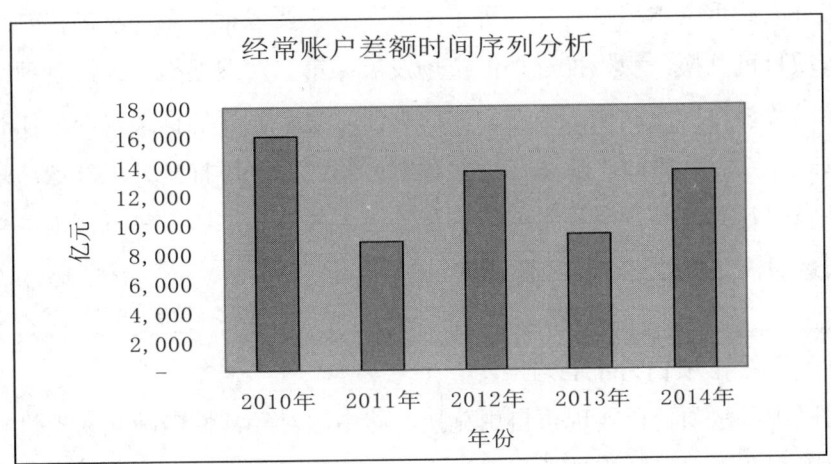

数据来源：国家外汇管理局网站

图6-1 中国经常账户差额时间序列分析

从资本项目看，2010年至2013年资本账户均为顺差，2011年达到最大，为352亿元，随后逐年减小。2014年，资本账户逆差，为-2亿元人民币。

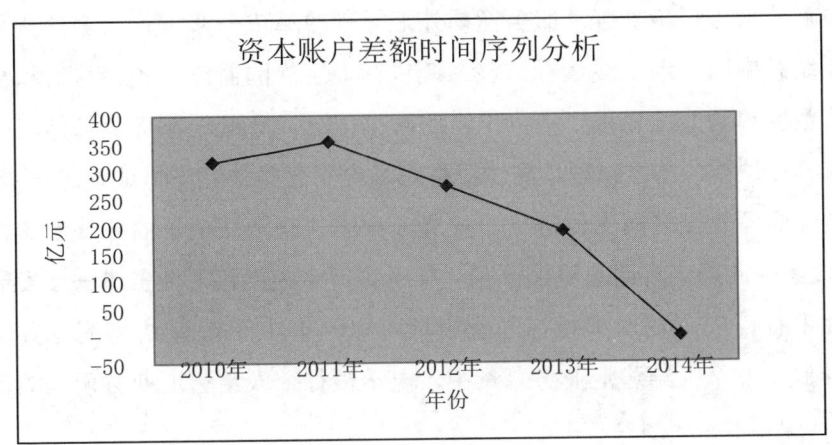

数据来源：国家外汇管理局网站

图6-2 中国资本账户差额时间序列分析

面对新的形势，以促进国际收支平衡为目标、以防范跨境资本冲击为前提，中国对外汇管理进行积极改革创新，主动适应国际收支和外汇形势的新情况，重点推进人民币资本项目可兑换等重大改革。主要包括：第一，加快推进人民币资本项目可兑换，积极推进外汇市场发展；第二，继续推动外汇管理简政放权，促进贸易投资便利化；第三，加快构建宏观审慎管理框架下的外债和资本流动管理体系，完善政策储备和应对预案；第四，严厉打击外汇领域违规经营和违法犯罪行为，保持对异常跨境资金流出入的高压态势；第五，推进外汇储备创新运用，完善外汇储备经营管理。

（一）经常项目外汇管理

人民币经常项目已实现可自由兑换，即中国对经常性国际交易支付和转移不加以限制，不实行歧视性的货币安排或多重货币制度，所有法规和规章都遵循这一原则。这有助于提供更加宽松的市场环境，吸引外商对华贸易和来华投资，同时推动中国的企业走向世界。

在人民币经常项目外汇管理方面：**货物贸易外汇管理改革成果进一步巩固。**货物贸易外汇监测系统进一步完善，专项监测指标增加，系统管理功能进一步丰富。企业负责人约谈制度进一步深入实施，风险提示函制度管理进一步完善，事中事后管理进一步加强。**服务贸易外汇管理改革进一步深化。**服务贸易外汇监测系统在中国各地上线运行。该系统包括多层次的监测、预警分析和全方位的分析数据等功能，提供了更为丰富的数据信息，有助于服务贸易外汇管理的后台监测、预警、主体管理。**支付机构跨境电子商务外汇支付试点进一步扩大。**跨境电子商务及互联网支付进一步发展，全国共有跨境电子商务外汇支付试点机构22家。四是个人用汇更加便利。**电子银行个人结售汇业务进一步发展。**中国农业银行、广东发展银行、平安银行可以开办电子银行结售汇业务，截至2014年底，在个人结售汇业务总量中，电子银行个人结售汇业务所占的比例已超过一半。

（二）资本项目外汇管理

人民币资本项目基本可兑换进一步加快，使用人民币的自由程度提高。实现人民币资本项目可自由兑换，更加方便国内个人跨境投资和境外机构投资者投资中国资本市场，有助于推动人民币国际化。

在人民币资本项目外汇管理方面：**资本项目重点领域改革进一步深化。**中国（上海）自由贸易试验区先行先试，外汇资本金结汇管理方式改革试点推行，跨境并购外汇管理改革深化。**资本项目外汇管理改革进一步推进。**通过对境内企业境外放款主体限制和放款条件限制的放宽，提高境内企业境外投资前期费用额度。推行外商投资企业外汇年检改革，取消强制审计要求等。**跨境证券投资业务管理进一步简化。**将人民币合格境外机构投资者（RQFII）有关投资额度调剂、资金延期汇入等由审批改为备案管理，以方便RQFII操作，促进投资额度有效使用。

（三）外汇储备经营管理

国家外汇管理局是中国外汇储备的管理机构，中国的外汇资产中绝大部分由外汇管理局经营管理，另外极小的一部分由交通银行和中国银行等商业银行代为管理。

目前，中国的外汇储备经营管理进一步完善。具体来说：第一，投资基准管理模式更加完善，投资策略和投资渠道更加多样化，各领域投资能力持续提升，取得了良好的经营效益；第二，外汇储备的应用更加多元化，外汇储备委托贷款平台不断完善，为服务实体经济发挥了积极、重要的作用；第三，风险管理进一步加强，风险管理的逻辑性、完整性和一致性不断提高，多维度风险评估体系更加完善；第四，机构管理能力不断提高，科学的人员管理体系更加完善，人才队伍更加专业化和精英化。

（四）金融衍生品领域的外汇管理法律法规体系基本建立

目前，我国初步建立起外汇管理的基本框架，修订完善并发布了《中华人民共和国外汇管理条例》《全国银行间外汇市场人民币对外汇期权交易规则》《境外直接投资外汇管理规定》《银行间外汇市场交易确认规则》等一系列法律、法规。注重从法律层面上引导外汇管理体制的各个方面，相较以前更加规范。但是，目前在外汇管理法律体系方面，还存在着一些问题，比如法规体系过于繁杂，立法层级效力低，某些法律法规效力不明的情况。

（五）改革外商投资企业外汇资本金结汇管理方式

外汇管理体制改革进一步深化，外商投资企业经营与资金运作更加便利。外商投资企业外汇资本金实行意愿结汇管理，企业可自由选择资本金结汇时机；明确外商投资企业资本金及其结汇资金的使用应符合外汇管理相关规定，对资本金使用实施负面清单管理；便利外商投资企业以结汇所得人民币资金开展境内股权投资；进一步规范结汇资金的支付管理，明确银行按照展业三原则承担真实性审核义务；明确和简化其他直接投资项下外汇账户资金结汇及使用管理；外汇局加强事中事后管理，进一步强化事后监管与违规查处。

（六）全国银行间外汇市场统一规范

目前，电子交易模式和互联网技术的不断发展，中国外汇市场通过采用新的交易方式来适应当今这个信息化时代。网络交易平台的建立为统一规范的全国银行间外汇市场的形成奠定了基础。市场竞争日益激烈，银行不断地推出新的金融产品来扩大自己的市场份额，其中就包括法律法规允许范围内的金融衍生产品。同时，交易方式和交易机制也在进一步创新，这大大提升了市场参与主体的参与积极性，同时有利于市场的多元化。2006年，全国银行间外汇市场引入了新的制度，比如国际通行的询价交易方式，做市商制度等，而且不断吸引实力雄厚的银行加入做市商队伍，加快金融创新，推出适应市场发展和满足不同类型客户需求的金融衍生产品，增强了市场价格发现的功能。而且全国银行间外汇市场还吸引了一大批优秀的、具备专业素养的优秀人才，为市场的进一步发展打下了良好的基础。

【案例】个人外汇资金大量流入结汇的监管

从近些年的统计数据看，个人渠道是外汇资金流入和流出的主要渠道。在个人外汇资金流入中，既有真正的合法资金，比如境外务工人员劳务报酬等，也有违规异常资金。这些资金兑换人民币的主要方式有借用他人身份证、护照，或者伪造凭证单据等，目的是将外币转换成人民币后进入中国股市、楼市等以获取人民币升值收益。这些资金的流入会造成中国国际收支不平衡，给经济的持续、健康、稳定发展带来冲击。

对此，中国对管理方式进行了创新，建立健全监管系统，对外汇资金的流入进行了有效的监管。具体采取的措施有：第一，建立个人结售汇年度总额管理模式，对个人年度购汇和结汇总额设定上限标准，在上限标准之内的，凭本人有效身份证件直接在银行办理；而超过上限的，经常项下凭本人有效身份证件和相关证明材料经银行审核后办理，资本项下须经必要的核准。这样有利于对大额结汇、购汇行为的监管。第二，建立个人结售汇管理信息系统，记录个人办理结售汇业务的详细信息，并进行准确统计和判断，进一步提升监管效率。以上措施的出台有利于实现对个人结售汇业务的逐笔监测和重点跟踪，对个人结售汇行为的有效规范，以维护我国经济的持续发展。

三、Q&A

（一）如何看待中国外汇储备适度规模的问题？

答：外汇储备并不是越多越好。中国既不追求外汇储备的规模庞大，同时也不追求国际收支的长期顺差。中国的经常项目和资本项目连续多年保持顺差，而国际收支"双顺差"会带来外汇储备的增加，反映了中国经济的长期持续稳定增长，这是由当前中国经济所处的发展阶段和特点决定的。

当前充足的外汇储备，有利于中国金融环境的稳定和中国经济的持续稳定的发展。中国是一个发展中的大国，即使按照传统的适度规模的指标衡量，也需要保持一定规模的外汇储备。

（二）中国为什么连续六个月减持美国国债？

答：美联储退出量化宽松，美元进入升值周期，人民币对美元微弱贬值，造成中国国际收支顺差减少，趋于平衡，经常性贸易顺差占 GDP 比重 2% 左右，达到相对理想的状态。通常来说，美债会随着新增外汇的减少而减少。而且，中国的用汇需求增加，2014 年仅出境游就形成 1000 亿美元的逆差。企业海外投资的用汇也在增加，企业愿意更多地持有美元，对美元资产的需求上升。

中国减持美债和更多的企业在国外投资、更多人国外消费紧密相连。这种资产形态的变化是中国希望的。从前由于人民币币值单边上扬，央行不得不持有大量外汇，而央行的目标是藏汇于民，如今终于出现了好的迹象。人民币对美元有升有减，人民币市场汇率趋近于均衡，进而摆脱从前人民币对美元单边升值的不利情况。之前中国具有大规模的外汇储备，这就要求对外汇储备的增长速度进行控制，这跟中国的初衷相一致。美元升值，导致更多人不愿意去结汇，也就是说不愿意将自己手中持有的外汇兑换成人民币，从而减少了外汇储备。但也应注意，中国外贸的状况不是很好，出口创汇能力不像过去那么强。而外汇储备在国外有更多的通道，资本走出去、海外并购、投资增加。此外，美债到了赎回期限也可能会造成中国减持美债。

（三）未来中国外储投资有什么变化？

答：中国所持有的美债、外汇储备增长速度放缓，甚至可能不再增加。而海外直接投资增加，海外并购、投资加快会成为趋势。由于中国成为资本净输出国，更多的资本外流，外汇储备增量可能会减少。减持美国国债可以看作是一种全球资产的再分配，钱流出到海外可以有更多种的用途，不仅仅是用于购买债券。

人民币汇率形成机制改革之后，人民币更加国际化，市场供求是汇率的决定条件。美元汇率也是市场化的。中国外汇市场的情况是决定中国是否要减持美债的关键条件。但是在将来，中国不会一直减持美国国债，依然会持有很多的美债。从前期的数据看，中国持有美债的数量降到第二，而日本第一，持有的美债数量与中国差别并不大，比中国多7亿。

中国如果要做出调整也需要相当长时间。美元是当今世界主要储备货币，欧债状况不如美债，欧洲也在实行量化宽松政策，总体来说美国的经济状况相对好一些。美国国债不仅会带来风险，也代表着国家实力。然而能够肯定的是，中国将会加大海外投资，更好地使用外汇资产，迎来一种新常态。

第七章
新兴的互联网金融

一、互联网金融——中国金融业的新兴力量

　　中国金融业的改革是全球瞩目的大事,尤其是利率市场化、汇率市场化和金融管制的放松。而全球主要经济体每一次重要的体制变革,往往伴随着重大的金融创新。中国的金融改革,正值互联网金融潮流兴起,在传统金融部门和互联网金融的推动下,中国的金融效率、交易结构,甚至整体金融架构都将发生深刻变革。

　　随着信息通信技术和互联网的发展,互联网金融信息对金融市场的影响已经越来越不容忽视。某一个新事件的发生或者是网络上对某支股票的热议都在很大程度上左右着金融实践者们的行为,同时进一步影响着股市变化的趋势。另一方面,在金融市场中,传统的金融市场的影响因素同样发挥着巨大的作用。

　　在中国,互联网金融的发展主要是监管套利造成的。一方面,互联网金融公司没有资本的要求,也不需要接受央行的监管,这是本质原因;从技术角度来说,互联网金融虽然具有自身优势,但是要考虑合规和风险管理(风控)的问题。

　　从政府不断出台的金融、财税改革政策中不难看出,惠及扶持中小微企业发展已然成为主旋律,占中国企业总数98%以上的中小微企业之于中国经济发展的重要性可见一斑。而从互联网金融这种轻应用、碎片化、及时性理财的属性来看,相比传统金融机构和渠道而言,则更易受到中小微企业的青睐,也更符合其发展模式和刚性需求。

二、互联网金融的主要业态

(一)众筹

众筹大意为大众筹资或群众筹资,是指用团购预购的形式,向网友募集项目资金的模式。众筹的本意是利用互联网和 SNS 传播的特性,让创业企业、艺术家或个人对公众展示他们的创意及项目,争取大家的关注和支持,进而获得所需要的资金援助。众筹平台的运作模式大同小异——需要资金的个人或团队将项目策划交给众筹平台,经过相关审核后,便可以在平台的网站上建立属于自己的页面,用来向公众介绍项目情况。

(二)点对点网络信贷(P2P)

P2P (Peer-to-Peerlending),即点对点信贷。P2P 网贷是指通过第三方互联网平台进行资金借、贷双方的匹配,需要借贷的人群可以通过网站平台寻找到有出借能力并且愿意基于一定条件出借的人群,帮助贷款人通过和其他贷款人一起分担一笔借款额度来分散风险,也帮助借款人在充分比较的信息中选择有吸引力的利率条件。

两种运营模式,第一是纯线上模式,其特点是资金借贷活动都通过线上进行,不结合线下的审核。通常这些企业采取的审核借款人资质的措施有通过视频认证、查看银行流水账单、身份认证等。第二种是线上线下结合的模式,借款人在线上提交借款申请后,平台通过所在城市的代理商采取入户调查的方式审核借款人的资信、还款能力等情况。

(三)第三方支付

第三方支付(Third-Party Payment)狭义上是指具备一定实力和信誉保障的非银行机构,借助通信、计算机和信息安全技术,采用与各大银行签约的方式,在用户与银行支付结算系统间建立连接的电子支付模式。

根据央行 2010 年在《非金融机构支村服务管理办法》中给出的非金融机构支付服务的定义，从广义上讲第三方支付是指非金融机构作为收、付款人的支付中介所提供的网络支付、预付卡、银行卡收单以及中国人民银行确定的其他支付服务。第三方支付已不仅仅局限于最初的互联网支付，而是成为线上线下全面覆盖，应用场景更为丰富的综合支付工具。

（四）数字货币

除去蓬勃发展的第三方支付、P2P 贷款模式、小贷模式、众筹融资、余额宝模式等形式，以比特币为代表的互联网货币也开始露出自己的獠牙，以比特币等数字货币为代表的互联网货币爆发，从某种意义上来说，比其他任何互联网金融形式都更具颠覆性。在 2013 年 8 月 19 日，德国政府正莺承认比特币的合法"货币"地位，比特币可用于缴税和其他合法用途，德国也成为全球首个认可比特币的国家，这意味着比特币开始逐渐"洗百"，从极客的玩物，走入大众的视线。也许，它能够催生出真正的互联网金融帝国。

比特币在中国也炒得火热，但也跌得惨烈。无论怎样，这场似乎曾经离我们很遥远的互联网淘金盛宴已经慢慢走进我们的视线，它让人们看到了互联网金融最终极的形态就是互联网货币。所有的互联网金融只是对现有的商业银行、证券公司提出挑战，将来发展到互联网货币的形态就是对央行的挑战。也许比特币会颠覆传统金融成长为首个全球货币，也许它会最终走向崩盘，不管怎样，可以肯定的是，比特币会给人类留下一笔永恒的遗产。

（五）大数据金融

大数据金融是指集合海量非结构化数据，通过对其进行实时分析，可以为亘联网金融枫构提供客户全方位信息，通过分析和挖掘客户的变易和消费信息掌握客户的消费习惯，并准确预测客户行为，使金融机构和金融服务平台在营销和风险控制方面有的放矢。

基于大数据的金融服务平台主要指拥有海量数据的电子商务企业开展的金融服势。大数据的关键是从大量数据中快速获取有用信息的能力，或者是从大数据资产中快速变现利用的能力。因此，大数据的信息处理往往以云计算为基础。

万德、恒生电子、同花顺等金融信息服务提供机构,在中国2014年以来的大牛市以来频频亮相,让公众初步见识了大数据在金融交易中的巨大作用。

(六)信息化金融机构

所谓信息化金融枫构,是指通过采用信息技术,对传统运营流程进行改造或重构,实现经营、管理全面电子化的银行、证券和保险等金融机构。金融信息化是金融业发展趋势之一,而信息化金融机构则是金融创新的产物。

从金融整个行业来看,银行的信息化建设一直处于业内领先水平,不仅具有国际领先的金融信息技术平台,建成了由自助银行、电话银行、手机银行和网上银行构成的电子银行立体服务体系,而且以信息化的大手笔——数据集中工程在业内独领风骚,其除了基于互联网的创新金融服务之外,还形成了"门户""网银、金融产品超市、电商"的一拖三的金融电商创新服务模式。

但是近年来,以微众银行为代表的纯线上银行也异军突起,开始在信息化金融机构领域分一杯羹。

(七)金融门户

互联网金融门户是指利用互联网进行金融产品的销售以及为金融产品销售提供第三方服务的平台。它的核心就是"搜索比价"的模式,采用金融产品垂直比价的方式,将各家金融机构的产品放在平台上,用户通过对比挑选合适的金融产品。

互联网金融门户多元化创新发展,形成了提供高端理财投资服务和理财产品的第三方理财机构,提供保险产品咨询、比价、购买服务的保险门户网站等。这种模式不存在太多政策风险,因为其平台既不负责金融产品的实际销售,也不零担任何不良的风险,同时资金也完全不通过中间平台。

三、中国代表性的互联网金融机构

（一）蚂蚁金融服务集团

蚂蚁金融服务集团正式成立于 2014 年 10 月，专注于服务小微企业与普通消费者。该企业与在美上市的阿里巴巴有着关联关系。

基于互联网的思想和技术，蚂蚁金服致力于打造一个开放的生态，与金融机构一起，共同为未来社会的金融提供支撑，实现"让倍用等于财富"的愿景。蚂蚁金融服务集团旗下品牌有：支付宝、芝麻信用、蚂蚁小贷、余额宝、招财宝等。

从 2003 年，支付宝担保交易首度在淘宝网推出，到 2014 年，蚂蚁金融服务集团正式成立，可以说，马云从自己熟悉的电商领域起步，走了一条农村包围城市的曲线救国之路，不知不觉，蚂蚁金服已经成为横跨众多金融业态的叠融控股集团。

（二）京东金融

"（京东东金融）对一切金融牌照都感兴趣。"负责京东金融战略研究和内部管理工作的京东金融副总裁姚乃胜如此阐述着京东金融的野心。

独立于 2013 年 10 月的京东金融，在不到两年时间内以极其迅猛的速度完成布局，俨然已有互联网鱼融大鳄之势。目前，京东金融现已建立七大业务板块，努别是供应链金融、消费金融、众筹、财富管理、支村、保险以及证券，陆续推出服务商家的投融资（网商贷、京保贝、京小贷）、众筹等；在个人用户方面，则推出白条（京东自条、索东钢镚）、众筹（产品众筹、股权众筹、轻众筹）、理财等，在牌照方面，京东已拿下支付、小贷、保理、基金销售支会结算等多张金融牌照。

可以说，在金融业态的拓展上，京东的步伐在某些领域已经超越了蚂蚁金福，可以预见，这两家中国的电商龙头，在互联网金融领域还有一场恶斗。

（三）陆金所

陆金忽，全称上海陆家嘴国际金融资产交易市场股份有限公司，平安集团旗下成员是中国最大的网络授融资平台之一，2011年9月在上海注册成立，注册资本金8.37亿元，总部设在国际金融中心上海陆家嘴。

陆金所旗下网络投融资平台2012年3月正式上线运营，是中国平安集团打造的平台，陆金所结合全球金融发展与互联网技术创新，在健全的风险管控体系基础上，为中小企业及个人客户提供专业、可信赖的投融资服务，帮助他们实现财富增值。截至2014年1月未，注册用户已逾570万。

陆金所是上海唯一一家通过国务院交易场所清理整顿的金融资产交易信息服务平台。

陆金所的服务范围包括：金融产品的研究开发、组台设计、咨询服务，非公开发行的股权投资基金等的各类交易相关配套服务，金融和经济咨询服务、市场调研及数据分析服务，金融类应用软件开发，电子商务，会务服务，商务咨询，财务咨询《不得从事代理记账》等。

陆金所目前是中国备家艘P乎台中声誉最好的，依托平安集团的强大信誉支撑，我们期待它在中国互联网信贷领域开发出一条好的道路。

四、Q&A

（一）外国人是否可以开设支付宝账户

答：可以。步骤如下：

1. 打开支付宝首页点击注册；

2. 点击【个人账户】，地区或国家系统默认选择【大陆地区】，点击下拉框选择用户所在地区，输入邮箱地址和验证码，点击【下一步】；

3. 填写手机号码，输入手机接收的验证码，点击【下一步】；

4. 接收并填写校验码后，点击【确定】；

5. 填写信息（不同国籍填写的信息不一样），点击【确定】；

6. 注册成功。可以在网上购物，但不可以充值、查询收入明细、收款金额不能使用。

Chapter 1 Overview of China's Banking Industry

1.1 History of China's Banking Industry

This chapter is a comprehensive description of China's banking industry, considering its leadership in China's financial industry, its large scale of assets, its staff number and its leading status in China's financial system. It's worth to mention that "banking industry" in this chapter refers to financial institutions of bank deposits in *Coding Standards for Financial Institutions* promulgated by The People's Bank of China*. According to this coding standard, "bank" is defined as a business entity that legally accepts deposits, grants loans and deals with settlements. With respect to the sphere of business of the special banking industry. I will not elaborate on this topic as it is already widely addressed in many other text book publications.

The new Chinese banking system was established by The People's Bank of China in 1948 when The People's Bank of China started to take over and reform the miscellaneous financial institutions from previous years. Between 1948 and 1979, The people's Bank of China was the only bank, serving both as an administrative institution and as an economic entity for banking services.

The period between 1979 to 1994 witnessed the second stage of development of the Chinese banking industry. During this period, the Agricultural Bank of China,

---

* The People's Bank of China is the Central Bank of the People's Republic of China. The "Code of Financial Institutions" was promulgated by the Survey and Statistics Department of the People's Bank of China on May 25, 2010

the Industrial and Commercial Bank of China, the People's Construction Bank of China (now known as China Construction Bank) were established. These banks were in charge of specialized banking operations and specific banking business while the People's Bank of China specially performed the function of Central Bank. Meanwhile, other numerous commercial banks have sprung up, such as, Bank of Communications, China Merchants Bank, Shenzhen Development Bank, and others.

After 1994, policy-related services of the previously mentioned four specialized banks were gradually discarded. In 2004, those four banks were transformed to stock companies and went out to public offering (known as IPO, Initial Public Offering). In 2015 a series of reforms were completed, China's banking industry has maintained its profitability and developing momentum, and has been playing a pillar role in the Chinese financial system.

【Case】The Epitome of China's Banking Industry: A Fluctuant Century of Bank of China*

Founded in February 1919, Bank of China (BOC) orderly performed the specific function as a Central Bank, an international exchange bank and an international trade bank during 1912 to 1949. After the founding of the People's Republic of China (PRC), BOC served as a foreign exchange and trade bank for the new nation, responsible for national foreign exchange management, international trade settlement, overseas remittance and other non-trade foreign exchange business. In 1994, BOC was restructured as an exclusive state-owned commercial bank. In August 2004, BOC, Ltd was officially established. Later in June and July 2006, the company went public in the Stock Exchange of Hong Kong and Shanghai Stock Exchange, making it the first "A+H" listed commercial bank in China. In 2013, BOC was once again selected as an important bank in the global banking system, becoming the only financial institution in the emerging market economy to receive this accolade for three consecutive years. BOC has

---

* Obtained from the official website of Bank of China.

had the highest level of internationalization and diversification considering its services expansion to customers from 37 countries as well as Chinese mainland, Hong Kong, Macau and Taiwan. The bank mainly takes charge of commercial banking business including corporate financial business, individual financial business and financial market business. Also, the bank established wholly owned stock subsidiaries including BOC International Holdings Ltd, BOC Group Insurance Ltd and BOC Insurance Ltd, BOC Group Investment Ltd, BOC Investment Management Ltd and BOC Aviation Leasing Enterprise Pte. Ltd, which are responsible for investment banking, insurance, direct investment and investment management, fund management and aircraft leasing respectively. As a matter of fact, BOC is at the primary stage of mixed management.

The revolution of BOC reflects the development of the new Chinese banking industry. Since 1949, the role of BOC has switched from a specialized bank to an exclusive state-owned commercial bank, followed by a shareholding commercial bank through the introduction of strategic investors and public fund-raising. Also, BOC has diversified its business to investment, insurance, fund management and finance lease. Generally, the developing process of BOC is representative of China's banking industry.

1.2 Status and Development Level of China's Banking Industry

As illustrated previously, the banking industry is the core of the Chinese financial system. Figure 1-1 below tells us that RMB loans have all along been the mainstream financing method in China. Despite the decline in occupation from 80% in 2003 to 60% in 2014, its dominance has remained. Furthermore, loans accounted for an increasingly larger percentage. Entrusted loan refers to the capital provided by a bailor from legitimate sources. According to the bailor's designated prospective borrower, purpose, amount of money, time limit and interest rate, the entrusted business bank would grant loans as well as supervise the use and recovery of loan business. The bailor here refers to government departments, enterprises, institutions and individuals. This business takes advantage of the bank's credit channel, and it also belongs to the financing methods of banks.

Of course, from 2003 to 2014, the proportion of corporate bond financing scale and stock financing scale also significantly increased. Among them, the scale of corporate bond financing increased steadily from less than 2% in 2003 to close to 15%, in 2014 indicating the growth rate was huge. On the other hand, the share of stock financing increased or decreased alternately in the past 12 years, largely due to the suspension of IPO policy implemented by China's securities issuing regulators from time to time.

In general, the percentage of indirect financing scale represented by the banking industry decreased from 90% in 2003 to 80% in 2014. In spite of the dip, indirect investment remains dominant in Chinese social financing.

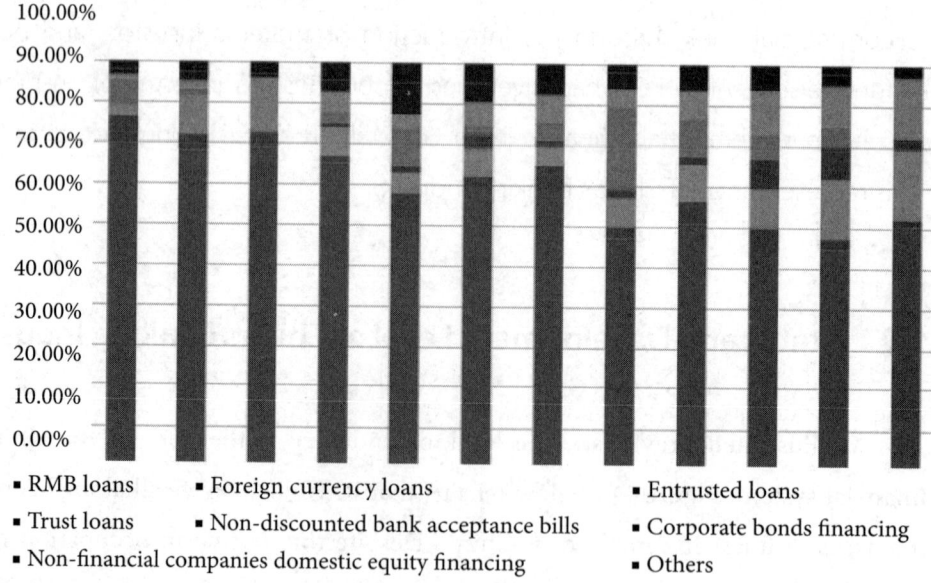

Source: PBC, NDRC, CSRC, CIRC, China Government Securities Depository Trust & Clearing Co., Ltd., China Association of Banks Market Dealers

Figure 1-1 Trends in the Proportion of Different Financing Modes in China's Social Financing Scale (2003-2014)

Chapter 1
Overview of China's Banking Industry

Then, what is the level of the domestically dominant China's banking industry at a global stage?

Table 1-1 below is an excerpt from the Forbes Global List of the Top 2000 global enterprises in 2015. As you can see, the four major banks in China ranked in the top four, followed by Warren Buffet's Berkshire Hathaway which ranked fifth. Therefore, China's banks have reached a relatively high level whether in terms of sales, profits, assets or market value.

Table 1-1   Excerpt of 2015 Forbes Global List of the Top 2000 Global Enterprises

	Corporation	Nation	Sales Volume	Profit	Assets	Market Value
1	ICBC	PRC	1,668	448	33,220	2,783
2	CCB	PRC	1,305	370	26,989	2,129
3	ABC	PRC	1,292	291	25,748	1,899
4	BOC	PRC	1,203	275	24,583	1,991
5	BHC	USA	1,947	199	5,346	3,548
6	JPM	USA	978	212	25,936	2,255
7	EMC	USA	3,762	325	3,495	3,571
8	Petro China Co., Ltd	PRC	3,334	174	3,877	3,346
9	GM	USA	1,485	152	6,483	2,535
10	WELLS FARGO	USA	904	231	17,014	2,783

Source: Forbes official website   Unit: 100 million USD

As is known to all, for the banking industry, it attaches importance not only to profitability and asset size, but also to the bank's Non-Performing Loan (NPL) ratio, provision coverage ratio, asset adequacy ratio and other indexes reflecting bank's ability to resist risks. To compare the various indexes of China's leading banks and other internationally renowned banks more comprehensively, we have demonstrated the comparison of the risk indexes between BOC, a major commercial bank in China, and that of the famous American Citibank. The comparison is based on the international status of BOC which has been selected as a major bank in the global banking system for three consecutive years. Additionally, the business framework and assets condition are representative among China's banking industry.

Table 1–2   Risk Indexes Comparison Between BOC and Citibank

	BOC	Citibank
Total Assets (100 million USD)	24,583	18,830
NPL (Non-performing Loans) Ratio (%)	1.18	1.5
NPL Provisioning Coverage Ratio (%)	187.6	168
Tier-one Ratio(%)	11.35	13

Source: BOC, Citibank annual report, estimation by reporters

As is indicated in Table 1–2 above, BOC excels Citibank in terms of assets scale, non-performing loans and provision of non-performing loans. However, the tier-one ratio of Citibank is higher than that of BOC. Generally, the indexes in these two banks are about the same, indicating that the Chinese banking industry is standing at the top in profitability, total assets and risk control.

1.3   Major Types of Banks in Chinese Mainland

According to the information provided by the regulatory administration in China, the banks in China can be categorized into the following nine types:

Table 1–3 Types of Banks in China

Type	Property	Quantity	Representatives
Policy Bank	Founded and financially supported by the government for the complementarity of administrative policies on economy and financing.	3	CDB /EIBOC/ ADBOC
State-owned Commercial Bank	Wholly state-owned commercial banks which introduced multiple shareholders before shareholding reform.	5	ICBC /BOC/CCB/ ABC/BOC
National Joint-stock Commercial Banks	A more varied background of shareholders. Consisting of regional governments, big SOEs and private sector companies, the branches spread around the country.	12	CIB/CCB/HXB/ CMB/, etc.
Urban Commercial Bank	Controlled by regional governments, the banks' administrative areas are confined to a small urban area	About 140	Rizhao Bank / Bank of Jiujiang / Bank of Ningbo
Rural Commercial Bank, Rural Ccredit Association, Rural Credit Union Funds	A mainstream financial institution mainly distributed in counties and rural areas in China.	About 300 rural commercial banks and about 1,400 rural credit cooperatives that have not been restructured	Xiamen Rural Commercial Bank /Beijing Rural Commercial Bank
Village Bank	A new type of financial institution in Chinese rural areas which is a commercial bank within an independent legal entity. Compared with rural commercial banks, it has shorter decisive chain, smaller scale and better penetration on lower tier cities.	About 1,500	Ningxia Zhongning Qingyin Rural Bank/ Commonwealth Bank of Australia (Lankao) Village Bank

(Continued)

Type	Property	Quantity	Representatives
Bank with Foreign Capital	Branches and subsidiaries of foreign banks in China.	46	HSBC China / Standard Chartered China
Postal Saving Bank	Created as a part of the business of the China Post Company. Its peculiarity is that it had previously operated as a remittance business of the State administration and was the largest bank of branches in China with branches in almost all cities and townships in China.	1	China Postal Savings Bank
Finance Company	According to the classification of the People's Bank of China, financial companies belong to deposit banking financial institutions most of which belong to large enterprise groups. They aim to strengthen centralized management of enterprise groups' funds and improve the efficiency of the use of enterprise groups 'funds, and provide financial management services for the members of enterprise groups.	186	Wuliangye Finance Company/ Zhonghai Petroleum Finance Company

Source: Edited by the author of this paper.

All these kinds of financial institutions will be introduced in detail one by one in the following pages.

1.3.1 Policy bank

China's policy banks, not for profit, specifically engage in policy financing activities directly or indirectly in the specific business fields in line with the government's social and economic policies or intentions, acting as the government's tools for economic development, social progress and macroeconomic management tools.

In 1994, China established the three major policy banks, namely, the China Development Bank (CDB), the Export-Import Bank of China (EIBOC) and the Agricultural Development Bank of China (ADBOC), all directly under the leadership of the State Council. Each of the three banks has its own specific responsibilities.

The main responsibilities of the EIBOC are to expand the import and export of electromechanical products, complete sets of equipment and high-tech products in China, promote enterprises with comparative advantages to carry out foreign contracted projects and overseas investments, promote the development of foreign relations and international economic and trade cooperation, and provide financial services. From 2010 to 2014, the EIBOC issued a total of RMB 3.2 trillion in loans to support the import and export of USD 1.46 trillion.

The main responsibilities of the ADBOC are to raise funds based on the national credit, undertake the agricultural policy-oriented financial business stipulated by the State, act as the proxy for the allocation of funds for supporting agriculture and serve the agricultural and rural economic development. From 2004 to the end of 2014, the ADBOC issued RMB 4.78 trillion in loans and storage loans for grain and cotton oil, and each year it supported the purchase of grain accounting for about 60% of the total grain output of the same year.

The CDB mainly provides financial services for medium and long-term development of the national economy mainly through medium and long-term credits and investments and other financial services. It provides financial support to key areas of economic construction such as infrastructural construction, shantytowns reconstruction, new urbanization and support for enterprises aiming for global expansion. By the end of 2017, the CDB's total loans to railways, highways and electricity exceeded RMB 5.2 trillion, supporting 60% and 30% of the total mileage of the country's railways and highways respectively, with a total of over RMB 8 trillion in loans for urbanization.

During the development of policy banks, many of the original policy-oriented businesses gradually evolved into commercial competitions. Policy banks suffered some controversies and confusion due to the unclear boundary between commercial businesses and policy-based businesses. In 2015, the Chinese government repositioned policy banks at the policy and functional levels, re-emphasized the orientation of policy functions, returned policy banks to their original jobs and prepared for the development of policy-based banking law.

1.3.2 State-owned commercial bank

State-owned commercial banks, also known as state-controlled large commercial banks, refer to commercial banks directly controlled by the State (Ministry of Finance, Central Huijin Corporation) and now include Industrial and Commercial Bank of China, Agricultural Bank of China, Bank of China, China Construction Bank, Bank of Communications.

Industrial and Commercial Bank of China was established in 1984. As one of the largest commercial banks in China, it has ranked among the top 500 in the world for several years. In 2010, the Banker magzine ranked banks by Tier-one capital. ICBC ranked 16th in the World Bank 1000 and was nominated for the Fortune Global 500 in the past few years. It was rated by the U.S. "Far East Economic Review" as Top 10 High Quality Products (Services) in China. On April 18, 2013, the Forbes Global Top 2000 list was released. ICBC (Industrial and Commercial Bank of China) overtook ExxonMobil to become the world's largest company.

Founded in 1951, ABC is one of the most powerful state-owned commercial banks in China. It was the first state-owned commercial bank established in New China and an important part of China's financial system, with its headquarters set in Beijing, ranking the 8th "Top 1000 World Banks", Moody's credit rating of A1.

Bank of China is one of the oldest commercial banks in China, the full name of which is Bank of China Limited. It is one of the major four state-owned commercial banks in the Chinese mainland (excluding Hong Kong, Macau and Taiwan) and rankes third in size. Bank of China was approved by President Sun Yat-sen on January 24, 1912 and officially opened on February 5, 1912. It was reorganized by the Huobu Bank established by the Qing government in 1905 (renamed as Ta Ching Government Bank) since 1908, responsible for the consolidation of the currency system, the issuance of currency, the consolidation of the State treasury and the exercise of the powers of the Central Bank. Bank of China has successively become the national central bank, the international exchange bank and foreign trade professional bank. Its business scope covers commercial banks, investment banks and insurance fields. Its subsidiaries include BOC Hong Kong, BOC International and BOC Insurance. These financial institutions provide comprehensive and high-quality financial services to individuals and corporate clients globally. In terms of core capital, Bank of China ranked 10th in 2008 among the Top 1000 World Banks according to London's *The Banker* publication, also ranking among the Fortune 500 companies.

China Construction Bank is a state-owned commercial bank featuring short-term and long-term credit businesses. Headquartered in Beijing, China Construction Bank operates in China and major international financial centers. China Construction Bank ranked 29th in the ranking of the Top 1000 World Banks according to *The Banker*, ranking by Tier 1 capital.

Founded in 1908, Bank of Communications is one of the oldest banks in China since the modern era and one of the first issuance bank branches in modern China. As one of China's top five state-owned banks, Bank of Communications is also one of the major integrated financial service providers in China and is becoming a large banking group with commercial banks as the mainstay, inter-market and internationalization. Its business scope covers commercial banks, investment banks, securities, trusts, financial leasing, fund management, insurance, offshore financial services and many other fields.

1.3.3 National joint-stock commercial banks

At present, there are 13 representative joint-stock commercial banks in China. Compared with state-owned commercial banks, joint-stock commercial banks have stronger institutional competition, a more complete staff incentive mechanism and a higher level of corporate governance. Specifically, there are several differences as follows.

In terms of organizational structure, due to its long history and many employees, the state-owned commercial banks have multi-layered branches and more levels, including the headquarters — tier one branch — tier two branch — sub-branch — tier two sub-branch. However, joint-stock commercial banks focus on the improvement of efficiency on their establishment, it is common to set branches directly at the prefectural and municipal level under the head office to manage the business in a large area, and to be more effective and efficient in organizational structure than state-owned commercial banks.

In terms of the market reaction mechanism, the state-owned commercial banks are separate from specialized banks. The presidents often have administrative ranks, in the market reaction mechanism, state-owned commercial banks are born out of professional banks, and executives often have administrative levels, so the decision-making mechanism is more similar to that of the administrative agencies, but it also has a slow response, similar to large institutions. It tends to be conservative in decision-making. The joint-stock commercial banks are more market-oriented, front-line business staff have more flexibility in decision-making power, while the decision-making chain is also shorter than that of the state-owned banks.

In the salary incentive system, the wages of employees of state-owned commercial banks show a relatively average level compared with the joint-stock commercial banks, and at the same time, they are lower than the joint-stock commercial banks in absolute terms. Therefore, in China, joint-stock commercial banks and state-owned banks play a slightly different role. Large state-owned banks are reputable, but they are also slow to adapt to the problems of the market, the joint-stock commercial banks are small in U-turn transactions, and have a stronger Catfish Effect in the market.

1.3.4 Urban commercial banks

Urban commercial banks are an important component and special group of China's banking industry. Its predecessor was the urban credit cooperative established in the 1980s. Its business orientation at that time was to provide financial support to SMEs (Small and Medium Enterprises) and pave the way for local economy to improve. From the early 1980s until the late 1990s, urban credit unions across the country thrived. However, with the development of China's financial industry, urban credit cooperatives gradually exposed many problems of risk management during their development. Many urban credit cooperatives were also gradually transformed into urban commercial banks, providing financial services to local economy and residents.

In the mid-1990s, China set up urban commercial banks based on the city credit cooperatives. Urban commercial banks were formed under the special financial historical conditions of China and were the product of the central financial authorities in purging urban credit cooperatives and defusing local financial risks. By the end of 2004, there were 169,000 employees and a total output of RMB 1,455.2 billion, accounting for 6.27% of the total assets of the nation's banking financial institutions and 27.7% of the total assets of the national joint-stock commercial banks. By May 2012, there were a total of 137 urban commercial banks across the country, nearly 10,000 outlets, all over the country provinces, municipalities and autonomous regions. By the end of 2004, there were 169,000 employees with a total output of 1,455.2 billion *yuan*, accounting for 6.27% of the total assets of banking financial institutions and 27.7% of the total assets of joint-stock commercial banks in China.

After more than a decade of development, commercial banks in cities have gradually developed and matured significantly. Although their degree of development varies greatly, a considerable number of commercial banks in cities have already completed their shareholding reforms and gradually digested the non-performing assets through various means, in order to reduce the non-performing loan rate, change the business model, the local possession, which has accounted for a considerable market share. Among them, there is a rapid development such as Bank of Shanghai, which has appeared at the Top 500 World Banks. Urban commercial banks in China are gradually developing into banks with a considerable number of them, increasing the size of the banking sector, with the five state-owned joint-stock commercial banks, postal savings banks and twelve joint-stock commercial banks together to form a multi-level pattern of China's banking industry.

1.3.5 Rural commercial banks, rural credit cooperatives and rural mutual funds

Rural Commercial Banks are joint-stock local financial institutions under the jurisdiction of farmers, rural industrial and commercial households, a business law person and other economic organizations.

At present, China has established about 303 rural commercial banks and about 210 rural cooperative banks. The total assets of rural banking institutions account for 41.4% of the total rural cooperative financial institutions. In addition, there are 1,424 rural credit cooperatives that have reached or nearly reached the conditions for the formation of rural commercial banks. Through the reform, the governance model of rural credit cooperatives has undergone fundamental changes. The longstanding problem of insider control has been effectively solved. The institution itself has formed an endogenous driving force for further deepening the reform of institutional mechanisms.

1.3.6 Village banks

Village Banks refer to the financial institutions funded mainly by local and foreign financial institutions, non-financial institutions and domestic natural persons approved by the China Banking Regulatory Commission in accordance with relevant laws and regulations. The banks provide financial services for farmers and farming industry to develop rural economy. Different from other bank branches, village banks are a first-class corporate body. Up to December 2014, there were 1,547 village banks in China.

1.4 Development Trend and Prospect of China's Banking Industry

As China's financial industry continues to deepen its internal and external opening, China's banking industry is also actively taking countermeasures. At the regulatory level, the implementation of the deposit insurance system and the gradual liberalization of mixed operation are expected to further raise China's risk-control ability and competitiveness. As the major market, all commercial banks are also constantly exploring the mode of mixed operation. In recent years, financial holding groups such as Ping An and Everbright Bank have emerged in various financial forms such as banking, insurance, securities and trust. The latest trend is that insurance companies and even private equity funds as well as e-commerce companies are also beginning to seek into the field of banking, mixed operation has emerged a new model, such as Minsheng Bank, Chengdu Rural Commercial Bank of Anbang Insurance Group, and MYbank initiated by Alibaba.

1.4.1 Deposit insurance system

The deposit insurance system is a kind of financial security system. It refers to the establishment of an insurance institution by the qualified deposit-taking financial institutions. Each deposit institution as an insured person pays insurance premiums according to a certain deposit ratio, and establishes a deposit insurance reserve. When a member institution faces a business crisis or faces bankruptcy, the deposit insurance institution provides financial assistance to the deposit taker or makes partial or full deposit directly to the depositors so as to protect the interests of depositors, safeguard bank credit and stabilize the financial order.

China formally implemented the deposit insurance system in January 2015. The maximum limit for deposit insurance is RMB 500,000. In fact, China has had an invisible deposit insurance system for a long time. The establishment of a visible deposit insurance system can better manage the public's expectation of deposit safety and help state-owned banks to compete with other banks on a more equitable basis.

In China, the deposit insurance institutions include deposit-taking banking financial institutions such as commercial banks, rural cooperative banks and rural credit cooperatives established in China. Branch offices set up by the above insurance institutions outside of China and branches of foreign banks in China are not listed insured institutions.

This figure is calculated by the People's Bank of China on the basis of the deposit status at the end of 2013 which can cover up to 99.63% of depositors' total deposits.

Sources of compensation for deposit insurance include: premiums paid by the insured, property distributed in the insurer liquidation, proceeds from the use of deposit insurance funds by deposit insurance fund managers, and other legitimate income.

Uninsured deposits include interbank deposits with financial institutions and deposits with senior insurers in insurance institutions. Insurance institutions pay premiums, the applicable rates vary, as determined by the deposit insurance fund management agencies. The premium has to be paid every six months.

The high profits of China's banking industry have been widely criticized by the public. For this reason, China's financial reform has initiated the marketization of interest rates. On one hand, the interest rates are determined by the financial institutions within a certain range; on the other hand, it has liberalized the pace of private capital in organizing banks to be involved in competition. However, these reforms will bring a new problem. In the event of bankruptcy by radical banks, depositors' deposits are at risk of loss.

In the past, China's bank deposits were implicitly guaranteed by the government. Such a comprehensive system encouraged the banks with less stringent risk control and posed moral hazard. The introduction of the deposit insurance system could reward and punish bad banks. On the premise that depositors' interests were basically protected by small and medium-sized banks as well as private banks at their own risk, more in line with the principle of market-oriented reforms.

1.4.2 Mixed operation trend and financial holding platform gradually formed

Up until today, China's financial regulation still adopts the mode of separate supervision. The People's Bank of China is responsible for the formulation and implementation of monetary policy. The Banking Regulatory Commission, the Securities Regulatory commission, and the Insurance Regulatory Commission are respectively responsible for banking, securities and insurance regulation.

However, at the operational level, China's financial industry is in fact developing into a mixed industry. After the well-known US *Financial Services Modernization Law* was passed, the U.S. financial institutions mainly operate banks, securities, and other securities in the form of subsidiaries of financial holding companies and insurance business; in other words, the financial holding company model is the main way for the U.S. financial "mixed operation". In fact, Article 20 and Article 32 of the *Banking Law* of 1933, which was explicitly repealed by the *Financial Services Modernization Act* of 1999, will no longer prohibit commercial banks and securities institutions from indirectly engaging in the business of each other's affiliates. However, Article 16 and Article 21 have not been abolished. That is to say, commercial banks and securities institutions are still not allowed to directly engage in business with each other.

In contrast, in China, the banking industry has actually involved other businesses in the financial industry through sole-funded subsidiaries. By setting up a fund management company, it directly engages in asset management or consignment of various wealth management products. The bank is deeply involved in the asset management business. By establishing a Hong Kong-based investment bank similar to the U.S. "Twentieth Company" (such as BOC International), it has returned to the Chinese mainland and engaged in various types of investment banking indirectly.

From a financially practical point of view, the mixed operation will surely promote the mixing of supervision. In fact, there are many discussions in the academic field around this topic. However, there are also voices that the current three-party regulatory pattern in China has formed the so-called "regulatory competition" model, conducive to the formation of a mutual restraint situation. As for the future, we will have to wait and see the outcome.

In the vigorous staking course of the banking industry, a batch of financial holding companies gradually emerged in China. The most famous are Ping An Group, Everbright Group, CITIC Group, China's top five state-owned banks and twelve national joint-stock commercial corporations. In recent years, banks have also arranged financial holding companies through the acquisition of brokerage firms, trust companies and self-construction. At the same time, companies such as Anbang Insurance Co., Ltd. and Jiuding Investment Co., Ltd. have also emerged as a result of the rapid development over the past few years. They are often referred as a *de facto* financial holding platform for companies across several financial formats. Even Alibaba Group, Jingdong Group, a well-known electricity supplier in China, IT companies such as Tengxuan and Baidu also have subsidiaries of banks, funds and insurance to different degrees.

For example, Alibaba Group's affiliate Ant Financial Holdings Fund has a fund company called Tianhong, an online insurance company Public Security, and MYbook. Alibaba's financial services career has risen from the ground almost overnight. The ever-increasing fierce competition shows that China's financial industry has entered the "Warring States Period".

1.5 Q&A

1.5.1 In China how can people find bank branches, and how is the network coverage rate?

In large and medium-sized cities in China, including Beijing, Shanghai, Guangzhou and Shenzhen, as well as provincial capitals, financial institutions are very densely situated. State-owned commercial banks and major national joint-stock commercial banks are well located, and there are also considerable local commercial banks.

For residents in China's ordinary cities, we suggest that state-owned commercial banks be selected to handle their business. Ordinary cities in the eastern region are also basically covered by branches of joint-stock banks. However, for ordinary central cities and outlets in the central and western regions. There are mainly state-owned commercial banks.

For China's counties and townships, it is advisable to choose either Agricultural Bank of China or China Postal Savings Bank to conduct business. The outlets of these two banks can basically cover all counties in China. In addition, there are also local agricultural banks.

1.5.2 In China, in how many places can consumers pay with credit card? Do they need to bring a lot of cash?

In the Chinese cities, credit card payment can be basically realized in larger places such as restaurants and supermarkets, while in small-sized retail outlets, it is suggested to ask the shopkeeper whether they can pay by credit card. In China's urban areas, self-service banking equipment is also widely distributed, but it should be noted that cross-bank withdrawals will have a fee.

If you go to China's counties and townships, it is recommended to carry a certain amount of cash, generally, there are less self-service banking equipment in counties.

1.5.3 Do Chinese credit cards need a password? Is the credit card used universally?

In China, whether you are using a credit card or a debit card, you need to enter your password. Now you can use the "flash payment" in some areas. This payment method does not require a password, but the popularity of this payment method is still very low. Chinese consumers basically do not use checks for consumption, and the issuance of checks is more complicated in China.

1.5.4 Does China's banking service support English?

Most of China's banking services do not support English. Most of the communication uses Chinese. It is recommended to learn some basic Chinese words in this context, such as "save money", "withdraw money" and "exchange RMB".

1.5.5 How can foreigners open a bank account in China's bank?

You only need to bring a valid personal passport that is valid during the period of the endorsement to open an account at a bank branch. Such a bank account can enjoy normal deposit, withdrawal and transfer services.

It is worthy to note that, if customers want to use the bank account to buy bank financial products, insurance, funds, they need to provide proof of personal work in China.

Chapter 2　Overview of China's Non-bank Financial Industry

By the end of 2014, there were 121 securities companies in China, out of which 22 were listed securities companies, 153 stock companies and 95 fund management companies. Figure 2-1 shows the number of operating agencies in China's securities and futures industry from 2004 to 2014.

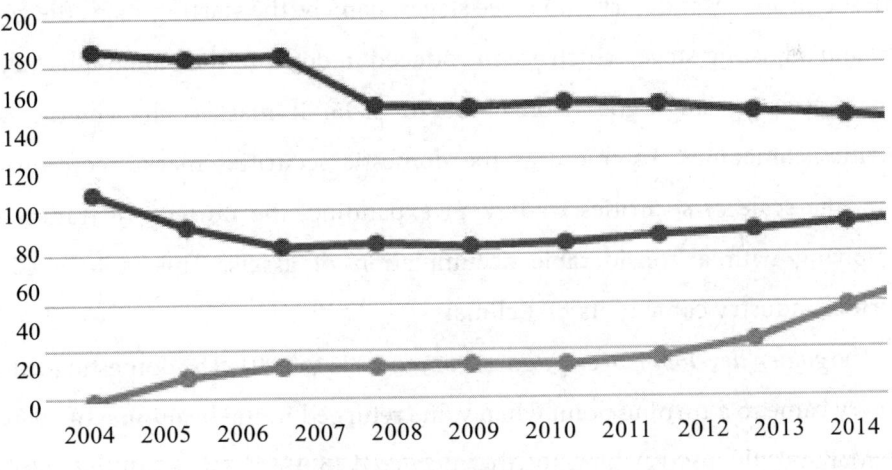

Source: China Securities Regulatory Commission

Figure 2-1　2004-2014 Changes in the Number of Securities and Futures Institutions

It can be seen from the figure that in the past ten years, the fund industry in China has been developing steadily. The number of fund companies has risen steadily while the number of securities and futures companies has not changed much or even declined slightly. This is mainly due to the fact that the internal integration between brokers has been constant, and the development of the industry continued to give birth to a stronger anti-risk ability and more capital brokers, a good example to illustrate this is the merge between Shenyin Wanguo Securities and Hongyuan Securities, which is a powerful combination.

2.1 Securities Industry

The securities business in China appears as early as 1980s when commercial banks set up overseas started to trade securities. In 1988, the first securities trader, the Securities Company of Shenzhen Special Economic Zone was established. Looking back at the history of the securities industry, we can categorize the domestic securities industry into three stages, namely, the starting stage, the golden stage and adjusting stage, which are introduced in detail in the paragraphs below.

The *starting stage* goes from 1988 to 1995. It marked the emergence of securities companies. Later on, as the domestic securities market continued to boom, the scale of securities trade kept expanding, the number of traders kept multiplying with a considerable accumulation of assets. This is how China's securities industry came to its first climax.

The *golden development stage* goes from to 1996 to 2001. The domestic securities industry came to a turning point when value returned in the beginning of 1996 and the "March 19th" market blowout that occurred in 1999. Later on, the securities industry began its bull market expansion. Domestic securities had new traits when market prosperity facilitated the development of stock market.(1) Securities firms generally had a large increase in operating profits; (2) Local securities firms with good assets, enterprise development strategy and advanced management technology have sprung up and quickly emerged in the competition. Many securities firms even achieved the purpose of scale expansion and business expansion by merging and reorganizing the securities business department of trust companies. According to the law, the mode of separate operation of China's financial industry is marked by the formal implementation of the Securities Law on July 1, 1999; (3) By 2001, more than 40 stock-holding or holding securities firms were set up, while as many as 100 listed companies had participated in the development of stock-holding, thus shareholding securities companies became very popular.

The *adjusting stage* goes from 2001 to present. After the over-two-year bull market period, the domestic securities bubble constantly swelled, as a result, the stock market suffered from strong sluggishness, causing a bear market period that started in July 2001. Moreover, the Chinese entry to the WTO in December 2001 dramatically altered the domestic industry, starting a process of globalization and internationalization that penetrated every corner of the Chinese industry. During this period, the development of securities traders had the following characteristics: large shrinking of business, increasing plunge, and the risk of securities became gradually greater.

The development of the securities industry in China has attracted worldwide attention since the beginning. In particular, since the release of the *Opinions of the State Council on Promoting the Reform and Opening up and the Stable Development of the Capital Market,* a series of reforms and institutional innovations carried out in the Chinese capital market. The implementation of the split share structure reform has effectively improved the stock market. The operating mechanism of the entire capital market and the impact of the macroeconomic environment solved a number of institutional constraints for the development of China's securities market. The future development of China's securities industry seems to be reaching a climax of sustained and healthy development thanks to the implementation of the risk control index management approach with the core capital as the center of the China Securities Regulatory Commission. The future development of the securities industry is bound to move forward in the direction of diversification of profitability models, standardization of management and operation, gradual development of development and internationalization of industry competition.

2.1.1 The composition of China's securities market

China's securities market consists of the main board market, the small and medium board market, the GEM market (Growth Enterprises Market), the new third board market and some over-the-counter markets (such as Beijing Equity Exchange Center), which will be described in detail in Chapter 4.

2.1.2 China's securities market trading rules

2.1.2.1 Open a trading account

According to current laws and regulations, if an investor wants to engage in securities trading, he must first apply to the securities registration company to open a securities account, this will allow the investor to participate in the secondary securities market. The investor also has the option to do an online subscription, for which he should apply for the opening of a capital account for security companies (exchange members), and deposit the transaction funds. The securities registration company will provide each investor with securities custody, registration and delivery services, as well as agency trading, agency clearance and cashier services. Identification verification rules also apply for the investors to open an account.

2.1.2.2 Commission trading

According to current laws and regulations, each investor who trades securities must be entrusted to a securities company with an official membership; that is, investors' trading orders are first reported to the securities company. Securities companies will then enter the client's transaction instructions input to the computer terminal via their intra-market transactions net or trading system; the securities company computer terminal will sync this transaction with the host computer of

Chapter 2
Overview of China's Non-bank Financial Industry

the stock exchange. Once the transaction is ready for liquidation, the delivery and transfer process take place.

Each trade order or statement should include the following:
- Shareholder account and password
- Order number and time (contract number and specific time of the transaction, six digits)
- Trading distinction (0 to buy, 1 to sell)
- Stock code (usually 4 digits)
- Number of delegates (in lots*)
- Commissioned price (market or limit)
- Validity period of the commission (valid on the same date)
- Other content, such as the client's funds account number, ID number and others

2.1.2.3 Indoor bidding

Once the client's trading instruction is entered into the host computer system, the transaction will go through a bidding process. There are two types of auction bidding methods: collective bidding and continuous bidding.

Collective bidding is mainly applied to the stock market opening price and daily opening price. According to this bidding method, the Stock Exchange shall set the auction time within the stipulated time (9:15 to 9:25) before the formal opening of the market on each business day (the closing price of the Shenzhen Stock Exchange is also determined on the set auction, and closing bidding time is 14: 57-15: 00 each trading day). The host computer matching system will only store the order without matching the deal; at the official opening, the host matching system will process all the entered order prices and quantities to create the opening price. The principle of matching transactions is as follows:

---

* In China, one lot refers to 100 shares.

- At the price which the maximum volume can be realized
- Buying-in at a higher price and buying-off taking the application at a lower price
- Buying in and off, taking at the same price as the one of the party who made the original deal

When two or more declared prices meet the above conditions, the Shanghai Stock Exchange makes the deal with the smallest volume of the undecided declared price for the transaction; there are still two or more prices to make the minimum undeclared price in accordance with the above conditions. The middle price would be set for the transaction. Shenzhen Stock Exchange will then take the price from the previous closing for this transaction. All transactions in the set auction are traded at the same price.

After the auction is over, the exchange will start its official trading in the morning and the trading system will enter a continuous auction until the close of the trading day.

Continuous bidding is the process by which both buyers and sellers continuously offer to buy and sell according to the bidding principle of price priority and time priority. According to this principle, the bidding price at each point in time is higher than or equal to the bidding price, that is, the price is matched to the order of price. At each equivalent transaction price point, if there is a time difference between sales and purchase orders (first reporter transactions) those who cannot be traded will be waiting for the opportunity to make a deal, this means that the remaining party will have to wait for the transaction to take place.

2.1.2.4 Liquidation and transfer

Securities trading liquidation refers to the securities buyers and sellers through the securities brokers in the Stock Exchange for sale after the transaction, through the transaction clearing system for transaction funds payment and receipt process. According to the transaction settlement system practiced in China, on the day the securities dealers dealt with securities transactions, the securities dealers should first conduct a liquidation transaction with the exchange after the close of the market and pay off the difference in the amount of securities traded on the securities according to the difference settlement rules. Then, each securities firm needs to settle the amount of each investor's trading securities. However, due to the prevailing practice of credit settlement, each investor has immediate settlement of the funds in his account at the exact same time the trade is warranted. The securities sold, then available for sale separate from other securities, and those who buy the securities have their funds deducted from their account. There is no overdraft purchase. This rule has actually formed the T+0 system of liquidation.

Transfer of securities refers to the market of buyers, sellers and brokers in the Stock Exchange, it also refers to the securities registration authority for the transfer of securities rights and registration process. In the Chinese registration and transfer system, the investor shall complete the transfer formalities before the next business day and the delivery order should be provided. If a statutory holiday falls on that day of the transaction, the transfer date shall be postponed until the next working day. This is known as the T+1 rule. Under this rule, securities bought on a business day can only be sold on the next business day.

According to the current laws and regulations, China's B-share transaction rules are not completely equal to the A-share liquidation rules. B shares transactions may apply T+3 rules.

2.2 Bulk Trading System

China's stock exchanges in both Shanghai and Shenzhen have stipulated a system of block trades, and the stock exchanges in both places have block trading counters. According to China's securities trading rules, all transactions of 500,000 shares or more stock can apply to the trading blockbuster. The blockbuster counter will receive the application, afterwards the receipt of the transaction will be stored without the immediate match at the end of the direct bidding transaction day, a unified matching transaction will be made according to the average transaction price of the stock on that day. That is to say, the actual bidding system adopted by China for bulk transactions is a collective bidding system.

2.1.3 Opening up of China's stock market
2.1.3.1 B shares

The official name of B shares is RMB special stocks. It is a foreign-capital stock that is denominated in Renminbi, which is subscribed for and traded in foreign currencies and listed on the stock exchanges in the PRC (Shanghai, Shenzhen). The registration of the B shares of a company and its listing should take place in the Chinese mainland.

2.1.3.1.1 Opening an account

Investors who need to buy and sell B shares in Shanghai Stock Exchange, should first open their B shares accounts.

Steps for opening a B shares account:

Step One: Applicants with a valid ID card, can go to the original foreign exchange deposit bank for, cash deposits and foreign currency deposits, that are placed into B shares margin security firms accounts that are located in their same city. The domestic commercial bank issues a voucher for the domestic individual investor and a statement to the securities institution.

Step Two: Open a B-share capital account with a securities institution based on the applicant's own valid ID card and the voucher received on step one. The minimum amount for opening a B-share fund account is USD 1000.

Step Three: Use the newly opened B-share capital account to the securities business institutions to apply for the opening of B shares account.

2.2.1.1.2 Comparison of B shares and A shares

B shares are not physical stocks. They rely on paperless electronic bookkeeping to implement the delivery system of "T+3" with the limit of up and down (10%). The participating investors are residents and foreigners in Hong Kong, Macao and Taiwan and hold Chinese mainland residents can also invest in legal foreign exchange deposits.

A shares are for domestic investors to invest in stocks, B shares for overseas investors to invest in stocks. B shares are denominated in Renminbi, but also in foreign currency. Both A shares and B shares are listed on the Shanghai or Shenzhen exchanges.

A shares are also known as RMB ordinary shares, tradable shares, public shares, ordinary shares. Refers to those registered and listed in Chinese mainland common stock. They are subscripted and traded in RMB.

A shares are not physical stocks, they are subject to electronic paperless accounting and the implementation of "T+1" delivery system, up and down (10%). These are restricted to investors in Chinese mainland's institutions or individuals.

2.2.1.1.3 Ways in which domestic residents and overseas investors invest in B shares

- Documents are submitted for account opening in different ways

When applying for the opening of a B-share securities account, residents in Chinese mainland shall use their valid personal identification documents and bank deposit vouchers of more than USD1,000 to apply to brokers that have the qualification of opening accounts for B shares.

However, overseas (non-resident) investors only need to obtain their permanent residency rights overseas only by their valid personal documents (foreign passport, foreign ID card, Chinese passport + proof of permanent residency) and thus they can be treated as domestic residents.

- Different deposit and withdrawal methods

Investors use B-share securities accounts to handle foreign exchange capital accounts (i.e.: B-share margin accounts) at the brokerage offices. Domestic residents deposit their cash or cash deposits transferred from banks into B-margin deposits. Overseas (nonresidents) shall deposit the foreign exchange currency remitted from abroad or the legal cash deposit of a domestic commercial bank into the B share capital account.

When the deposit is withdrawn, the domestic resident shall first make the funds in the B-share margin account back to the domestic commercial bank and withdraw it to the bank, and the funds returned to the bank shall be regarded as foreign currency cash and shall not be paid abroad; while the overseas investors (non-resident) can be remitted abroad to pay, or deposited in Chinese mainland to open a valid foreign exchange account.

- Domestic B shares investors in Shanghai need to implement designated transactions

Domestic B shares investors in Shanghai take B shares accounts at the same time, the designated transaction has been completed, as the only trading point of trading securities, investors can only be specified in the securities trading business transactions, liquidation, settlement. To change the designated transaction, you must first cancel the designated securities in business department, and then go to the other securities business department to re-apply for the specified transaction.

- Foreign investors in Shanghai buying and selling B shares "can buy everywhere, sell everywhere"

Different from domestic residents, overseas investors are reflected in buying and selling the B shares of the Shanghai stock market: they are readily available for sale everywhere. That is, the B shares bought in any different securities business department with the same securities account may also be sold at any securities business department.

The balance of shares is reconciled by the clearing member on a monthly basis. However, no matter what B shares are bought by the sales department, the cash dividends of the shares issued here are still in their designated clearing members. All relevant inquiries, reporting of losses, rights and interests acquisition, freezing, thawing and non-trading transfer shall be settled at the designated settlement member handle.

Finally, as far as B shares investors are concerned, they are open to all foreign countries. They can be both institutional investors such as investment funds and non-resident individuals. At present, they are only open to domestic residents and are not yet open to legal persons.

2.1.3.2 QFII & RQFII

QFII (Qualified Foreign Institutional Investors) is an English abbreviation for eligible foreign institutional investors and QFII mechanism refers to the foreign professional investment for institutions to invest in the domestic qualification system.

As a transitional institutional arrangement, the QFII system is a special channel for an orderly and a prudently open securities market in countries and regions where the capital account has not yet been fully liberalized. Under this system, QFII will be allowed to import and exchange a certain amount of foreign exchange funds into the local currency and invest in the local securities market. Through a special account under strict supervision and administration, various capital can be converted to foreign exchange remittances including dividends and bid-ask spreads after gains have been audited, in fact, it is a limited opening up of foreign securities market.

QFII is a transitional system in which a country introduces foreign capital and opens its capital markets to a limited extent under the condition that currency cannot be completely freely convertible, and the capital account has not yet been opened up. Such a system requires foreign investors to enter the securities market of a country, must meet certain conditions, get the approval of the relevant departments of the country after the passage of a certain amount of foreign exchange funds and converted into local currency, through strict supervision of the special account invested in the local stock market.

The essence of the QFII system is a kind of creative capital controls. Under this mechanism, any person planning to invest in domestic capital markets must separately deal in securities through a qualified institution so as to facilitate the government's supervision and control over foreign exchange with a view to reducing capital flows, especially the short-term "hot money" for the domestic economy and securities markets impact. Through the QFII system, management can restrict and guide the foreign capital entry necessary to make it compatible with the country's economic development and the development of the securities market, control the impact of foreign capital on the economic independence of the country, and suppress the influence of foreign speculative hot money on the domestic economic impact, promote the internationalization of capital markets and promote the healthy development of capital markets.

RQFII (Renminbi Qualified Foreign Institutional Investors) refers to Renminbi qualified overseas investors. It refers to the system of qualification of foreign professional investment institutions to invest in China. RQFII and QFII have the following important differences.

QFII is a qualified overseas institutional investor. After the review by the CSRC, foreign institutional investors may exchange foreign exchange for RMB within the amount allowed by the SAFE (State Administration of Foreign Exchange) for domestic investment.

RQFII is a foreign institutional investor of RMB, with a quota less than that of QFII, also known as Small QFII. It is a system where overseas institutions make domestic investment in RMB. The main difference between RQFII and QFII is the difference between the currency used, RQFII uses Renminbi and QFII uses U.S. Dollars.

2.3 Futures Industry

The development of China's futures industry has undergone a long and tortuous process which can be summarized as the following stages: the initial founding, rectification and governance and the stage of olderly development. The specific points are as follows.

The initial founding period. In the 1980s, the price fluctuation of agricultural products gradually increased, and the dual-track system of the price of means of production was gradually inclined to marketization. Because of the deepening of economic system reform, the market mechanism plays an increasingly important role. In March 1988, the State Council of China demanded active development of various types of wholesale markets and exploration of futures trading. From that date on, China started a long period of exploration of futures trading practices and rectified the normative period.

In mid-October 1990, with the approval of the State Council, the highest state administrative organ, Zhengzhou grain wholesale market officially launched a futures trading mechanism, which laid the foundation of China's futures market. However, driven by the demonstration effect of industry interests, the unchecked proliferation of underground futures trading, good and bad practitioners being mixed up, and the lack of relevant laws and regulations, various futures exchanges emerged in China, which resulted in the superficial economic prosperity of China's futures market.

Rectification and governance period. As China's futures market expanded blindly, the State Council made its first rectification of the futures market in 1993. After another five years, the futures market was rectified for the second time. As a result of the first rectification, fifteen exchanges were designated as pilot exchanges. In the second rectification in 1998, the number of futures exchanges was reduced to 3 and futures contracts were kept at 12. Higher access standards for futures companies were required in the following year (1999) with their registered capital needing to be more than or equal to 30 million *yuan*. In the last year of the 20th century, self-regulatory organizations of China's futures industry came into being.

Therefore, these two reforms promoted the improvement of self-management ability of the futures market, maintained the survival of the futures market, which begun to enter a standardized and orderly track. A relatively independent futures industry was basically developed.

The stage of olderly development. The clean-up and reorganization in the 1990s provided the external conditions and foundations for the city under the rule of law, it also highlighted the decline of the market and the weakening of both the trading volume and the trading volume of futures. It was only after 2003 that the industry started to regain vitality and entered the track of healthy development. Through the analysis in Figure 2-2, we can conclude that the total volume of futures market in 2000 was 53.618 million hands, less than one tenth of that in 1995, while from the beginning of 2003, both volume and turnover began to climb gradually ushering in the second spring for China's futures industry!

At present, there are Zhengzhou Commodity Exchange (hereinafter referred to as ZCE), Dalian Commodity Exchange (referred to as DCE), Shanghai Futures Exchange (referred to as SFE) and China Financial Futures Exchange (referred to as CFFEX). As of the end of 2013, the futures and commodities traded in the market increased from 24 in 2012 to 25 in 2013 (of which the iron ore futures were traded on the DCE on October 18, 2013). This covered a large number of industries and fields, forming a relatively complete system of commodity futures. The establishment time and major varieties of the four domestic commodity exchanges are shown in Table 2-1. Here is the introduction of the futures exchanges.

(A) Zhengzhou Commodity Exchange (ZCE). By the end of 2012, there are 209 members in ZCE, including 42 non-futures companies and 167 futures companies. ZCE had a total turnover of 347 million contracts traded in 2012, decieased by 14.61% year-on-year, the total turnover of 17.36 trillion *yuan*, decieased by 48.04% year-on-year, Its acumulative turnover volume throughtout the year accounted for 23.93% of the total market share, and the turnover 10.15%.

In 2012, ZCE stepped up the establishment of the system in order to gradually improve its membership service function. Firstly, the transaction settlement system was upgraded to meet the business requirements and complete the service functions of members. Secondly, in terms of basic building modules of information system, efforts were made to step up the construction of Futures Building and disaster preparedness system for other locations, the construction of computer room infrastructure in the technology center and the construction of data protection projects in three centers and two regions. In order to further improve the future terminal construction and cooperation with room internet service members, and to provide members with safe and reliable quality, the member-end internet service network upgrade project was launched.

In terms of self-regulation management, ZCE, taking the actual situation of the futures market into consideration, gradually improved business rules, strengthened daily monitoring, and strictly investigated and dealt with daily irregularities. In 2012, it handled more than 80 abnormal transactions.

(B) Dalian Commodity Exchange (DCE). As of the end of 2012, DCE has 178 members, including 163 members of futures companies and 15 non-futures companies. 2012 is the year that the scale of trading in DCE achieved a historic high. The trading volume and open interest reached record highs. In 2012, the turnover volume of DCE was RMB 633 million, an increase of 119% over the same period of last year; the turnover increased by 97% year on year to reach RMB 33 trillion; in the ranking of global derivatives exchanges in 2012, DCE occupied the 11th place. The number of investor accounts has increased by 13% to a total of 1,568,000 accounts.

In terms of business innovation, DCE officially launched the multi-level commodity market construction project. One way is to start the construction of the multi-level commodity trading service platform. A special working group has been set up by the DCE, and its personnel have been sent to India, Chongqing and Tianjin for field investigation and research. A multi-level market construction scheme with strong operability has thus been formed and entered the stage of approval. Second, the preparatory work for the listing of options has been put on the agenda. Thirdly, with a view of facing the international market and focusing on the future, we have strengthened our research on the extension of trading time, multi-currency settlement, cash settlement, contract plug-in and other business innovation projects, and have worked out a preliminary report.

With respect to market services, in 2012, DCE, in accordance with the requirements of improving its work style, getting closer to the society and the market, conducted in-depth research at the grass-roots level, listened extensively and thoroughly to the opinions and suggestions of its members, enterprises and investors. On the basis of this, it has improved its business rules, launched its services for the "three rural issues" and enterprises, and actively explored innovative means of service with the result that the market outlook and image of Exchange have changed a lot. The first way is to adapt to market changes and actively improve business rules and systems. The second way is to provide better services for the activities in rural areas and service industries. DCE will continue its well-known market services such as "industry congress", "thousands of villages and tens of thousands of households" and "tens of thousands of factories and enterprises", actively carry out various training and marketing activities in order to guide more enterprises to make scientific use of the futures market. The third way is to cultivate institutional investors and talents in the futures industry. In October 2012, the first phase of the financial laboratory independently developed by DCE was successfully launched. This new tool, by integrating R&D strategy, experimental simulation, remote counseling and other functions, adapts to the development direction of integration of R&D and investment of futures companies and is thus an important innovation of market service mode.

(C) Shanghai Futures Exchange (SFE). As of the end of 2012, there were 208 SFE members, of which 161 were futures companies, accounting for 77.4% of the total, while 47 were non-futures companies, accounting for 22.6% of the total. In 2012, the overall trading volume of SFE was stable, mainly due to the fine-tuning of the national monetary policy. Also, a repeated downward adjustment of transaction fees greatly reduced the transaction costs of investors and other factors.

In terms of market services, SFE has always been making efforts to refine existing varieties of products, improving the management of hedging and reducing the standard of service charge. Secondly, it has optimized the delivery operation mechanism and made a forward-looking exploration on the basis of the research of the establishment and layout of delivery warehouses in the international futures market. Third, it has improved the quality of market services. Under the leadership of SFE, we have held face-to-face talks with members and representatives of investors in various districts, listened to their opinions and suggestions, and offered training for senior managers and analysts.

Regarding information technology innovation and development, SFE, in 2012, not only guaranteed the safety of technical system operation, but also maintained the leading position of technical system in the industry. First, the annual evaluation of information security grade protection has been completed, and the pass rate has increased by 2 percentage points compared with 2011. Second, the network monitoring and application performance analysis system has been optimized integrating equipment management, performance management, fault management, configuration management and other functional modules, which obviously improved the speed of support. Thirdly, we persist in carrying out emergency drills and have successfully completed the joint emergency drills of information security in the industry organized by the China Securities Regulatory Commission (CSRC). Fourthly, we are accelerating the construction of a new generation of trading systems and have established a time measurement mechanism that is accurate to microseconds, basically reaching the international first-class level. Fifth, the network consulting project has been launched, and the planning of network communication platform has been unified. At present, the system evaluation has been finished and the investigation of the network status of foreign advanced exchanges has also been completed.

(D) China Financial Futures Exchange (CFFEX). The number of members in the stock index futures market increased steadily in 2012. By the end of 2012, CFFEX had a total of 146 members. This includes 70 trading members, 15 full settlement members and 61 transaction settlement members. Stock index futures in 2012 ran smoothly for 243 trading days, with a total of 127,000 accounts, and 113,000 clients involved in the transactions.

CFFEX attaches great importance to technical safety work and regards it as the foundation for the exchange to survive. In 2012, by continuously improving the level of safety operation, we kept the system operate safely without any accidents throughout the year. First, we have strengthened the optimization and transformation of the technical system and successfully completed the simulation of treasury bond futures and the transformation of the production system. Secondly, the hierarchical guarantee system of technology has been constructed. The 19 information systems of the exchange have been classified, and the standards and procedures of safeguard are defined, so as to further improve the level of operation and maintenance management. Third, we have promoted the establishment of a new generation of system by holding more than 70 seminars to complete the system construction organization and promotion programs.

2012 also saw CFFEX make significant breakthroughs in international exchange and cooperation. Remarkable progress was made in expanding channels of foreign exchange and strengthening exchanges and cooperation with foreign institutions. First, through outbound visits, invitations and participation in international conferences, we have further expanded our channels of foreign exchanges, and have smoother contacts with overseas futures exchanges and well-known financial institutions. The second progress was to join the World Federation of Exchanges and have established a basic platform for international cooperation for CFFEX.

In terms of internal construction, the Exchange, by insisting on building Party organizations on the basis of development, has carefully planned, orderly promoted and continuously deepened the Party building work of CFFEX. First, we planned the Party building work from a long-term and strategic perspective with the focus on the current work. Secondly, we laid stress on the establishment of relevant rules and regulations and improved the level of democratization and institutionalization of the work of the Party committee. Third, we paid attention to the appointment of full-time personnel. Fourth, we strengthened honesty and self-discipline to ensure the construction of a clean and honest Party and clear responsibility. Table 2-1 summarizes the representative trading products of CFFEX.

CFFEX currently offers trading in Treasury Futures and Stock Index Futures. Here we will outline the trading rules for China's financial futures. We can determine China's Financial Futures Trading Rules as follows:

1. Margin trading rules

According to this rule, China has 8% margin trading rules for securities and futures trading. Securities and futures traders can trade one-sided securities and futures commodities with a par value of 8% margin; the law allows futures brokers based on the 8% basis Additional margin, according to the futures market practice, the margin ratio should not exceed 15%. It can be seen that the margin trading rules are two-fold. On the one hand, the financial futures exchange will apply to all futures brokers engaged in securities and futures trading and receive a trading margin of 8% of the transaction amount. On the other hand, the futures broker will charge its clients Trading margin of 8% or more.

2. The day without debt settlement rules

According to the rules, the financial futures exchange shall promptly notify all its futures trading members and complete the settlement of liabilities with them at the close of the day, and the futures trading member shall settle with the customer again based on the result of the futures transaction settlement, the settlement results should be promptly notified to the consumer in accordance with the agreement. When the client has been put on this position, the contract will constitute a liability to the futures trading member. The futures trading member has the right to request the client to replenish the trading margin and take responsibility for the exchange with its own funds.

3. Forced liquidation rules

According to the rules, when there is not enough margin for trading members of futures exchanges, they should promptly add margin or open their own positions. If the member fails to increase the margin or to liquidate himself within the time limit prescribed by the futures exchange, the futures exchange shall forcibly liquidate the contract of the member and forcibly liquidate the relevant expenses and losses incurred to be borne by this member. When the client's margin is insufficient, it shall promptly be increased or he should open his own account. If the client fails to timely increase the margin or open his own position within the time prescribed by the futures company, the futures company shall forcibly liquidate the contract of the client and the relevant costs and losses incurred by the forcible liquidation shall be borne by the client.

4. Daily mark-to-market rules

In connection with the above rules, China also adopts the daily mark-to-market rule in the practice of futures contract law. Under this rule, a futures broker has the right to require all its clients to have fixed office locations, fixed office workers, fixed contact numbers around their futures companies. Legal notice of daily settlements is official as long as the futures company is in agreement with the fixed contact on the customer side. At the expiration of the contractual period, the futures company has the right under the terms of the contract to infer the client's meaning.

5. Clearing member rules

China implements a system of hierarchical settlement of futures trading. Under this system, the parties engaging in securities and futures trading are only the trading members of the financial futures exchange. Any party that wishes to engage in securities and futures trading must pass through an authorized futures broker and the relationship between the client and the futures broker is a specific brokerage contractual relationship. On the other hand, according to China's "Futures Trading Regulations", the daily settlement with the Financial Futures

Exchange must be its clearing members, futures companies that do not have the financial futures clearing membership must be through clearing members and financial futures exchange settlement; financial futures exchange clearing members are divided into general clearing members and special clearing members of two. General clearing members will have their own funds and take their own risk on behalf of all its clients and the financial futures exchange settlement, and special settlement members and financial futures exchanges can represent only a limited number of customers. All the financial futures exchange clearing members are required to pay the financial futures exchange risk reserves, and all their clients transactions to the financial futures exchange negative settlement guarantee.

6. Risk control rules

According to the regulations of China's "Futures Trading Regulations", when an abnormal situation occurs in China's futures market, the futures exchange may, in accordance with the authority and procedure stipulated in its charter, decide to take the following emergency measures and immediately report to the futures regulatory authority of the State Council:

(1) Increase the proportion of margin

(2) Adjust the range of price limit

(3) Limit the maximum positions of members or customers

(4) Temporarily stop trading

(5) Forced to lighten up

(6) Take other urgent measures

(7) Price daily limit rules and fuse mechanism

(8) Limit positions and large positions reporting rules

(9) Risk reserve rules

(10) Mandatory lighten up disposal rules

Table 2-1 Highlights on the Representative Transactions of Various Futures Exchanges in China

Exchange Name	Established Time	Futures Species
Zhengzhou Commodity Exchange	1990.10.12	Hard wheat, cotton, sugar, refined terephthalic acid, rapeseed oil, indica rice, methanol, etc.
Dalian Commodity Exchange	1993.2.28	Yellow soybean, corn, beans cypress, soybean oil, palm oil, linear low-density polyethylene, polyvinyl chloride, etc.
Shanghai Futures Exchange	1998.8.1	Copper, Aluminum, Zinc, Gold, Wire, Natural rubber, rebar, fuel oil, etc
China Financial Futures Exchange	2006.9.8	Treasury bonds, stock index futures (Shanghai and Shenzhen 300, Shanghai 50, etc.), stock options

Source: the official website of the exchanges, summarized by the author.

2.4 Fund Industry

China's fund industry has generally gone through three stages of development.

2000-2007: Initial stage of collective development. In 2000, the domestic fund industry was still controlled by the "old ten". At that time, the number of fund companies was small and the market was more concentrating. Basically, the total size of the top five fund companies accounted for more than half of the market. During the following seven years, from 2000 to 2007, the domestic fund management industry was booming. The number of fund companies increased at an average rate of six per year. The number of fund companies increased from the "old ten" in 2000 to 57 by the end of 2007.

2008-2012: Stagnation. From the beginning of 2008, due to the financial crisis, the regulatory authorities had basically suspended the approval of the fund industry licenses. From 2008 to 2010, basically no fund companies were established, but in 2011, the fund industry was further liberalized and the amount of companies increased to 70 in 2012. During this period, because of the strict industry regulation and the poor market of capital market, the competitiveness of the industry has decreased compared with bank financing and trust companies. The concentration of the industry has not changed much, basically maintained at about 30% (the top five companies) and about 50% (top 10 companies).

Since 2013: The industry has entered a new stage of development. After the financial innovation in 2012, especially after the promulgation of the new *Fund Act*, the barrier of fund industry has been lowered, the investment scope has been greatly widened, and the innovation of new fund products has emerged in an endless stream. Since then, the set-up of the fund industry has undergone great changes. Tianhong Fund is widely favored by the market for its product of "Yu'e Bao". Its monetary fund scale reached 570 billion *yuan*, accounting for 15% of the total fund management scale. As it promoted the company to the top rank, it made the top five fund companies account for 40% and the top 10 57% in scale.

Judging from the changes in the net worth of various funds over these years, in the initial stage of the fund industry, the industry was mainly composed of closed-end funds and hybrid funds. With the arrival of bull market, aggressive stock funds have gradually become the mainstream of the market, accounting for 50 percent during the peak. In recent years, the stock market has underperformed, so investors turned to choose low-risk products. The scale and share of fixed-income products Represented by the monetary funds have substantial growth. The monetary funds reached a quarter of the whole market share in 2012. Even though the stock funds declined about 20% in 2013, hybrid funds maintained about one-fifth of the whole market share. From the perspective of future trends, combining the experience from the developed countries, investors who have different risk preferences are going to prefer stock funds with risk-return characteristics (representing high-risk and high-yield) and monetary funds (representing low-risk and low-yield). However, hybrid funds are positioning more obscurely, and the characteristics of the investment are not significant, thus, hybrid funds are gradually marginalized.

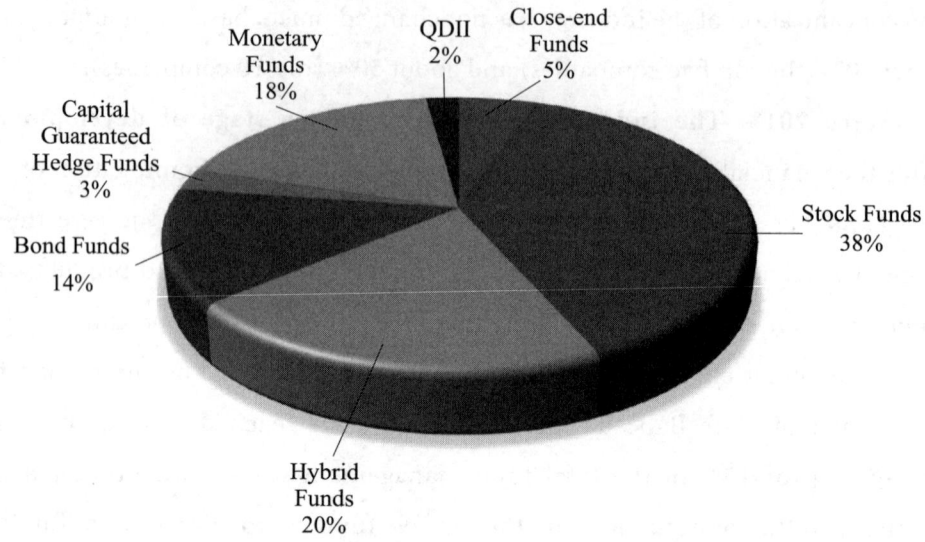

Source: Asset Management Association of China

Figure 2-2 Various Types of Fund Assets Account for Market Share

In recent years, China's fund industry is also constantly innovating.

Innovation in scope of funds' investment. As the China Securities Regulatory Commission has already defined the scope of funds' investment, the innovation mainly lies in the refinement of investment scope and the restriction on the proportion of investment. After the refinement of scope, more sector funds and industry funds appeared as equity funds and bond funds. More specifically-divided funds appeared, such as pure debt funds and subdivision bond funds of convertible bond funds. After setting different proportions of stock investment, innovative products as total funds, preference-debt allocation funds and life-cycle funds with positions changing with the dates of the market emerged. Moreover, QDII (Qualified Domestic Institutional Investors) funds, after the refinement, were divided into themed QDII and regional

Chapter 2
Overview of China's Non-bank Financial Industry

QDII. Also after the innovation of index funds, a fund tracking the composite index of stocks and bonds was created. Recently, with the acceleration of innovation, there has been a fund for investing in gold commodities, taking an important step toward innovation in the scope of investment.

Table 2-2 A Summary of Innovation in Scope of Funds' Investment

Innovation	Theme Type	Example of Specific Funds
Sector Equity Funds	Emerging industry theme, medicine theme, Consumption theme and so on	Emerging industries from CIFM, health and medical care from CUAM
Subdivision Bond Funds	Pure debt funds, convertible bonds funds and financial management funds	Pure debt funds from BOCIM, convertible bonds funds from BAM
Innovation in Proportions of Stock Investment	Total funds, preference-debt allocation funds	Macro strategy from Fullgoal Fund and so on
Themed QDII Funds	REITs, Resource QDII	REITs from Lion Fund Management, Global commodity from XinCheng Fund
Commodity Funds	Gold Exchange Traded Fund	Gold Exchange Traded Fund from HuaAn Funds and so on
Composite Stock-bond Index Funds	Composite stock-bond index funds	Growth stock from Yinhua Fund

source: The official websites of the fund company, edited by the author

The refinement of the investments' range gives investors various options to choose implemental products which have more certainty of risk and return. In the short term, innovative products have not brought significant scale expansion to fund companies, but in the long run, personalized products and completed product lines will enhance the competitiveness of fund companies, which will contribute to the development of scale economy.

Innovation in modes of operation. As for the mode of operation, funds have gone through a long course, ranging from closed to open, and then to the combination of various modes, like closed/regularly open/semi-closed/ETF (Exchange Traded Fund) and so on. Enclosure manner of bond funds can better avoid the impact of redeeming capital, in order to obtain returns with higher certainty. As a result, closed-ended debt bases, regular-open debt bases and debt-based bonds leading by rates are introduced. Take a high-yield fund from Fullgoal Fund as an example, the fund establishes a quarterly restricted open-ended period and an annual free-floating period. During the free-floating period, redeeming funds will not be charged, while in the restricted open-ended period, redeeming funds need to be charged, and the fee is going to be 1% of the redemption. In addition, during the restricted open-ended period, if the net amount of redemption exceeds a certain percentage (initially 10%) of the fund's assets, the applications of redemption on that day will be partially confirmed according to a certain percentage to ensure that the capital scale of the fund will not be greatly affected. Except for closed and semi-closed debt bases, the important innovations in modes of operation also include graded funds, ETFs and so on. Graded funds allocate fund returns to meet the needs of investors with different risk preferences. The ETF funds directly link the index funds with the price of a basket of stocks, thus improving the tracking efficiency of the index funds. Some ETFs have become the object of securities margin trading and have laid the foundation for fund companies to expand their scale.

Table 2-3 Innovative Examples of the Mode of Funds' Operation

Innovation	The Main Type	Examples of Specific Funds
Regularly Open-ended Debt Bases	Regular open-ended debt bases, regular semi-opened debt bases, debt-based bonds leading by rates	One-year fixed open-ended funds from ChinaAMC, and stable income fund from HuaAn Funds Management

Innovation	The Main Type	Examples of Specific Funds
Active Liquidation Fund	Funds which meet the conditions of active liquidation with absolute return features	One-year fund from Rongtong Funds Management
Graded Funds	Structured index, active structured stock, structured bonds	Graded growth Enterprise Index from Fullgoal Fund
Close-ended Debt Bbases	Close-ended debt bases	All-seasonal return funds from ICBC, credits and benefits from China Merchants Bank
Cross-market ETF	Cross-market ETF and cross-border ETF	CSI 300 Index ETF from Harvest Fund
Currency ETF	Currency ETF	Quick money from China Universal Asset Management

Source: Asset Management Association of China.

Innovation in service. Compared with product innovation, fund companies also introduced service innovation to strengthen their competitive edge.

Customize account. The inability of fund companies to provide fund products which their investors need is a culprit accumulated over the years in the industry. Most of the fund products are standardized, pursuing relative returns, but what investors need are absolute returns, and most fund investors do not have the professional knowledge of fund investment as well as lack of professional guidance in the timing and selection of the fund. Based on this, Harvest Fund has set up an "Return Center for Investors" where professionals provide "customized accounts" services to investors. According to the risk level, the "customized accounts" are divided into "aggressive combination", "calm and steady combination" and "easy money combination". Investors using the "custom account" service will have their money directly taken care of by a manager.

Monetary fund T+0. Another service that has emerged in recent years is the T+0 service. Monetary funds are one of the good types of fulfilling investors' risk preferences and absolute return demands at the same time. However, because its liquidity is slightly worse than monetary funds and lack of publicity, although T+0's return rate is much higher than that of bank deposits, it is not familiar with the majority of investors, so the scale did not grow and develop in the past years. Since 2012, various forms of T+0 services have emerged in money-based funds. Many currency-based funds can redeem T+0 funds in certain channels, such as banks, or online direct sales channels. The capital of redemption is partially composed by banks and fund companies. On the basis of the service, the liquidity of the monetary fund moved closer to the demand deposits of the banks, which provided the basis for the monetary funds to compete for the market of the banks' demand deposits.

Innovation in channels. Sales channels have always been the focus of competition in fund companies. Historically, the main channel of sales funds has been the bank. In recent years, third-party channels have been gradually shedding their stakes. With the issuance of third-party payment licenses, third-party sales have shown their advantages. The most typical is Tian Hong Asset Management and Alipay's cooperation. Alipay's users can purchase currency-fund named "increase profit" fund directly through the Alipay, which not only provide good liquidity (the balance of Yu'e Bao can be consumed on Taobao), and its purchasing threshold is pretty low (1 *yuan* to buy), also Alipay itself has a vast customer base and sedimentary funds. According to media reports, since June 13, 2013, when Yu'e Bao was available for customers online to early September, the scale of capital has had nearly 50 billion *yuan*.

2.5 Insurance

Thirty years ago, there was only one insurance company in Chinese market —People's Insurance Company of China. The insurance businesses are all planned targets. Today, the insurance market has exceeded 100 entities, and the market size increased by more than 1,500 times. In the past 30 years, there have been two highlights in China's insurance industry. First, the insurance industry has maintained an average annual growth rate of 30% in 30 years, making it one of the fastest growing industries in the country. Second, in Chinese financial industry, regardless of the opening time, the determination of the act of opening and the pace of the opening up, put the insurance industry at the forefront. During the 30 years of reform, the insurance industry has played an increasingly important role in promoting social stability and development of financial society.

2.6 Trust Industry

Trust, along with banking, securities, and insurance, is one of "the four pillars" of the financial industry. Its original meaning is "entrusted by the people, on behalf of people to make financial management". "Trust" refers to the clients who entrust their property rights to an assignee based on the trust they have in the assignee. The assignee, on behalf of clients' will or in his own name, will then manage or dispose the property, for the benefit of his client or for any specific purpose.

Trusts have a history of 3,800 years in the world, and it is praised as having infinite economic activation, because they are connected with the money market and the capital market. They are attached to the industrial market and can be financed and invested. In the words of Scott, an American authority in the trust topic, "the scope of trust's application can be compared with that of human's imagination."

China's trust industry started in Shanghai in the early 20th century. In August 1921, the first specialized trust and investment institution, China Commerce and Trust Corporation, was established in Shanghai. In 1935, the Central Trust Agency was established in Shanghai. From 1949 to 1979, financial trusts were not able to develop under the highly centralized planned system of economic management.

In October 1979, China International Trust & Investment Corporation, was established. Since then, various forms of trust and investment companies have been set up from the PBC to various specialized banks, competent departments of industry and local governments. By 1988, the number of trust companies were at the peak, there were more than 1,000 in total in the market, and their total assets reached more than RMB 600 billion, accounting for 10% of the total financial assets.

At the beginning, China's trust and investment companies were mainly engaged in bank-like businesses. We can say that this is where the real trust and investment business started. For instance, JinXin Trust & Investment Co., Ltd. issued the first mutual fund called "JinXin Trust" in Zhejiang Province in 1992, and it also launched the "personal-public entrusted deposit" business in August 1995. However, due to the lack of legal norms and management experience of trust and investment companies, in 1999, before PBC's fifth reorganization of trust industry, there were only 239 remaining companies in the market.

In 2015, China's trust industry assets finally achieve a reversal in the second quarter of this year after experiencing an embarrassing decline of quarter-on-quarter growth rate for seven times. Public information shows that by the end of the second quarter, the size of the national trust assets had exceeded RMB 15 trillion, an increase of 27.16% over the same period the year before.

China Trustee Association released *A review of the development of China's trust industry in the second quarter of 2015*, which shows that by the end of the second quarter, trust assets managed by the country's 68 trust companies reached RMB 15.87 trillion. Compared with RMB 14.41 trillion by the end of the first quarter of 2015, quarter-on-quarter growth of trust industry is 10.13%, an increase of 27.16% compared with the second quarter of 2014. This is also the first time since the third quarter of 2013 to the first quarter of 2015 that the growth rate of the trust assets recovered after suffering a total of seven-consecutive-quarters drop quarter-on-quarter, marking this as the beginning of the "RMB 15 trillion era" of the trust industry.

2.7 Q&A

2.7.1 Can foreigners or foreign companies set up wholly foreign-owned or foreign-controlled securities investment consulting firms in the Chinese mainland?

Regarding the relevant provisions of the establishment of foreign-funded securities investment consulting company, they should be in alignment with relevant provisions of CEPA Supplementary Agreement IX and XII, "Hong Kong securities companies that qualify as overseas shareholders of foreign-invested securities companies and securities companies that have the conditions for setting up subsidiaries in the Chinese mainland are permitted to set up joint-venture securities investment consulting companies in the Chinese mainland. As a subsidiary of the Chinese mainland securities companies specializing in securities and investment consulting business, the shareholding ratio of Hong Kong securities companies can reach as high as 49%. In a number of reform pilot zones approved by the Chinese mainland for 'first pilot in financial reform', Hong Kong and Macao securities companies are allowed to hold more than 50% of shares in joint venture securities investment consulting firm."

2.7.2 How can offshore banks apply for the qualifications of RMB qualified foreign institutional investors?

If the bank (Institution) wishes to apply for eligibility of RQFII, it should satisfy:

(1) The registered place and the principal place of business are in Singapore's

financial institutions.

(2) Qualifications in asset management business obtained from the securities regulatory authority in Singapore and asset management business implemented.

The rest of the requirements should be implemented in accordance with the *Methods on Pilot Scheme for Domestic Securities Investment of RQFII* and the relevant laws and regulations. The banks which meet the above requirements of Singapore Commercial Bank can apply for RQFII qualification. According to the provisions, applicants should submit documents to the China Securities Regulatory Commission through domestic commercial banks which have qualified foreign institutional investors' custodian qualifications. If there are any problems encountered in the process of application, offshore banks can consult to the custodian or the relevant regulatory agencies.

Chapter 3   Money Market in China

3.1   An Overview of Money Market in China

Since 1998, with the changes in the means of monetary control by the Central Bank and the improvement of economic monetization and financial marketization, great progress has been made in the development of the Chinese money market. The main achievement is that three major sub-markets, including the inter-bank borrowing market, the inter-bank bond market and the commercial paper market as well as the development of the money market are accelerating. At present, the interbank borrowing market has become the main place where financial institutions manage their positions. The inter-bank bond market has become the main platform for the open-market operations of the Central Bank. The commercial paper market has become an important way for enterprises to do short-term financing and banks to improve liquidity management and risk avoidance. According to statistics, in 2014, the accumulated turnover of inter-bank market lending and borrowing, bonds and bond repo amounted to RMB 302.4 trillion, increasing 28.5% over the same period of last year. Among them, transactions of inter-bank lending and borrowing market were RMB 37.7 trillion, increasing 6.0% compared to last year; transactions of bond repo were RMB 224.4 trillion, which increased 41.9% over the same period of last year; the spot transaction volume was RMB 40.4 trillion, decreasing 3.0% from the same period of last year.

By the end of 2003, the number of members in the inter-bank lending market was 616, increasing 80 from the beginning of this year. The number of members in the bond market was 2,895, which is an increase of 1994 from the beginning of the year. In 2003, the total amount of commercial paper issued by enterprises was RMB 2.77 trillion, rocketing 72.7% over the same period of last year. The accumulative discount and rediscount papers were RMB 4.44 trillion, up 91% over the same period of 2003. At the end of 2003, the balance of issued commercial papers before the due dates was RMB 1.28 trillion, increasing 73.5% over the same period of last year; the balance of papers and rediscount reached RMB 893.4 billion, up by 69.7% over the same period of last year.

The above shows that the development of the money market in China is indeed at an accelerating stage of growth, with an annual substantial increase, which is rare in both developed and developing countries. However, geometrical growth only shows a superficial phenomenon. To study the actual situation of the development of China's money market, it is necessary to examine it in many aspects. After doing an in-depth study of the background of formulation, framework of policy making, operation mode and incentives mechanism of operation in China's currency market, a preliminary conclusion can be drawn: currently, the money market in China is still in a primary stage of development at best, with a low degree of openness, market-oriented approaches, uneven structural development and backward technological facilities.

3.2 Inter-bank Borrowing Market

The inter-bank borrowing market is a market for financial institutions to regulate short-term and temporary positions between themselves. It is an important part of the money market. It is not only an important means of implementing liquidity management, but also an important base for the Central Bank to formulate and implement monetary policy.

The inter-bank borrowing market has the following characteristics: first, the financing period is relatively short. The longest duration of inter-bank borrowing funds in China is four months for inter-bank borrowing funds are mainly used for short-term and temporary financial needs of financial institutions. Second, participating institutions basically have deposit accounts at PBOC, and the main transactions in the market are excess funds that financial institutions depositing on the account. Third, inter-bank lending and borrowing is basically a credit lending. Lending activities are conducted among financial institutions. The market accesses are more stringent, and financial institutions mainly rely on their credits to participate in lending and borrowing activities.

As one of the key financial reform projects in China, the inter-bank market started from the 1980s. It experienced three stages: initial stage, rapid development, and standardization.

1986–1991 was the initial stage. At that time, the inter-bank market developed rapidly. However, there were also some problems: the institutional chaos among funds lending business of organizations, the irrational use of borrowed funds, the excessively high interest rate and the prolonged period of time. Especially in 1988, because some regional financial institutions violated the provisions on the borrowing of funds and used the funds to invest in fixed assets, which could not be recovered at maturity. In accordance with the instructions of the State Council, the People's Bank of China carried out a rectification of the irregularities in the inter-bank lending market, abolished the financing companies, restricted the access of non-bank financial institutions to the lending market, before imposing a cap on the lending rate, and strictly stipulating the main body of the lending, the duration of the lending and the use of the lending funds. However, the effect of these measures was not obvious. The trading volume of the lending market did not decreased significantly. From 1989 to 1991, the trading volume was 220 billion *yuan*, 237 billion *yuan* and 292.7 billion *yuan* respectively. In the same period, the People's Bank of China also issued the Trial Measures for Inter-bank Borrowing

Management. For the first time, the management of inter-bank lending market was systematically regulated in the form of special laws and regulations, which made the inter-bank lending market standardized and developed to a certain extent.

1992–1995 was a period of development and clarification. Since 1992, there have been some increases in the inter-bank market, but there are also many problems at the same time: the qualifications of market access in this market are barely no use, the scope of market participants is greatly expanded. Even some individuals participated in this process. The interest rates were arbitrarily raised, some of which were as high as 150% per month, and even as high as 200% in some southern cities. With the lengthening of the borrowing period (even up to five years), a large amount of borrowing funds was used for real estate investment, fixed assets investment, development zone projects and speculation in stocks. This chaotic situation seriously affected the healthy development of China's borrowing market and interfered with the normal operation of the financial market. Thus, in 1993, the People's Bank of China issued a series of rules and regulations. The Interim Measures for the Management of Lending and Loaning Funds promulgated by the Central Bank on February 15, 1994 stipulated more stringent provisions on the types, quantity, duration, uses and trading subjects of lending and borrowing. Thanks to this rectification, the market order of inter-bank lending improved significantly, market irregularities were greatly reduced, and the lending market began to get on the right track. In 1994 alone, the volume of interbank lending reached about 500 billion *yuan*, while in 1995 it exceeded trillion *yuan*. In 1993, the People's Bank of China implemented a series of rules and regulations to rectify the inter-bank market. As a result, the order of the inter-bank market has been significantly improved, gradually getting the market back on the rails.

From 1996 until today, we can talk about the period of scale development. On January 4th, 1996, the People's Bank of China released the nationally unified inter-bank lending and borrowing rate, that is, the weighted average interest rate of the inter-bank market in China, and abolished the limitation of inter-bank lending and borrowing rate from June 1st, which means the lending rate was fully liberalized, and change from regulated interest rate to the market-oriented interest rate has been achieved. From the money market's term structure of trading, in 2000, the inter-bank market's term structure has undergone fundamental changes, the proportion of inter-bank lending and borrowing within seven days (including overnight) has risen to 71.4%. This shows that the inter-bank market has become an important venue for regulating short-term positions among financial institutions. At the end of 2006, a total of 703 financial institutions entered the national inter-bank lending center, which ushered in a historic breakthrough in the lending market. Compared with ten years ago, the size of institutions increased by 12.8 times at the end of 2006; the total amount of borrowing and lending in 1998 was less than 200 billion *yuan*, but in 2006 it exceeded 2 trillion *yuan*. Since 1996, China's inter-bank lending market has been running well, and there has been no further extreme chaos and disorder. The market lending rate has also increased considerably.

Table 3–1   China's Inter-bank Lending Aamount from 2000 to 2008

Years	2000	2001	2002	2003	2004
Total Amount of Inter-bank Lending and Borrowing (100 Million *Yuan*)	6,728.07	8,482.05	12,107.26	22,220.33	13,616.56
Years	2005	2006	2007	2008	
Total Amount of Inter-bank Lending and Borrowing (100 Million *Yuan*)	12,303.93	21,483.66	106,284.5	150,491.8	

Source: Collected from the statistics of the Chinese Academy of Social Sciences' Institute of Finance and Banking.

However, there are still many obvious irregularities and defects in the current interbank lending market in China. First, although the interbank lending market in China has taken shape, it is not a normative monetary market in terms of operation mechanism and management system. At present, only banks and non-bank financial institutions are allowed to participate in market lending, and non-financial institutions are not allowed to enter. Moreover, the proportion of short-term lending over one month is too large, which has the nature of short-term loan to a large extent. The short-term funds, especially the position compensation, at the grass-roots level of commercial banks, have not been given enough attention to. The operational objectives of inter-bank lending are obviously deviated, and the phenomenon of long-term use of short-term funds is serious. Also, the lending market business is mainly managed by administrative means, and has not really broken away from the planned and administrative constraints.

Secondly, the market-oriented degree of inter-bank lending market is not high, which affects the standardized development of inter-bank lending market. The state-owned commercial banks are in the transition period of operation mechanism, and their credit operation has not become really market-oriented, so their lending business is not always in the need of balancing positions but, to a large extent, has the nature of seeking credit funds, and is mostly used to fill the credit gap. Many other financial institutions that do not have the amount of borrowing and lending capital are engaged in other businesses such as securities repurchase and stock investment in the name of borrowing and lending due to the lack of necessary restraint and supervision in the market, which has affected the normal development of the borrowing and lending market.

Third, the liberalization of inter-bank lending rates does not reflect the real relationship between supply and demand of market funds, so it is difficult for the central bank to regulate with its monetary policy. According to the data of inter-bank lending rate on September 20, 1996, the interest rate of daily to 3-month lending is 11.34%~11.768%, while the central bank's three-month lending rate is 9.72%, and the commercial bank's six-month lending rate is 9.18%, with the margin exceeding more than two points. This made it possible for commercial banks and other financial institutions in the process of adjusting their operating mechanism to avoid regional risk and transfer funds, and also facilitated some banking institutions to collect funds from the Central Bank illegally.

At present, after many rounds of rectification, the inter-bank market in China has the following features:

1. The inter-bank market is a unified market.

2. The unified national inter-bank market consists of primary transaction networks and secondary transaction networks. The first level network regard 15 head offices of commercial banks in China, 35 financing centers consisting of national financial trust and investment companies, and ones that affiliated to each branch of the People's Bank of China as their members of network. The secondary network takes 35 financing centers as the core, consisting of branches of commercial banks in various regions, non-bank financial institutions as members of network.

3. The types of inter-bank lending are classified into the following two types: position lending and short-term lending, and various business are divided into different types. It can not only meet the temporary turnover needs of the borrowers, but also meet the needs of short-term working capital.

4. The inter-bank lending rate is formed through the market price bidding.

5. The object of inter-bank lending is strictly regulated. Non-bank financial institutions can only lend through positions funds. Short-term funds or borrow through position funds are forbad. Bank institutions can borrow or lend through position funds and short-term funds.

China Foreign Exchange Trade Center accepts the leadership and supervision of the People's Bank of China and the State Administration of Foreign Exchange, which is a market of intermediaries that provide trading and clearing services for the trading of foreign exchange among financial institutions. Its mission is to provide foreign exchange trading system, organize the sale and purchase of foreign exchange instruments, and handle foreign exchange settlement transactions and the related confidence services.

China Foreign Exchange Trade Center adopts membership system as its organization form. Any financial institution authorized by the SAFE to operate a foreign exchange business may apply to become a member. As a member, the Central Bank Open Market Operations Office also participates in foreign exchange transactions. Members can handle self-operated foreign exchange trading and act for foreign exchange trading within the scope prescribed by the state. However, for self-operated business of foreign-funded financial institutions and non-bank financial institutions, according to the current state regulations, only can one-way sold out foreign exchange, but cannot handle business of purchasing foreign exchange.

At present, in the foreign exchange market, there is only one business type —spot foreign exchange for transaction. There are four currency codes for transaction, including RMB, the Hong Kong dollar, the Japanese yen, and euro four currencies. Pilot projects on changeover from forward foreign exchange transactions to an intangible market are under way.

In 1998, People's Bank of China approved the entry of some foreign-funded banks that operate RMB business in Pudong, Shanghai into the national inter-bank lending market. This is another important measure taken by China to gradually and systematically implement the financial opening-up.

Approved foreign banks are: Industrial Bank of Japan, Dai-Ichi Kangyo Bank, Citibank, the Standard Chartered Bank, Hong Kong and Shanghai Banking Corporation, Credit Agricole Corporate and Investment Bank, Sanwa Bank and Bank of Tokyo-Mitsubishi.

It is understood that since the RMB business was started in Pudong, Shanghai in April, 1997, foreign banks' RMB borrowing and lending was carried out through the Shanghai Financing Center. After a year of operation, the conditions for foreign banks to enter into the national inter-bank lending market have now matured.

After these eight foreign banks' entry into the market, they can make use of the computer networking system provided by the National Inter-bank Lending Center to make RMB inter-bank lending transactions with other members, and increase the bond trading and repurchase operations as well as gain access to statistics of national currency market, the background, credit status and other information of each trading member through the network.

The approval of foreign banks to enter the national inter-bank lending market will be conducive to a reasonable clutch of foreign-funded banks' positions. Liquidity management also helps the central bank to keep an accurate picture of their transactions through the computer network and monitor their money market operations immediately.

In 2005, the PBC released the announcement named "The Rules for Approving the Access of Banking Financial Institutions to the Nationwide Inter-bank Borrowing Market," which stipulates:

Article 10 When applying for access to the inter-bank borrowing market, the headquarter of a foreign-funded commercial bank with the corporation institute established within China or a foreign-funded commercial bank branch with the corporation institution established outside China shall submit an application therefore to the local office of the People's Bank of China which shall make a preliminary examination and then submit the application level by level to the headquarters of the People's Bank of China for approval.

Article 11 To apply for access to the inter-bank borrowing market, a foreign-funded commercial bank shall submit the following materials to the local office of the People's Bank of China:

1) An application for access to the inter-bank borrowing market

2) A photocopy of the financial license

3) A photocopy of the business license

4) An approval document issued by the banking regulatory institution under the state council to the foreign-funded commercial bank for its engaging in RMB

business

5) The articles of association

6) The internal control system for capital management

7) The balance sheets and profit and loss statements for the past two years

8) Particulars on the department and personnel who take charge of the capital operation

9) Other materials as may be required by the People's Bank of China.

Article 12 A foreign-funded commercial bank with the bank as a corporation established within China, which has been approved by the PBC to engage in the inter-bank RMB borrowing business, shall carry out its business in the name of the bank as a corporation, with no branches being allowed to engage in inter-bank borrowing business.

3.3 Bond Repo Market

Bond repo is a kind of short-term financing and margin trading conducted in the bond market, that is, the bondholders as the seller and the buyer in the bond trading agreement signed by both parties were regulated to repurchase that bond at a fixed time and price via bilateral agreement and agreed to pay interest rate which was calculated via bilateral agreement. It is easy to see that the agreement is a repurchase agreement for the seller and a reverse repo agreement for the buyer. Therefore, the bond transaction is essentially a transaction in which the seller obtains short-term loans from the buyer by using the bonds as collateral. Treasury bills are the main targets of transactions in repo agreements, and others include corporate bonds, bank acceptance bills and commercial paper. At present, the repo business set up by the Shanghai Stock Exchange uses a standardized method of mortgage financing, that is, regardless of the type of bonds, universally calculating upon the denomination value of the holding amount of bonds for financing and securities lending business.

Bond repo, as an important transaction mode in the money market, provides a very effective means for the development of the national debt market, open market services of the Central Bank and the adjustment of the structure of financial assets by various commercial and financial institutions according to their needs.

3.3.1 The development of China's bond repo market

Since the national treasury bond repo started relatively late in 1989, the State has allowed treasury bills to be circulated in the market and has developed rapidly. Especially since 1993, with the expansion of the securities market, the need to revitalize funds of the financial institutions and active treasury bond market, the treasury bond repo has developed rapidly, becoming one of the indispensable trading varieties in the bond market. On-floor trading (standardized repo designed by exchanges and approved by government authorities within a stock exchange or equity futures) is growing rapidly due to the simplified bond repo set-up and the sound trading mechanism of on-floor trading. Including the Shanghai Stock Exchange, the Shenzhen Stock Exchange, the STAQ (Securities Trading Automated Quotations) system, the Tianjin Stock Exchange, Wuhan Trading Center and other securities trading center, many securities trading places have opened this business.

With the improvement of the mechanism and the investor's investment awareness, the repo market has become increasingly active. The volume of the repo business increased rapidly. In particular, the SSE's bond repurchase business implemented full coupon value mortgage and adhered to the principle of being both active and standardized. In addition, the orderly development of the repurchase market coupled with its high returns and low repurchase business fee, strong security, and others, make it more attractive to investors. In 2014, the settlement volume of spot bonds and repo transactions in the bond market was RMB 352.55 trillion, anincrease of 30.03% from the same period of previous year, an increase of 28.98 percentage points from the growth of 2013. Among them, the total settlement volume of cash securities in the whole market was 40.61 trillion *yuan*, down 6% from the previous year; the total settlement volume of repurchase transactions in the whole market was 311.54 trillion *yuan*, up 36.88% from the previous year, or up 16.2 percentage points. On the other hand, the bond repurchase transactions of each stock exchange accounted for a larger share of the bond transactions in the securities market. In 1995, the total amount of repurchase transactions in Tianjin Stock Exchange Center was more than 68 billion *yuan*, accounting for 90% of the total amount of treasury bond transactions in the whole market; the total amount of repurchase transactions in Wuhan Securities Center was 150 billion *yuan*, accounting for 45% of the total amount of treasury bond transactions in the whole market; and the total amount of repurchase transactions in STAQ system was 104.7 billion *yuan*, accounting for 90% of the total amount of Treasury.

Table 3–2　Distribution of Inter-bank Pledged Repo Period in 2000

Repurchase Types	Denomination Value (100 Million Yuan)	Proportion	Settlement Volume (Per Transaction)	Average Delivery Volume (Ten Thousand Yuan/ Per Transaction)
R001	578,270	63.02%	90,293	64,044
R002	13,954	1.52%	2,184	63,891
R003	132,464	14.44%	21,302	62,184
R007	125,405	13.67%	32,649	38,410
R014	44,051	4.80%	11,448	38,479
R021	7,379	0.80%	2,521	29,270
R1M	8,812	0.96%	2,985	29,522
R2M	3,666	0.40%	984	37,260
R3M	2,491	0.27%	655	38,033
R4M	415	0.05%	91	45,651
R6M	592	0.06%	182	32,510
R9M	93	0.01%	25	37,220

(Continued)

Repurchase Types	Denomination Value (100 Million Yuan)	Proportion	Settlement Volume (Per Transaction)	Average Delivery Volume (Ten Thousand Yuan/ Per Transaction)
R1Y	54	0.01%	14	38,645
All	917,647	100.00%	165,333	55,503

Data Source: http://www.chinabond.com.cn

Bond repurchase is a flexible way of financing and securities trading. Due to the fact that it has just started in China where the management is not experienced, and the relevant laws and regulations are not perfect, the OTC (Over The Counter) repurchase business between financial institutions outside the exchange is not standardized, and has caused some problems.

First, the period is too long to have created risks. According to the usual practice of the repurchase market, the repurchase period should not exceed one year. But now, the so-called bond repurchase business undertaken by some traders is more than one year. This extension of repurchase period can neither meet the needs of the financiers for short-term financing, nor bring safety to the investment of the securities brokers, which is not conducive to the traders to adjust the types of transactions according to the term structure of interest rates and standardize trading behavior. Second, obtain credit by deception in the name of borrowing and repurchasing. According to the regulations, the financier should sell the bond to the financing side at spot price, and then buy back the bond at contract price when the repurchase period expires. However, at present, some securities are repurchased without holding the corresponding bond. In fact, this is the practice whereby securities traders exploit the loopholes of the regulation that the issuance and sale of treasury bonds can issue bonds on behalf of custody; in other words, they issue corporate bonds in the name of false repurchase of Treasury bonds; it violates the national credit and is a kind of short selling prohibited by the state;

this kind of behavior not only deceives the financiers, but also disrupts the normal order of the financial market. Thirdly, arbitrarily raise interest rates to increase inflation. Because of the imperfection of the restraint mechanism in the previous period, some companies have changed bond repurchase into a means of obtaining national credit by deception to raise funds for their own units by raising interest rates, and then used the funds raised as investment in fixed assets, stocks, futures and loans to enterprises. The annual interest rate of bond repurchase bonds issued by them not only exceeds the floating range of the interest rate of corporate bonds stipulated in the Regulations on Corporate Bonds, but also is much higher than the yield in the secondary market of spot bonds and the coupon rate of newly issued bonds. From the perspective of financing, this practice of arbitrarily raising interest rates seriously violates the national regulations on the unification of interest rates in financial markets and is an unfair competition. It also seriously affects the issuance of treasury bonds in the primary market by the Ministry of Finance and disrupts the normal state financial deployment. From the perspective of investment, this behavior confuses the money market and capital market, not only increases the risk of repurchase market, but also invisibly expands the credit scale, increases the inflationary pressure, and intensifies the speculative degree of stock market and futures market.

3.3.2 Foreign institutions participating in China's bond repo market

In 2015, PBC issued the "Notice on Clearing Offshore RMB Securities and Overseas Participating Banks in Debt Repurchase in the Inter-bank Bond Market" (aka the "Notice"), approving the liquidation of offshore RMB business and the offshore participating banks in conducting bond repo transactions in inter-bank bonds market. The "Notice" shows that offshore RMB clearing banks and participating banks that have been allowed to enter the inter-bank bond market can carry out bond repo transactions, of which the repo financing balance is no more than 100% of the total amount of the bonds they held, and the repo funds can be transferred overseas to use. Offshore RMB Business Settlement Bank refers to the institutions that carry out the RMB clearing business in the overseas regions (including Hong Kong, Macau and Taiwan) that have established offshore RMB settlement arrangement. The overseas participating banks refer to those companies that conduct cross-border RMB settlement business in accordance with the relevant provisions Hong Kong, Macau, Taiwan commercial banks.

Access to the vast inter-bank bond market is the ultimate appeal of many agencies, because the best-selling products on the market are all here, such as treasury bonds, policy bank financial bonds, short-term commercial paper, medium-term votes and so on. Accelerating the development of the inter-bank bond market is also a policy that follows the internationalization of the RMB and accelerates the opening up of capital accounts. "The high-level requirement of the internationalization of RMB is that international investors invest in RMB-denominated assets."

3.4　Paper Market

In modern financial market, paper refers to a written debt issued by an enterprise or an individual that reflects the credit relationship between a creditor and a debtor. As means of payment and circulation, paper can be transferred. Paper can also be discounted and rediscounted as a financing instrument, equivalent to loans without strict rating approval. It is convenient and quick, and is also called semi-direct financing. In western developed countries, the act of papers is the main mean by which the enterprises pay and raise funds in the market. As a sub-market of the money market, the paper market plays a fundamental role in a country's financial market and plays an irreplaceable role of other markets.

3.4.1 Development of China's paper market

China banned commercial credit for a long time, so there was no commercial paper. Since China did not form the corresponding bills acceptance and discount business, naturally, there was no paper market.

1982-1994 is the stage of promoting the usage of bills. Chinese bill business started from 1981. In that year, Shanghai and other places began to try out the business of acceptance and discount of commercial bills of exchange. At the end of 1984, the People's Bank of China promulgated the Interim Measures for Acceptance and Discount of Commercial Banks, which encouraged commercial credit between industrial and commercial enterprises to be billed. In 1986, the People's Bank of China promulgated the Trial Measures for Rediscount. But the business was basically in a state of suspension before 1994. It was not until the end of 1994 that the Central Bank, in conjunction with relevant departments, proposed to promote the use of commercial bills of exchange in the credit sales of some industries and varieties of commodities and to open acceptance, discount and rediscount of bills. Only then did the bill business really begin.

From 1995 to September 1999, the systematical construction stage of bill market took place. With the promulgation of the *Negotiable Instruments Law of the People's Republic of China* in 1995 as a symbol, the laws and regulations on bills business were initially established and gradually improved. The rediscount policy was relatively adjusted. During this period, the rediscount rate was greatly reduced, and the generation mechanism of the rediscount rate was improved and perfected.

The bill market has been rapidly evolving since October 1999. During this period, the bill business has been rapidly growing and its total business volume has doubled. From 1999 to 2002, the amount of issuance and acceptance of commercial bills was constantly updated. In 2002, the amount of commercial bills issued nationwide reached 1,613.9 billion *yuan*. The discount amount of bills handled by financial institutions increased from 240 billion *yuan* to 2,100 billion *yuan* (including partial discount), an increase of 31 times and 7.7 times respectively. During the same period, the amount of outstanding commercial bills increased from 159.5 billion *yuan* to 750 billion *yuan*, and the discount balance of bills increased from 54.7 billion *yuan* to 574.3 billion *yuan*, increasing by 37 times and 95 times respectively.

Table 3-3   Market Size of Bank of China Acceptance Bill Since 1995

Years	Balance of Acceptance Bills (100 Million *Yuan*)	Balance of Bill Discount (100 Million *Yuan*)	Balance of Rediscount Rate (100 Million *Yuan*)
1995	865	150	322
1996	1,285	505	416
1997	1,335	581	337
1998	1,595	547	331
1999	1,873	552	502
2000	3,676	1,535	1,256
2001	5,110	2,795	655
2002	7,347	5,200	68
2003	12,776	8,167	766
2004	15,000	10,000	33
2005	19,600	13,800	2
2006	22,100	17,200	18

Data Source: Wind Consultative System

3.4.2   The present condition of China's paper market

1. The prototype of paper specialization institutions emerged.

At present, China has initially formed two modes of intermediary institutions for the bills market, which are mainly engaged in commercial bills trading and advisory services. One is the nationwide bill sales department set up by ICBC and the other is the bill discount window set up by each share-holding financial institution. Shanghai Pudong Development Bank, China Everbright Bank, Shanghai Bank, China Minsheng Bank have set up bill centers one after another. These specialized bills institutions handle bill business in a centralized manner, which is conducive to improving operational efficiency and reducing costs and risks.

2. Unified bill information platform starts to set up:

The "China Paper Net" established in June 2003, which launched a unified ticket market service platform in China to provide quotations and inquiries services for such transactions as the discard of financial instruments and the repurchase of bills. Through this platform, all network members can access or issue ticket business information from the internet, select the appropriate transaction objects, notes types and transaction methods. It is both expanding and enhancing the business spheres of financial institutions to achieve the sharing of information resources, at the same time, increasing the credibility and transparency of the transaction object, and improving the efficiency of the transaction in the bill market.

3. Introduce short-term financing bills with traits of commercial paper

On May 26th, 2005, the People's Bank of China launched the short-term financing bills for financial innovation products suitable for market players. The issuance of short-term financing bills has enriched the currency market varieties, which is conducive to changing the imbalance between direct financing and indirect financing, and also to improving the monetary policy transmission mechanism and the overall coordinated development of financial markets.

【Case】China's Central Bank Innovative Bills: "Central Bank Bills"

The Central Bank Bill is a short-term debt document issued by the Central Bank to commercial banks to regulate their excess reserve. The essence of the Central Bank Bill is the "Central Bank Bond", which is called

"Central Bank Bill", it is designed to highlight its short-term characteristics. Issued Central Bank Bills' shortest period is three months, and the longest period is only three years.

The Central Bank Bills are issued by the People's Bank of China in the inter-bank market through PBOC's bond issuance system. The issuance targets are primary dealers in the open market. At present, there are 48 first-tier dealers in the open market, including commercial banks, securities companies and so on. Among the 34 issued Central Bank Bills, except for competitive bidding, 19 issued bills through the pattern of non-competitive bidding sell themselves to nine bilateral bidding merchants including China Industrial and Commercial Bank, Agricultural Bank of China, Bank of China and China Construction Bank at the same time. As the Central Bank Bills are issued without distribution, other investors can only invest in the secondary market.

The role of the Central Bank bill is to enrich the operating tools of the open market and make up for the shortage of cash coupons in open market operations. After the Central Bank Bills are introduced, the PBOC can make use of bills or repurchases and their combinations to carry out "balancing control and bidirectional operations". The rolling operation of central bank bills increases the flexibility and pertinence of open market operations and enhances the effectiveness of implementing monetary policies. The second is to provide the benchmark interest rate for the market: the international community generally use short-term bond yields as the benchmark interest rate. However, judging from the situation in China, the vast majority of the treasury bonds issued by the Ministry of Finance is over three years, and the short-term treasury stock market is extremely small. Under the premise that the Ministry of Finance cannot form a short-term treasury bond rolling issuance system, the issuance of bills by the Central Bank can improve the market interest rate structure and form the market benchmark interest rate by using the set term of the bills while solving the problems of the open market operation instruments. Third, to promote the development of the money market: at present, there are few instruments in the Chinese money market. Due to the lack of short-term money market instruments, many institutional investors can only chase long-term bonds and bring long-term interest rate risk to the bond market. The issuance of Central Bank Bills will change the status quo that in Chinese money market, there are basically no short-term tools. As for institutional investors, the Central Bank Bills are providing an important instrument to have flexibility in the hands to swap positions and reduce short-term financial pressures.

3.4.3 Mechanism of foreign institutions participating in China's paper market

The Central Bank of China promulgated the "Regulations of the People's Republic of China Governing Foreign-funded Banks" in 2006. Since December 11th, 2006, foreign-funded banks can handle bill acceptance and discount business domestically.

The "Several Opinions of the State Council on Further Utilizing Foreign Capital" issued in 2010 indicated that foreign capital shall be encouraged to participate in the restructuring and merger of domestic enterprises by means of equity participation and acquisition, A-share listed companies shall be supported to bring in domestic and overseas strategic investors. Qualified foreign-invested enterprises shall be bolstered to publicly issue stocks, corporate bonds and medium-term notes within China to widen financing support of credit loan for foreign-invested enterprises. The scale of overseas subjects issuing RMB within China shall be steadily expanded. The pilot project in utilizing foreign capital to set up the minor enterprises guarantee companies shall be advanced and foreign businessmen encouraged to invest to set up investment enterprises, private equity and investment funds proactively utilized and exit mechanism perfected.

3.5 Treasury Bond Market

Short-term Treasury Bonds are government-issued financing instruments that provide credit guarantees for a period of less than one year. Like medium- and-long-term treasury bonds, short-term treasury bonds have dual functions of financial fund raising and monetary control. They are important instruments for the operation of the monetary policy of the Central Bank. At the same time, in the bond market, the issuance of short-term treasury bonds helps to form a complete and reasonable market benchmark yield curve, which helps to promote the formation of a market-based interest rate system. Short-term treasury bonds are also an important mean of treasury financing. Smoothing the fluctuation of the treasury cash flow to ensure the proper implementation of budgetary expenditures.

Before 2003, the scale of issuance of China's short-term treasury bonds was relatively small, and often interrupted in time. In 2003, the issuance of short-term government bonds accounted for about 10% of the total government bonds issued in that year and then increased year by year, reaching 23.89% in 2006. One-year government bonds also tended to stabilize.

However, there are still some problems in China's current issuance of short-term bonds: first, the types of short-term bonds are not rich enough; second, there is no regular, balanced and rolling system for the issuance of short-term bonds; third, the scale of issuance of short-term bonds needs to be further expanded to meet the needs of the Central Bank open market operations and treasury cash management.

3.6 Central Bank's Innovative Financial Instrument

3.6.1 Standing lending facilities

Drawing on international experience, the PBC set up a Standing Lending Facility (SLF) in early 2013. SLF is the normal liquidity supply channel of the PBC, whose main function is to meet the large liquidity needs of long-term financial institutions. The main targets are the policy banks and national commercial banks. The period is one to three months. The interest rate level is determined according to the regulation of monetary policy and the need to guide the market interest rate. SLFs are usually issued as mortgages. Eligible collateral includes bonds with high credit ratings, high quality credit assets and so on.

The objects of SLFs from PBC's branches include four types of local financial institutions such as city commercial banks, rural commercial banks, rural cooperative banks and rural credit cooperatives, which are local legal entities registered in China. The issuance is in the form of pledge.

Main features of SLFs are: first, initiated by financial institutions. Financial institutions can apply for SLFs according to their own liquidity needs; second, SLFs are "one-on-one" transactions between Central Banks and financial institutions, and third, SLFs' counterparties are widely covered, which often covers depository financial institutions.

3.6.2 Short-term liquidity operations

Short-term Liquidity Operations (SLO) is an open market operation. It can be seen as a necessary complement to regular operations in the open market, used at the exactly time when there is temporary volatility in the banking system.

SLO is mainly composed by short-term repurchase within seven days, and if meets the holidays, it may be appropriate to extend the operation period. It uses market-oriented interest rate bidding to operate. According to the needs of currency regulation and control, the PBC needs to consider comprehensively various factors such as the liquidity supply and demand in the banking system and the interest rate in the money market so as to flexibly determines the operation timing, operation scale, duration times and so on. In principle, this instrument is used during the intermittent period of regular operation in the open market.

3.6.3 Pledged supplementary lending

PSL, abbreviation for Pledged Supplementary Lending, as a new instrument of reserve policy, has two meanings: first and foremost, on the aspect of quantity, the new channel of basic money launching. Second, on the price aspect, the interest rate of financing obtained from the Central Bank through commercial bank mortgage assets can lead medium-term interest rate.

The PSL instrument is very similar to relending, which is a kind of unsecured credit loan, but the market tends to give the relending a certain financial stability meaning, that is, only when an institution has a problem, it will be re-lent. For various reasons, the Central Bank may upgrade its relending instrument to PSL. In the future, it is likely that PSL will largely replace re-lending facilities, but re-loan will remain in the PBC's policy tools basket.

In China, there are many credit deliveries, such as credit deliveries for infrastructure construction and people's livelihood expenditures, which are often guaranteed by the government with poor profitability. If commercial banks' independence pricing and complete commercial pricing based on the market interest rate, higher loan pricing will not meet this type of credit demand. The so-called mid-term policy of the Central Bank's PSL to guide the level of interest rates, to a large extent, aims at directly providing a portion of low-cost funds to commercial banks to guide the funds to invest into these areas. This can also serve to reduce the cost of this part of social financing.

3.6.4 Medium-term lending facilities

Medium-term Lending Facility (MLF) is a composite instrument issued by PBC to guide the volume and price. The operation of MLF is allowing Central Bank loans with quality bonds such as treasury bonds, Central Bank papers, policy financial bonds, high-grade credit bonds and high-quality credit assets as eligible pledges to get a three-month loan. Main funding channels are policy banks and national commercial banks.

3.7 Q&A

3.7.1 Can foreign investors invest in Chinese bonds?

The Chinese government has approved foreign investors in Hong Kong, London and Singapore to invest a total of RMB 274.6 billion (USD 45.2 billion) in the stock and bond markets through so-called RQFII program. This project allows RMB funds to raise funds overseas and then invest in domestic securities. An earlier QFII program starting in 2002 approved a total of USD 49.25 billion in quotas for institutional funds outside China and in 2012 allowed them to buy bonds instead of just stocks.

3.7.2 What are the attractiveness for foreign investors to enter the Chinese bond market?

High yields are attracting investors to Chinese bonds. 10-year Treasury bonds had returned traded 4.6% in the domestic market, and the offshore RMB-denominated bond yield was about 3.9%, while the yield of the ten-year Treasury over the same period, though higher in May, was only 2.93%.

3.7.3 What are the risks of foreign investors entering into Chinese bonds market?

Some of this high-return bonds in China's bond market need to be offset by a number of risks, including the local rating agencies' preference for giving the highest rating to almost all corporate's guarantees, the normality of modern capital markets, and the risk of default are not counted and so on. The Chinese bond market has not yet experienced a complete credit cycle, which means the bond market may fluctuate in the future. Although Chinese government bonds have higher return than other government bonds, the liquidity of Chinese government bonds is much lower than that of other major countries. Some investors choose to invest in Chinese bonds in the offshore market to get a higher yield than the local market. The interest rate hike in the United States also makes Chinese bonds discourage some investors.

Chapter 4 An Introduction to Capital Market in China

In general, a market with more than a year of investment activity is called a capital market. It includes more than one year in the securities market and bank credit markets. However, in China, capital market generally refers to the securities market, including the stock market, bond market and investment fund market.

Mature multi-level capital markets should be able to provide financing platforms and share-trading services to large, medium and small-sized enterprises at the same time. In terms of market size, this should be reflected in the "pyramid" structure. Since the establishment of the Shanghai and Shenzhen Stock Exchanges in 1990, China's capital market has formed a number of stock trading platforms including the main board market, the small and medium market, third board market (including the "New OTC Market" or "NEEQ", abbreviation for National Equities Exchange and Quotations), the property rights trading market and the equity trading market and so on, which set a prototype for developing multi-layer capital market system.

4.1 Stock Market

4.1.1 Main board market

The main board market is also called first board market. It refers to the traditional securities market (usually the stock market) and is the main place for issuing, listing and trading securities in a country or region. The mainboard market emerged earlier than the GEM market, and they are not only differentiated from each other, but also are important parts of the multi-layer capital market. Relative to the GEM market, the main board market is the most important part of the capital market, which to a large extent, is able to reflect the financial development, so, it is called "a barometer of the national economy". The main board sets higher standards for the issuer's operating period, the size of the share capital, profitability, minimum market value and other aspects. Due to its standards, most listed companies on the main board market are mature, large-scale enterprises, with greater capital size and stable profitability. Main board markets in Chinese mainland include the Shanghai Stock Exchange and the Shenzhen Stock Exchange.

Figure 4   Shanghai Stock Exchange

In general, the major stock exchanges in each country represent the domestic main board market. For example, the American Stock Exchange (AMEX) is the main board market in the United States; China's Shanghai Stock Exchange and Shenzhen Stock Exchange are China's main board markets. By order of the entry, the securities market can be divided into the new issue market and the trading market. The new issue market is also called the primary market, and the trading market is also called the secondary market. It is not a same concept with the main board market, the second board market, and the third board market.

4.1.2 Small and medium enterprise board market

SME board is a sub-board of the Shenzhen Stock Exchange for listing of small and medium-sized enterprises in order to encourage independent innovation, and set up a special gathered board for these companies. These companies generally have the characteristics of quick revenue growth, strong profitability and high content of science and technology, and the liquidity of the stock is good and the transaction is active, which is regarded as the future "Nasdaq" for China.

Small board is relative to the main board market, including the Shenzhen Stock Exchange and Shanghai Stock Exchange. Some companies cannot meet the requirements of the main board market, so it can only be listed on the SME board market, which is a transition of GEM market.

GEM is a second board market, which plays an important role next to main board market, represented by the NASDAQ market, which in China particularly refers to Shenzhen GEM.

4.1.3 Growth enterprise market

The GEM board is next to the main board market, represented by the NASDAQ market, which in China particularly refers to Shenzhen GEM. The threshold of listing, regulatory system, information disclosure, traders' conditions, risk of investment and other aspects are quite different from those of the main board market. Its main purpose is to support small and medium-sized enterprises, especially for high-growth enterprises, to establish a normal exit mechanism for venture capital investments and VC (Venture Capital) firms, provide a financing platform for national strategy for independent innovation in China and contribute to the construction of a multi-layer capital market system.

GEM, also known as the second board market, which is the second stock exchange market. In China, main board refers to the Shanghai and Shenzhen stock markets. The GEM refers to the stock exchange market that provides financing channels and growth space for SMEs and emerging companies that are temporarily unable to be listed on the main board. It is an important complement to the main board market and has an important position in the capital market. The GEM appeared in the United States in the 1970s and flourished in 1990s represented by Nasdaq, which had hatched a number of Fortune 500 companies like Microsoft. Thus far, there are more than 6,000 companies listed on the NASDAQ, while more than 2,000 companies have delisted. It can be said that the GEM board market is stock market with a low threshold, high risks, and strict regulation, and also an incubator or cradle of science and technology companies and growing enterprises.

4.1.4 New Third Board Market

4.1.4.1 Formation of "New Third Board" market

On July 16, 2001, in order to solve the problem of stock circulation of the original STAQ and NET listed companies, the China Securities Association launched an agent stock transfer system (the "Old Third Board"), which refers to the share transfer services provided by the securities companies for non-listed companies with their own or rented business facilities. The agent stock transfer system was small in scale, and the stock source was basically the companies registered in the original NET and STAQ systems that did not meet the listing conditions. At the end of 2001, "Narcissus" became the first listed company in China to withdraw from the mainboard. In order to solve the problem of share transfer of delisting companies, delisting companies were included in the pilot scope of agency share transfer since August 29, 2002. It can be seen that resolving the problems left over by history was an important task undertaken at the beginning of the establishment of the third board market. Another purpose of the third board is to undertake the delisting stock of the main board, thus playing a role in defusing delisting risk in a specific period, and making up for the structural defects of the securities market.

In order to change the backward situation of over-the-counter trade and provide more places for share transfer for high-tech growth enterprises, in January 2006, the share quotation transfer system of unlisted joint stock limited company in Zhongguancun Science and Technology Park (the "New Third Board") was officially launched, which became an important supplement to the domestic main board, small and medium-sized board and GEM market. On October 25, 2006, China Software and Beijing Times officially announced directional capital increase, which marked the formal opening of the gate of "New Third Board" financing. In 2010, in line with the explosive GEM's "three high" issuance—high priced issuance, high-profit issuance and superfund issuance, directional additional issuance of the "New Third Board" saw dramatic development. By 2013, the Securities Regulatory Commission announced that the State Council approved the expansion of the "New Third Board" and that the National Small and Medium-Sized Enterprises Share Transfer System Company (the "New Third Board Company") was formally established. In February 2013, "New Third Board" company issued business rules and supporting documents by which, except for the marked maker system, the "New Third Board" system rules were basically completed."

4.1.4.2 The role of the "New Third Board"

The "New Third Board" is a national securities trading place approved by the State Council and established in accordance with the Securities Law. It mainly serves the development of innovative, entrepreneurial and growing small and medium-sized enterprises. For non-listed companies, it is a platform for enterprise financing: the existence of the "New Third Board" makes the financing of high-tech enterprises no longer limited to bank loans and government subsidies, because more equity investment funds will take the initiative to invest because of the institutional guarantee of "New Third Board"; secondly, it can improve the level of corporate governance: according to the "New Third Board" rule, once a company in the park is ready to login to the "New Third Board", it must first carry out equity reform under the guidance of professional institutions, clarify the company's ownership structure and high-level responsibilities. At the same time, the "New Third Board" set up the information disclosure requirements of its registered companies in accordance with the listed companies, which promotes the standardized management and healthy development of enterprises, and strengthens the development potential of enterprises.

For investors, it is to provide a platform for value investment: the existence of "New Third Board" makes value investment possible. The second benefit is to reduce the risk of equity investment through supervision: the establishment of the "New Third Board" system, which makes the equity investment and financing behavior of registered companies incorporated into the trading system, subjects them to the supervision of the sponsor securities firms and the securities industry association. Thirdly, it has become a new way for private equity funds to withdraw: the establishment of share quotation transfer system has become a new way of capital withdrawal for private equity funds investing in "New Third Board" registered companies, and the registered companies have also become another hot spot of private equity funds.

4.1.5 National equities exchange and quotations

NEEQ is a national securities exchange market approved by the State Council and established under the Securities Law. It mainly serves the innovative, entrepreneurial and growth-oriented micro, small and medium-sized enterprises.

For non-listed companies, it is: first, a financing platform for corporate. The existence of NEEQ makes high-tech enterprises' financing no longer limited to loans from banks and government's grants, more equity investment funds will actively invest because of the protect provided by NEEQ system. Second, raising the level of corporate governance: in accordance with the rule of NEEQ, once a company is ready to list on this board, it must launch equity reform under the guidance of professional institutions to clarify ownership structure of company and responsibilities of top staff. At the same time, the requirements of the information disclosure of listed companies in the NEEQ are well set compared with listed companies, which has largely promoted standardized management and healthy development of enterprises and enhanced the potential of the enterprises' development.

For investors, it is: first, providing a platform for value investing. NEEQ makes the value of investment possible. Second, reducing the risk of equity investment through regulations. The establishment of NEEQ system has resulted the listed companies' equity investment and financing behaviors to be incorporated into the trading system and supervised by the host brokers and the securities associations. Third, it is a new way for private equity funds to withdraw. The establishment of the quotation of share transfer system has become a new way for capital withdrawal for companies that invest in NEEQ listed enterprises which have become another investment hotspot for private equity funds.

4.1.5.1 Regional equity trading market

Regional equity trading market is an important part of China's multi-layer capital market. By its very nature, the regional equity market is a private equity market in financial markets. Its activities are mainly equity, bond transfer and capital raising, while serving only specific regions. The regional equity market can play a facilitating role in the trading of small and medium-sized enterprises and create the ultimate capital of the enterprise, which makes up for the weakness of the real economy and has become an important part of the development of the capital market.

The operation mechanism of the regional equity exchange market is mainly accomplished through "one center, two resources, three types of agencies and four major sections". The "one center" referring to the regional equity trading center, is an important platform for the regional market trading. The "two resources" refer to the resources of the unlisted companies in the current regional equity market and the enterprise resources with the demand during the process of equity transfer.

Such resources can greatly enhance the development benefit of the enterprise and are the premise of equity financing, bond financing, and equity transfer. The "three types of agencies" mainly refer to the member institutions in the regional equity market, namely, recommendation agencies, strategic cooperation agencies and professional service agencies. These three types of agencies promote each other and guide each other, forming the basic core of the regional equity market. The "four major sections" includes equity transfer and financing, bond transfer and financing, equity registration and custody service, financial innovation business. The equity transfer and financing provide the foundation for the development of the enterprise and improve the capital structure and equity composition of the enterprise. Good debt financing broadens the channels for the development of enterprise's capital through the financing of some bonds or bond products. The equity registration and custody service is in accordance with the ownership of non-listed companies under the control of various indicators such as custody, ranking, change, transfer and other issues, to achieve the standardization of enterprise management content; for enterprises, other financial innovation business bring more opportunities for development through mortgages and financing private placement completed the product derivation under the regional equity market environment.

4.1.5.2 Over-the-counter market of securities companies

Over-the-counter transactions of securities companies refer to the transactions between securities companies and specific counterparties outside the centralized trading places or the acts of providing services for investors outside the centralized trading places. The products of over-the-counter transactions of securities companies include the basic financial products and financial derivatives issued or sold outside the centralized trading places approved, filed or endorsed by the relevant state departments or their authorized agencies. The "over-the-counter market" mentioned in the "Securities Company Over-the-Counter Business Code" is different from the "over-the-counter market" mentioned before. The term "over-the-counter market" mentioned previously mainly refers to the listing and transfer of shares of non-listed companies. At present, the over-the-counter market mainly provides liquidity for securities dealers themselves or for financial products sold on commission and the over-the-counter trading products are positioned as private products. In the early stage of the construction of the over-the-counter market, it mainly assisted in the innovation of asset management business, sold and transferred financial products of securities companies or acted a commission agent.

In terms of trading mode, securities companies 'over-the-counter trading business mainly focus on agreement trading, and will gradually try to carry out quotation trading or market maker trading mechanism in the future. The so-called agreement transaction refers to the bilateral quotation and point-to-point transaction between the two sides of the transaction; while the quotation transaction refers to the open intention quotation on the counter; the market maker transaction generally refers to the securities dealer offering the bilateral quotation for investors, such as a one-year financial product issued by the securities dealer's asset management, which cannot be redeemed. During this period, what if the investors are eager to use money? In this situation, securities firms make bilateral quotations based on the net value of the products at that time, and investor interested in transferring the products and the investor taking over them reach an agreement. The former receives funds, while the latter continues to hold the products with the specified span. These quotations are similar to those in the inter-bank market, which are all off-the-market models. However, the inter-bank market currently mainly deals with fixed income products such as bonds. At the present stage, securities companies' over-the-counter trading market mainly focuses on financial products and consignment financial products.

The over-the-counter market of securities companies is only a platform for quotation and transfer of unlisted private financial products, which is different from the exchange market and has the following characteristics:

First, the over-the-counter trading market of securities companies is clearly positioned in the private market, which is a platform for securities companies to issue, transfer and trade private products. Therefore, in the early stage of the construction of the counter market, we should attach great importance to risk control, with relatively low-risk products as the main part, and adopt the non-public transfer mode.

Secondly, the market is highly open and the transfer mode is flexible, which can provide diversified and even personalized services for investors. Transfer function and diversified investment and financing service function are the main function orientation of the counter market, which is a platform for providing liquidity as the main service content, rather than a trading place integrating multiple functions.

Thirdly, OTC customers are mainly institutional ones. Each securities company has formulated corresponding OTC appropriateness management system, worked out different investor access standards according to different products, and realized the matching between customers with different risk preferences and products with different risk levels by establishing customer classification and product risk rating system.

Fourthly, no membership system is adopted and transfer services are provided directly to investors, nor there are any brokers. The over-the-counter trading business will be dominated by agreement transactions, and try to carry out quotation trading or market maker trading mechanism without bidding transactions.

Fifthly, only risk assessment and control are carried out in product management, and no other access conditions are set. Products transferred into the market shall be examined and approved by the industry authorities or their authorized departments and units. The over-the-counter market shall only be controlled by risks. Private equity financial products suitable for the over-the-counter market subscription by qualified investors can be transferred over the counter.

Sixthly, real-time monitoring and management of transfers are carried out. Products, issuers and intermediaries are supervised by departments or units authorized or required by the regulatory authorities. Counter markets are coordinated and supported according to the requirements of the regulatory authorities. The over-the-counter market mainly provides transfer services, monitors the transfer behavior according to the requirements of the industry authorities, and regularly submits business reports to the competent authorities.

4.2 Bond Market

The current Chinese bond market consists mainly of the inter-bank bond market, the Shanghai and Shenzhen Stock Exchange bond markets and the commercial bank counter bond market. In 1997, when the PBOC established an inter-bank bond market and demanded that the whole nation's commercial banks should exit from the original exchange bond market, as a consequence, China's inter-bank bond market became the largest component of the current Chinese bond market and the main body of current bond market of China. From the total amount of bond custody, the stock of bonds and bond trading in the inter-bank market accounted for more than 90% of the total. The Shanghai and Shenzhen Stock Exchange bond markets are important parts of China's bond market. There are a large number of institutional and individual investors in the bond markets of the Shanghai and Shenzhen Stock Exchanges, which have activated our bond market. The Shanghai and Shenzhen Stock Exchange bond markets are composed of two parts: one is the bond retail market, in which the centralized matching transaction is implemented; the other is the wholesale bond trading market, which is composed of the bulk bond trading system and the national revenue trading platform. Commercial bank counter bond markets belong to the OTC bond market, which is the bond retail market, and also can be said derived from the inter-bank bond market, but most bond trading involved in are individual investors and a small number of institutional clients.

After several decades of development, China's bond market now contains a variety of financial products, which mainly are bonds, papers issued by PBOC, local government bonds, corporate bonds and short-term financing bonds and other types. In terms of bond's duration times, there are not only short-term bond products with a term of three months but also ultra-long-term bond products with a term of 30 years and 50 years in the Chinese bond market.

4.2.1 The update of overseas institutions participating in the inter-bank bond market

With the acceleration of RMB internationalization, more and more overseas regions are striving to become offshore centers of RMB. With its well-established circulation channels of RMB, Hong Kong and the Chinese mainland take their natural advantages to become the largest RMB denominated cities in the whole world and the largest RMB offshore market around the world.

With the continuous expansion of RQFII pilot area and the development of offshore RMB market, more and more types of overseas institutional investors have access to China's bond market. The RQFII pilot also extends from Hong Kong to offshore RMB markets in Singapore, London, Germany and South Korea, and offshore RMB market has also taken shape in these traditional international financial centers. With the trend, offshore RMB deposits, offshore RMB bond issuance, and financial derivatives based on RMB interest rates and exchange rates all develop rapidly. Foreign institutional investors showed great enthusiasm for becoming QFII and RQFII, or entering into the domestic inter-bank bond market as offshore RMB participating banks. Although compared to the large stock of the bond market, the new investment quota is still insignificant, it has changed the expectations of the participating institutions in the market and also added new counterparties options. In the future, the further increase of the number of overseas institutional investors and the continuous increase of the total investment amount will become an inevitable trend.

By the end of September 2014, 125 overseas institutions including Hong Kong and Macau clearing houses, overseas participating banks, overseas insurance agencies, RQFIIs and QFIIs were allowed to enter the inter-bank bond market, and the number of overseas institutional investors increased almost 23% compared with the end of 2013. Among them, there were 87 overseas participating banks and clearing banks, whose investors were increasing by nearly 9% as compared with the end of last year. A total of 30 RQFIIs have been approved by the PBOC, an increase of 43% over the end of 2013; QFII became the first qualified foreign institutional investors participating in the inter-bank bond market.

4.2.2 Characteristics of foreign institutions participating in China's bond market

From the perspective of overseas institutions investing in bonds, the total amount of bonds held by overseas institutions accounted for only about 1.74% of total market bonds by September 2014. Even the highest level of government bonds accepted by overseas institutions only accounted for about 2.42%. Although the various types of bonds held by overseas institutional investors make up an increasing share of the total inter-bank bond market, the overall amount is still less affected for the whole bond market. However, because overseas institutions are limited to be engaged in transactions in the secondary market, the limits are replied at the same time and the relatively consistent opening of accounts led to the overlapping of establishing positions periods and other factors, the problem of insufficient depth in the inter-bank bond market will be magnified in some months when a number of overseas institutions set up their positions in a concentrated manner. Also, the investment direction of overseas institutions has become an important benchmark affecting the market at that time.

Another notable feature is the relatively consistent preferences of investment of overseas institutions. Due to the lack of adequate understanding of China's credit market, overseas institutions generally regard government bonds and policy-oriented financial bonds as their priority in choosing investment instruments.

However, with the continuous standardization of credit market and the continuous development of credit rating, the mainstream credit products in the inter-bank market, including short-term financing bills and medium-term papers, have gradually become the investment targets of some overseas institutions. Except for the strict control of the overseas Central Banks for their own investment guidelines, which lead to their seldom access to credit products, other overseas institutions have shown a growing interest in credit products. It is worth mentioning that, as RQFII took the lead in piloting in Hong Kong, investors in the Greater China Circle including Singapore are familiar with the development of the domestic credit market in China. For credit bonds, short-term financing bills in short duration and ultra-short-term financing bills, as well as high rated bonds with international ratings, are preferred.

The third feature is the huge growth potential. Judging from the trading behavior of overseas institutions in the inter-bank bond market, the quantity of overseas institutions buying has continued to grow in recent years. Since the third quarter of 2013, due to the continuously higher return since the second half of last year and the acceleration of regulatory approvals, the number of purchases has shown a leap forward. Although, the ROI (Return On Investment) of 2014 is greatly rocking, the active trend of overseas institutions participating in the investment activities in the inter-bank bond market has not changed. With the approval of more overseas institutions in 2014, the growth potential of overseas institutions investing in inter-bank bond market remains huge and will continue to maintain a high growth rate.

It can be said that the overseas institutions investing in the domestic inter-bank bond market, to a certain extent, is an inevitable outcome of the development of the real economy and the financial environment in China, and it is an objective requirement for China to continuously promote the internationalization of the RMB. The scale of real economy in China has been growing and China needs to introduce more funds to invest in the domestic market. With the continuous development of cross-border trade in China, the scope of RMB settlement in cross-border trade is constantly expanding and the cross-border RMB direct investment business is deepening, so there is an urgent need for more RMB back-flow channels for overseas investors.

4.3 Financial Derivatives Market

4.3.1 Financial derivatives

There is no set definition for financial derivatives so far. Financial derivatives can be literally interpreted as new financial products deriving from fundamental financial products like bank credits, bonds and stocks, include forward foreign currency or RMB foreign exchange transactions, futures trading and foreign currency swap transactions. All of them have the following characteristics in common:

Virtual. As certificates of profit yield with relative independence, they themselves are worthless and their value is determined by price of underlying assets.

Leveraged. A margin system is commonly adopted in the financial derivatives trade before which both sides need to pay certain deposit amount. That explains why the trade has a leverage effect. The amount of deposit is proportional to the leverage effect while the risk is inversely proportional to that.

Risky. The highly leveraged nature result in concentration of risks which are increased by the virtual platforms and the unpredictability of the derivatives.

Contractual. Financial derivatives represent an agreement on future transactions, specifying the future rights and obligations of traders with a legal effect.

4.3.2 Current situation of China's financial derivatives market

The development of China's financial derivatives can be traced back to the time when warrants trade first appeared in June 1992 in Shanghai and Shenzhen Stock

Exchanges, followed by the successive emergence of financial derivatives such as government bond futures, foreign exchange futures and stock index futures which stopped trading due to illegal operation and lack of demand and other reasons in 1996. After the early practice of the 1990s and the subsequent serious reforms and China's accession to the WTO, the construction of its financial derivatives market got back on track with the gradual opening up of China's financial market, the exchange rate reform and the gradual deepening of marketization of interest rates.

As for RMB foreign exchange derivatives products, the inter-bank market officially launched the forward RMB foreign exchange trading business on August 15th, 2005. The inter-bank foreign exchange market for RMB and foreign currency swap business was officially launched in April 2006 and several other currencies that were added by the end of 2007. In March 2011, the RMB foreign exchange currency swap business was launched in the bank to customer market to improve the market structure of currency swaps. In April, the RMB foreign exchange option business was launched in the bank to customer market and inter-bank foreign exchange market to further enrich the foreign exchange market products. In addition, interest rate derivatives market has also been gradually formed. ICBC concluded the first bond forward trade with CIB (China Industrial Bank) in June 2005. RMB interest rate swap contracts were implemented in March 2006 and forward rate agreement in October, 2007. Starting from the establishment of China Zhengzhou Grain Wholesale Market, China's futures market has taken shape after going through the stages of early development, clean-up and rectification and normalization. There are four futures exchanges in China namely Dalian Commodity Exchange, Zhengzhou Commodity Exchange, Shanghai Futures Exchange and China Financial Futures Exchange.

As of early 2013, China's financial derivatives have enjoyed rapid growth and further enriched variety in the 21st century, especially since 2005. In terms of the types of RMB financial derivatives, interest rate derivative products include bond forwards, interest rate swaps and long-term interest rate agreements; foreign exchange derivatives include foreign exchange forwards, foreign exchange and currency swaps, foreign exchange options, equity derivatives include warrants, and more. Credit derivative products include inter-bank market Credit Risk Mitigation (CRM) tools. The number of the species of four major futures exchanges reached a total of 32. In addition, there are also a number of wealth management products that include structured derivatives linked to interest rates, exchange rates, stocks or indices, credits, commodities or commodities index.

In terms of the transaction scale, although China's financial derivatives were influenced in some way by the financial crisis sweeping the globe in 2008, it still showed some vitality after 2009. We can illustrate this with the fact that the trading scale of financial derivatives such as RMB foreign exchange, currency swaps and interest rate swaps has been maintaining steady and rapid growth. Take RMB foreign exchange derivatives as an example, the forward volume of inter-bank foreign exchange market was USD 88.6 billion; the inter-bank foreign exchange and currency swap business was a single big with a cumulative volume of USD 2.5 trillion, increasing by 42.5% over the last year, accounting for 96.4% of the RMB foreign exchange derivative market. The accumulated volume of nominal principal inter-bank foreign exchange options market reached USD 3.3 billion, with an year-on-year growth of 2.3 times. In the RMB interest rate derivatives market, the nominal principal volume of RMB interest rate swaps reached RMB 2.921 trillion, with an year-on-year growth of 8.45% in 2012.

4.3.3 Defects of domestic financial derivatives market

4.3.3.1 Few financial derivatives

Financial derivatives in the international financial market include futures, exchange rates, stock options, interest rate forward contracts, etc. However, there are only few derivatives in the domestic financial market, such as convertible bonds and warrants on the Shanghai Stock Exchange. The insufficient variety hinders the expansion of financial derivatives and the scale of investment in China.

The fact that RMB derivatives market is not active enough, and the participants of derivatives are not broad enough also restricts the development of China's financial derivatives market.

Financial derivatives are flawed in design. Compared with foreign financial derivatives markets, our customized derivatives have higher homogeneity, which leads to the coexistence of many products with the risk being expanded instead of transferred.

4.3.3.2 Decentralization of financial derivatives regulatory bodies

In theory, the supervision of financial derivatives should be a three-level supervision system established by the government, industry associations and exchanges. However, there is no clear responsibility of the regulatory authorities when the derivatives market was first established in China, so up to now there has not been a sound regulatory system. Each financial institution manages financial derivatives from its own point of view. The decentralization of regulators thus leads to the inconsistency and instability of policy and methods, which makes the supervision inefficient.

4.3.3.3 The legal system of financial derivatives supervision is not complete

At present, China's legislation on financial derivatives is relatively lagging behind. Firstly, from the point of view of development, the current laws and regulations related to financial derivatives are formulated by various regulatory bodies based on specific financial derivatives, and lack unified regulations to improve. The cross-domain risk of financial derivatives deprives them of corresponding legal protection when specific problems arise. Secondly, in the current laws and regulations, restrictive provisions are in the majority and incentive laws are less. Although these restrictive decrees play a positive role in preventing the expansion and spread of financial risks, they also restrict the expansion and development of the derivatives market.

4.3.3.4 Lack of market equilibrium price

At present, China's financial derivatives market is still in its infancy. The price of most financial derivatives differs greatly from the equilibrium price of the market. The price of financial derivatives is closely related to the price of basic financial products. This, plus the fact that China has strict control over financial prices and foreign exchange, the price of financial derivatives is largely controlled by the national policy. Moreover, the RMB cannot be converted freely under the current capital account, which leads to the price of derivatives not controlled by the market. Therefore, the price difference between the two has become the center of contention for speculators, which increases financial risk to a certain extent.

4.3.3.5 Lack of openness and transparency in information disclosure

For participants, accurate information is the prerequisite for making correct judgments. Therefore, financial markets must have a complete information disclosure system. The current information disclosure in China lacks openness and transparency, and cannot truly reflect the market situation of financial derivatives. Therefore, investors are not able to make rational judgments and expectations of the market, which has a negative impact on the development of financial derivatives transactions in China. Moreover, the transparency and publicity of information can reduce investors' risk, but wrong information will lead to wrong judgment of expectations, thus causing serious losses and even endangering the national financial system.

4.3.3.6 The quality of market participants is not high

Participants in financial markets are either individuals or institutions. At present, the quality of participants in China's financial derivatives market is generally low. Since they lack relevant theoretical knowledge and rational judgment on the expected judgment of financial derivatives, their blind investment and follow-up behavior have aggravated the instability and risk of China's financial derivatives market.

Chapter 4
An Introduction to Capital Market in China

【Case】 Review of the First Stock Exchange of Shanghai Stock Exchange

Shanghai Stock Exchange, China's first stock exchange, opened in the Chinese mainland since the founding of the People's Republic of China. It was formally established on December 19th, 1990 with the authorization of the State Council and approval of the People's Bank of China.

First public offering: Shanghai Feile Acoustics Co., Ltd

Shanghai Feile Acoustics Co., Ltd issued 10,000 shares to the public on November 18th, 1984, becoming the first public offering of stocks of new China. The initial par value was 50 *yuan* with corporate shares of RMB 0.3 million, the

internal staff shares of 7,000 making up the total shares of 10,000 and the total volume of the shares of RMB 500,000.

The First Stock Exchange Counter: Jing'an Securities Business Unit

The first securities counter trading point was established at the Jing'an Branch of ICBC Shanghai Trust and Investment Corporation, which was named as one of the "National Top Ten Economic News of 1986".

The First "Room for Big Clients": Room for Big Clients of Shenyin Securities Company in Shanghai

On December 19th, 1990, Shenyin Securities opened the first big room of Shanghai, with China's first generation of large individual securities investors appearing. The former Shanghai Shenyin Securities Company and the former Shanghai Wentworth Securities Company were merged into Shenyin Wanguo Securities Co., Ltd. on July 16th, 1996.

The First Loss-making Company: FAW Gold Cup

Gold Cup was the second stock from other provinces going public after Zhejiang Phoenix. However, since 1994, the performance of the companies kept falling sharply due to the unmarketable products, the poor level of localization and the low efficiency of input and output. In 1995, the net profit showed a loss of 254 million *yuan*.

The First Delisted Shares — "PT Narcissus" (Shanghai Narcissus Electric Appliance Co., Ltd)

On April 23rd, 2001 a memorable event happened in the history of China's securities development: "PT Narcissus" terminated the listing of its stocks, becoming the first delisted stock in China's securities market.

4.4 Q&A

4.4.1 What are the regulatory documents for reference for overseas investors entering Chinese capital market?

The basic complete of reform of non-tradable shares and the issuance of relevant regulations one after another including "Measures for the Administration of Strategic Investment in Listed Companies by Foreign Investors", "On the Relevant Issues Concerning the Opening of A-share Securities Account by Foreign Strategic Investors" and "Interim Provisions on the Takeover of Domestic Enterprises by Foreign Investors" give legal support for introduction of foreign investment in the capital market.

4.4.2 What are the paths for foreign strategic investors to enter China's capital market?

Before the non-tradable share reform, the ways for foreign capital to acquire listed companies mainly include the acquisition of non-tradable shares by OTC and indirect acquisitions (such as controlling majority-shareholding of listed companies). As the share-trading reform was basically completed, overseas strategic investors are able to enter China's capital market through directional issuance, transfer of on-site agreements, tender offer and issuance of directional convertible bonds.

4.4.3 How can foreigners open stock accounts in China?

According to the relevant regulations nowadays, foreigners cannot buy A shares directly in China while B shares are allowed to buy. However, foreigners can buy the fund of QFII companies allowed to enter China. With the funds raised, QFII company can buy A shares. Many of the big international investment banking financial institutions have Chinese QFII fund products.

Chapter 5 China's Financial Regulation and Financial Supervision System

Financial supervision involves a wide range of comprehensive content and covers rich theoretical knowledge as well as practical knowledge, which is increasingly scientific and standardized as time goes by. The in-depth study of the theoretical knowledge of the financial regulatory system will offer a theoretical basis for the development direction of China's financial regulation.

5.1 Overview of China's Financial Supervision

This part mainly introduces the history of China's financial regulation and the necessity of the current framework of China's financial regulation.

5.1.1 The history of China's financial regulation

First stage: planned economic management system (1949-1978)

From the founding of New China in 1949 to the introduction of the policy of reform and opening up in 1978, China implemented a strict system of planned economic management. At that time, there was almost no financial market in China with the People's Bank of China as the only bank responsible for both the credit business and financial supervision, which definitely formed a centralized financial supervision system.Although the "unified finance" was highly planned in nature, it played a very important role in the economic development in a special period of history.

Second stage: the People's Bank of China becomes a composite Central Bank (1978-1982)

At this stage, China has seen the successive establishment of four state-owned commercial banks, PICC, China International Trust and Investment Corporation and other financial institutions and the issuance of some administrative rules and regulations to regulate their business operations. As a composite Central Bank, the PBC undertakes both the function of making monetary policy and operating as commercial banks, also responsible for the supervision of financial institutions throughout the country. The main focus of its financial supervision is to cooperate with the supervision and inspection of the implementation of national financial policies, division of labor and rules and regulations by financial institutions, and to crack down on financial speculation and financial crimes. During this period, the financial supervision was more administrative than specialized, which means the PBC does not really perform its financial regulatory functions, strictly speaking.

The third stage: the People's Bank of China financial supervision system (1982-1992)

In September 1983, the People's Bank of China became an independent Central Bank whose financial regulatory responsibilities began to be specialized, marking the establishment of the Central Bank financial supervision model in China. However, China is still in the initial stage of the transformation of the planned economic system to the market economy system. As a result, there is a lack of obvious market supervision of financial institutions. The regulatory measures of the PBC mainly depend on the administrative system and power on the basis of administrative rules and regulations, Moreover, due to the excessive administrative interference and weakening of financial supervision power in the administrative organs of China's financial regulatory agencies, the financial supervision system in this period did not match the inherent requirements of the development of market economy. which still carries the characteristics of administrative regulation, rather than established by clear legal authority.

The fourth stage: regulatory pattern of separate operation by the Central Bank with other three commissions (1993-2015)

As a decision of the State Council, there was a Reform of the Financial System specifically in the functions of the Central Bank, the enhancement of financial supervision and separation of operations. Separate management of financial institutions according to different businesses was proposed, laying the foundation for the formation of a separate operations system. In 1998, the China Securities Regulatory Commission (CSRC) and the China Insurance Regulatory Commission (CIRC) were successively separated from the People's Bank of China, respectively responsible for the supervision of the securities, futures markets and the insurance industry. In 2003, the China Banking Regulatory Commission (CBRC) was established, responsible for the independent supervision of banking financial institutions. However, together with the establishment of the CSRC and the CIRC, the People's Bank of China maintained the financial supervision over the money market, anti-money laundering and credit information systems. This marked the official formation of the current separate supervision system and the actual transformation of financial supervision from "all in one" to "all in four". The formation of this pattern is conducive to strengthening the specialized management of bank industry as well as the emerging securities and insurance industries. It is conducive to preventing financial risks arising from the mixed operations in the period when the level of financial industry management in China is not high.*

5.1.2 Necessity of financial supervision

For the theory of the necessity of financial supervision, there are two major prevailing systems currently: the financial fragility theory and the public interest theory. The former theory illustrates the need for financial supervision due to

---

* *Research on China's Financial Supervision System Reform*, Deng Minghui

the instability within the financial system. Because of the higher leverage in the banking sector and the fact that more assets were opaquely allocated, as well as illiquid and more difficult markets, the public's uncertainty was exacerbated in the face of serious information asymmetry between depositors and banks. Moreover, inter-bank borrowing and its payment systems made their finances more closely intertwined, which made the payment difficulties of the banks contagious. This means that a bank's default on another one may affect the bank's commitment to its peer, as a result any bank failures or file for bankruptcy would soon be spread to others. In addition, the business failures involve many stakeholders and can be rapidly spread. Therefore, the banking industry does have high vulnerability and contagion. Once the financial crisis has triggered a run-off, it is easy to see a chain reaction of "technical bankruptcy". According to the public interest theory, financial markets may also experience malfunction which will lead to the failure to achieve "Pareto Optimality" in the allocation of financial resources. As a public product, financial supervision is a mean to reduce or eliminate market failure which is mainly manifested in natural monopoly, external effect and information asymmetry.

5.1.3 China's financial regulatory system (the Central Bank with other three commissions)

5.1.3.1 The current situation of China's regulation

The financial regulation refers to government's regulation on the main body of financial transactions through a specific agency, like the Central Bank. It is essentially a kind of government regulation institution with specific connotation and characteristics.

Financial supervision can also be divided into narrow sense and broad sense. In a narrow sense, it refers to the supervision and management of the whole financial industry, including all business activities of financial institutions in the financial market by the central bank or other financial regulatory authorities according to the authorization of national laws and regulations; in a broad sense, financial supervision is done beyond its narrow sense including as well the internal control of financial institutions.

Because of the differences in economy, society, history, traditions and cultures, all countries have adopted different financial regulatory systems, unchanged and without uniform mode. According to the concentration degree of the financial regulatory bodies' power and the distribution mechanism and their different levels, it can be divided into three categories including one tier supervision with one regulatory agency, one tier supervision with multiple regulatory agencies and two-tier supervision system with multiple regulatory agencies, three of which the latter one has more financial regulation power from the central authorities and less from local government.

(1) Single-line and single-head system

The single-line and single-head system is a centralized system, which means that from the central government to local regions, only a single financial regulatory agency is responsible for the supervision of all kinds of financial institutions. The representative countries of this type of model is the United Kingdom. Most developing countries also adopt such financial regulatory regimes.

(2) Single-line and multi-head system

The "single line" here refers to the centralization of financial supervision power in the central government. There is no uniform regulation on the number of regulatory bodies at the central level, but the responsibility usually lies in two or more institutions, while the local authorities do not have independent powers. Germany, Japan and other countries have this system.

(3) Dual-line and multi-head system

"Double-line" means that the power of financial supervision is concentrated in the central and local governments, which have supervision power over financial institutions (double-line). At the same time, at each level, several institutions exercise supervision functions (multiple). Federal countries such as the United

States and Canada mostly implement this regulatory system.

Among the three types, the later the system is, the smaller the central financial supervision power and larger the local financial supervision power will be.

Under the mixed operation, financial innovation blurs the boundaries of products and services provided by different financial institutions. The business of different financial institutions overlaps and their functions tend to be same. Therefore, the institutional supervision system is facing many problems, such as unfair competition, regulatory arbitrage, waste of regulatory resources and regulatory loopholes, so it is more suitable for functional supervision. In order to adapt to the development trend of financial business integration and avoid the defects of functional supervision in the overall supervision, comprehensive supervision emerged as the times require. Due to the development of mixed operation, the trend of merging three major financial services--bank, securities and insurance into a single financial institution is obvious. The supervision of these financial groups must be carried out on the basis of merger to achieve effective supervision so as to manage and control the risks of the entire financial system. The outbreak of the financial crisis has fully exposed the inherent conflict between protection of financial consumers and prudent regulatory objectives, and has also made the regulatory authorities of various countries realize that paying attention to the interests of financial institutions but neglecting the effective protection of consumer's interests will destroy the foundation on which the financial industry depends and affect the stability of the financial system.

Currently the one tier supervision with multiple regulatory agencies is adopted in China. This regulatory authority is highly concentrated in the central government, while multiple regulatory agencies at the central level are established to supervise different financial institutions. All of above led to the formation of the main pattern of separate regulation in China. Under the current regulation system of "Central Bank with other three commissions", the PBC is mainly responsible for formulating and implementing monetary policies to safeguard financial stability;

the CBRC supervising banks, financial asset management companies, trust and investment companies and other deposit-taking financial institutions; and the CSRC supervising the securities and futures companies, securities investment fund management companies, securities registration and clearing companies, futures clearing agencies and securities and futures investment advisory bodies; the CIRC overseeing both the insurance and non-insurance agencies established by overseas insurance institutions.

5.1.3.2 China's financial regulation system

"Central Bank with other three commissions" is the major component of China's financial regulation and control system. The term "Central Bank with other three commissions" is the short name for the four financial management and supervision departments including the People's Bank of China, the China Banking Regulatory Commission, the China Securities Regulatory Commission and the China Insurance Regulatory Commission which form the pattern of China's separate regulation of finance industry. The framework of the system is shown as below:

- The People's Bank of China (macro-control)
- The People's Bank of China is a department of the State Council and the Central Bank of the People's Republic of China. It is a macro-control department under the State Council's leadership that formulates and implements monetary policies, maintains financial stability and provides financial services.
- CBRC, CSRC and CIRC (Industry Regulation)
- The China Banking Regulatory Commission (CBRC) is a directly-subordinate institution under the State Council. Under the authorization of the State Council, it uniformly supervises and manages banks, financial asset management companies, trust and investment companies and other deposit-taking financial institutions to safeguard the legitimate and steady

operation of the banking industry.

- The China Securities Regulatory Commission (CSRC) is a directly-subordinate institution under the State Council. It supervises and manages the securities and futures markets in the country in a unified manner and the authorization of the State Council, maintains order in the securities and futures markets so as to guarantee its lawful operation in accordance with laws and regulations under the authorization of the State Council.

- The China Insurance Regulatory Commission (CIRC) is a directly subordinate institution under the State Council. Under the authorization of the State Council, it performs its administrative functions, supervises and manages the national insurance market in accordance with the laws and regulations and maintains the lawful and steady operation of the insurance industry*.

---

* The People's Bank of China: *National Financial Textbook*, Beijing, China Financial Publishing House, 2014.

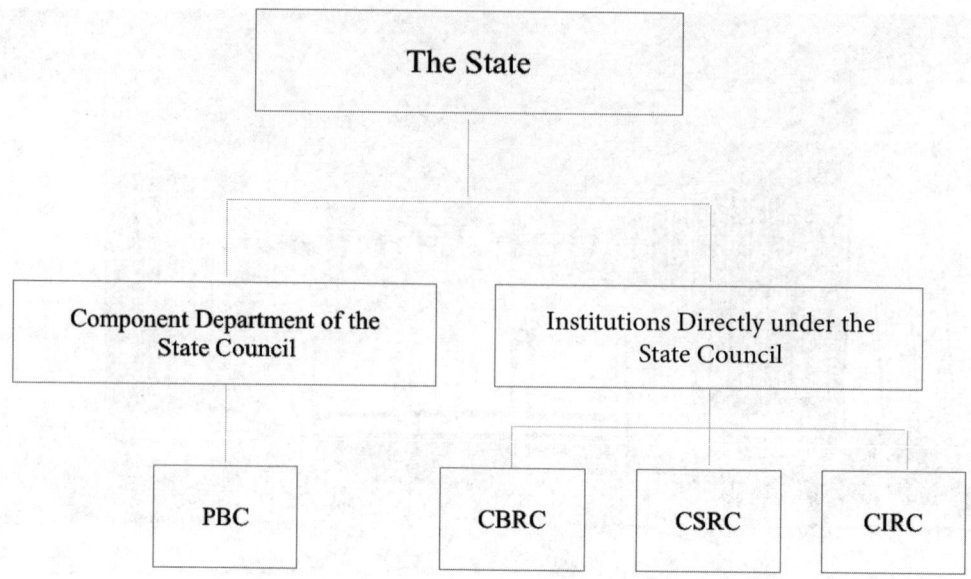

Figure 5-1　Chinese Financial Regulation System

5.2　The People's Bank of China

The People's Bank of China is the Central Bank of the People's Republic of China. Its main functions are to formulate and implement monetary policies, safeguard financial stability and provide financial services.

5.2.1　Formulating and implementing monetary policies

Monetary policy is the general term for the People's Bank of China's adoption of monetary policy tools to adjust its monetary supply and demand so as to achieve the goal of macroeconomic regulation and control. The elements of monetary policy also include the intermediate goal of monetary policy, the operational objective of monetary policy, monetary policy instruments and the monetary policy transmission mechanism. The ultimate goal of China's monetary policy is to maintain the stability of the currency value and thus promote economic growth.

In order to achieve the monetary policy objective, the People's Bank of China has comprehensively used various tools such as open market operations, reserve deposits, refinancing and rediscounts, standing loan facilities, short-term liquidity adjustment instruments and interest rate policies, and others. Meanwhile, the PBC also improved its macro-prudential policy framework and play its counter-cyclical regulation effect.

5.2.2 Maintaining financial stability

Finance is the core of the modern economy. Once there is financial market turmoil, the entire economy and society will be greatly affected. Historically, stock market disasters, bank failures and financial crises are commonplace. The consequences of the financial crisis often stagnate economic growth and cause social turmoil.

As the Central Bank of China, the PBC undertakes the important responsibility of guarding against and resolving systemic financial risks and safeguarding the country's financial stability. By monitoring and assessing financial risks, tackling potential risks in the financial sector, promoting the reform and development of the financial sector, strengthening the construction of a financial safety net, taking on the function of the lender of last resort, the PBC maintains the liquidity of the financial system and ensures the smooth operation of the financial system. The PBC has integrated tools such as interest rate and exchange rate policy, open market operations, capital account management, loan repayment and payment system support as well as institutional arrangements such as macro-prudential regulation, regulatory coordination mechanism, protection of financial consumer rights and interests, to create a good environment for financial institutions, steady operations of market as well as to maintain the overall stability of the financial system.

5.2.3 Providing financial service

In many eyes, the PBC is only a State organ that formulates and implements monetary policies and maintains financial stability, it is perceived as an institution that is far away from the daily life of people. This is not the case. The PBC also provides financial services to the whole society which are closely linked to the lives of ordinary people.

The RMB generally used by people is printed and distributed by the PBC. Every transfer or remittance made between different banks passes through the clearing system set up by the People's Bank of China. When you go to a commercial bank to apply for a loan, you also need to provide a credit certificate with the credit information system set up by the People's Bank of China.

The PBC offers far more than just these financial services. It manages the State treasury, the country's foreign exchange reserves and gold reserves, statistics, financial data and organizes anti-money laundering efforts.

5.3 China Banking Regulatory Commission

Banking financial institutions mainly include banks, financial asset management companies, trust and investment companies and other deposit-taking financial institutions. Due to the fact that China is an indirect financing-based country with high savings rate of residents, effective supervision and management of banking financial institutions play a crucial role in China's financial industry.

The CBRC mainly performs its duties of general supervision with the main purpose of uniformly supervising and managing banks, financial asset management companies, trust and investment companies and other deposit-taking financial institutions so as to safeguard the lawful and steady operation of the banking industry. The banking regulatory approach consists of three main components: the regulatory authority's general supervision, the deposit insurance system and the lender of last resort system. China's Lenders of Last Resort System is implemented by the People's Bank of China. The deposit insurance system has not yet been completed. The regulatory authority's general supervision is implemented by the CBRC.

5.3.1 The basic duties of the CBRC

5.3.1.1 Market access regulation

Banks are a highly profitable industry, so people are motivated to invest in banking. However, the banking industry is a high-risk industry. The characteristics of its debt management determine that banks must give priority to "safety". The bankruptcy of banks will make the depositors suffer losses and lead to a "domino effect", triggering a series of chain reactions. In order to prevent risks, all countries and regions tend to restrict market access to banks especially for private capital banks while strengthening their supervision of banks.

Market access refers to regulatory measures for examining the opening of banking institutions, blocking unqualified applicants outside the banking gate, which is the first line of defense to ensure the stability of the banking sector. Therefore, the CBRC's main responsibilities include formulating and promulgating rules and regulations governing the supervision and administration of banking financial institutions and their business activities in accordance with laws and administrative regulations; and managing the qualifications of directors and senior managers of banking financial institutions.

【Case】The Establishment of Private Banks

Since 2014, the CBRC has piloted the first batch of private-owned banks and put forward the framework suggestion for piloting private banks. With the agreement of the State Council, the pilot projects have achieved initial results. In the practice of market access, private capital mainly enters the banking industry through such measures as launching and setting up, subscribing for new shares, transferring equity, mergers and acquisitions and reorganization. In March 2014, the CBRC announced the pilot list of the first batch of five private banks and officially started pilot projects of private banks. In accordance with the principle of voluntary will and commercial sustainability, the CBRC actively coordinated with the initiators to improve the preparation plan. Five factors were taken into account in pilot selection criteria:

1. Institutional arrangements that assume the remaining risks
2. Good bank qualification and anti-risk ability
3. Terms of agreement stipulating shareholders to accept regulation
4. A differentiated market positioning and specific strategies
5. Legally feasible recovery and disposal plan.

The first batch of five pilot private banks reflects the operating characteristics of serving small and medium-sized enterprises, the principle of "agriculture, rural areas and farmers" and the community. Among them, Tianjin Jincheng Bank adheres to "public deposit of public loans"; Zhejiang Online Commercial Bank "small deposit of small loans"; Shenzhen Qianhai Weizhong Bank "personal savings and small loans", while Shanghai Huarui Bank and Wenzhou Commercial Bank "specific area" business model.

In July 2014, the CBRC approved the establishment of WeBank, Wenzhou Commercial Bank and Tianjin Jincheng Bank; in September 2014, the CBRC approved the preparation of Shanghai Huarui Bank and MYbank. Among them, WeBank and Shanghai Huarui Bank were approved for operation in December 2014 and January 2015, respectively. Wenzhou Commercial Bank and Tianjin Jincheng Bank were approved for operation in March 2015.

The significance is to change the banking market competition structure, strengthen the banking market, cultivate a modern management system of banking institutions. Private capital's initiative of the establishment of financial institutions such as small and medium-sized banks stimulate the enthusiasm and creativity of non-governmental capital in financial services. It is a powerful complement to financial resources, conducive to diversifying the ownership structure of financial institutions and further enhancing the market vitality of financial institutions.

5.3.1.2 The scope of business of validation financial institutions

The supervisory authority's supervision over the scope of banking activities means that once a financial institution is established, it should engage in financial activities in accordance with the permitted business scope and shall not be offside from this frame of work. For example, the *Commercial Bank Law of the People's Republic of China* stipulates that commercial banks may operate some or all of the following businesses: absorbing public deposits, issuing short-term, medium-term and long-term loans, settling domestic and foreign settlements, accepting and discounting bills, issuing financial bonds, issuing, cashing and selling government bonds as agents, selling and purchasing government bonds, financial bonds, inter-bank lending, buying and selling foreign exchange by itself or as an agent, engaging in bank card business, providing letters of credit services and guarantees, operating agent payments and agent insurance business, other businesses approved by the banking regulatory authority under the State Council. The scope of business shall be subject to the provisions of the charter of commercial banks and shall be submitted to the banking regulatory authority under the State Council for approval. With the approval of the People's Bank of China, commercial banks may operate foreign exchange settlement and sales business.

5.3.1.3 Conducting audit check on the operation of financial institutions

Audit check on the operation of financial institutions mainly include on-site supervision and off-site supervision. On-site supervision refers to the supervisory authority's unannounced on-the-spot inspection of the bank whose function is to prevent the bank from concealing the truth for knowing in advance that it needs to be inspected. Off-site supervision refers to the analysis of the operation status, risk management status of the banks by using certain technical methods according to various regulatory and financial data and reports submitted by supervisory authorities to the banking financial institutions to evaluate the risk status of financial institutions in banking industry. Effective combination of the two supervisors can effectively control banking risks.

5.3.1.4 Handling of problematic financial institutions

Due to the contagion effect of financial risks, the problems of individual financial institutions are likely to trigger systemic risks which means the handling of troubled financial institutions is particularly important. For example, the CBRC has the power to take over or reorganize a banking financial institution that has or may have a credit crisis that seriously affects the lawful rights and interests of its depositors and other customers. It also has the power of revoking banking institutions that have illegal operations and mismanagement.

5.3.2 Development and regulation of foreign-funded banks

In order to adapting to the new situation of economic globalization, implementing a more proactive strategy of opening up and improving a mutually beneficial, win-win, diversified, balanced and safe and efficient, open and economical system, the China Banking Regulatory Commission ordered the banking sector to open up to the outside world in an orderly manner, adhered to the principle of expanding opening up and strengthening supervision simultaneously and paying equal attention to prudential regulation and optimization services, guarding against opening up risks through supervision and improving the open environment through optimization of services so as to promote China's overall improvement in the open economy in the banking sector. Therefore, the development of foreign banks in China also faces new opportunities.

First, China's economic development has brought new opportunities. China's economic development has entered a new normal, changing from high-speed growth to medium-to-high speed of growth. Economic growth has become more stable and its momentum has become more pluralistic. Its economic structure has been continuously optimized and upgraded with more stable development prospects. The government has vigorously simplified its administration and decentralized power, relaxed market access, expanded the opening up of the service sector to the outside world and opening up of inland and border areas, which further release market vitality. The new normal will bring new opportunities for development of foreign banks in China.

Second, the deepening of the opening up of the banking industry will bring new opportunities. The CBRC thoroughly implemented the party Central Committee's overall plan on building a new open economy based on the actual economic and financial development in China and the development trend of international banking, so as to accelerate the continuous expansion and deepening of the banking industry's opening to the outside world on the basis of fulfilling China's commitments to the WTO and provide a favorable policy environment for the development of foreign banks in China. The implementation of the latest liberalization policy and future policy trends will all provide new opportunities for foreign banks to participate in the Chinese market. First, the Regulation of the People's Republic of China on the Administration of Foreign-funded Banks was revised so that starting January 1st,

2015, foreign banks will implement three measures to further expand opening up: firstly, the minimum number of working capital requirements for domestic branch of a foreign-funded legal person bank would be canceled. Secondly, the requirement of setting up a representative office before the establishing foreign-funded bank business operative institutions. Thirdly, the requirement for foreign-funded banks to apply for operating RMB business would be reduced from three years to one year and requirement of making two consecutive years of profit would also be canceled correspondingly. Also, through continuous cooperation with relevant countries and regions under the framework of bilateral arrangements in accordance with the principle of mutual benefit, the bank will continue to improve the level of opening up to the outside world. Finally, starting from March 1st, 2015, the banking sector in Hong Kong and Maucao will be further liberalized adopting the pre-establishment national treatment (PENT) with a negative list for the first time in accordance with the latest arrangement of the Chinese mainland, Hong Kong and Maucao on setting up a more compact economic and trade relationship. In addition to the restrictive measures listed in the negative list, the banking institutions in Hong Kong and Maucao will enjoy the same treatment as those in the Chinese mainland market in Guangdong province, further expanding their development potential in the mainland. The cooperation between the mainland and Taiwan's banking sector is constantly expanding. Supported by preferential mainland policies, the banking industry in Taiwan has accelerated its pace of entering the mainland market in recent years. By using its own advantages, Taiwan's banking industry has actively provided services for the economic and financial development across the Taiwan Strait and laid the foundation for its own development of next stage. At the same time, China's economic reform has entered a comprehensive and deepening stage with opening up to the outside world constantly expanding. The new policies and measures in the process of reform and opening up as well as the constantly improving market-oriented business environment will provide more space and opportunities for foreign-funded banks to develop in China.

Chapter 5
China's Financial Regulation and Financial Supervision System

A good foundation for development is conducive to seizing new opportunities. After more than 30 years of development, the network of foreign-funded banking institutions in China continues to expand with the business rapidly increasing. In the past five years, the CAGR (Compound Annual Growth Rate) of total assets of foreign-funded banks has reached 23%, and the financial services capability has been continuously strengthened, which has played a useful role in supplementing and promoting China's banking industry.

In terms of the distribution of outlets, at of the end of 2014, 41 foreign-funded legal person banks and 97 foreign bank branches were set up by foreign-funded banks in 69 cities in 27 provinces (municipalities and autonomous regions) in China, bringing the total number of operating agencies to 1,000. In addition, 182 representative offices were also set up by 158 banks from 47 countries in China. Under the supervision of the China Banking Regulatory Commission, branches of foreign-funded banks have gradually expanded from coastal provinces and major cities to inland provinces and second and third-tier cities in the northeast, central and western regions. Network functions also tend to be more diversified, paying more attention to close to China's market demand. Some foreign banks have set up small and micro enterprise franchise branches, county branches and off-shore branches to provide more suitable special financial services for small and micro enterprises, county economy and new rural construction, contributing to the local economic construction and development.

At the same time of rapid development, foreign-funded banks in China maintained a steady growth as a whole. The overall capital adequacy ratio has remained at over 15% in recent years. With good asset quality and the controllable liquidity risk, laying a good foundation for the next step.

Playing a comparative advantage is conducive to seize new opportunities. In terms of providing differentiated services, foreign banks have conducted trade financing, structured finance, international trade settlement, foreign exchange transactions and derivatives transactions, cash management, wealth management and other areas of special financial services relying on the parent bank's global network resources, multinational management experience and product technology advantages in combination with the needs of China's market. We have developed financial products and services that are suitable for our market in areas such as consumer finance and small and medium-sized enterprise finance to help SMEs and individuals solve their financing problems. Foreign banks and Chinese banks work together to complement each other in areas such as credit card, liquidation, currency swap, asset securitization, cross-border services, RMB cross-border use, overseas mergers and acquisitions, and multinational operations to provide clients with more comprehensive financial services to promote China's financial market with international standards.

When it comes to supporting the "going global" of Chinese-funded enterprises, foreign-funded banks make use of the global network to help Chinese-funded enterprises to gain an in-depth understanding of overseas markets, study and formulate strategic plans; provide various types of financial services such as trade financing, commercial loans, cash management, payment and settlement to customize personalized products for Chinese-funded enterprises; use their knowledge and understanding of environmental protection, labor and community laws and policies to help Chinese-funded enterprises fulfill their social responsibilities overseas and establish a good corporate image.

During the development of RMB cross-border use, foreign banks actively participated in integrating cross-border RMB business into their key development strategies and actively explored cross-border RMB settlement, cross-border investment and financing, RMB QFII (RQFII) custody, and the issuance of RMB loans in the offshore market , issuance of RMB financial bonds, issuance of RMB corporate bonds on behalf of clients, and being market makers who participate in the direct exchange of RMB with other currencies. The sustained and healthy development of China's economy, the further promotion of reform and opening up and the comparative advantages of foreign banks will provide foreign banks more opportunities and room for development in the Chinese market.

5.4 China Securities Regulatory Commission

The CSRC, is a directly-owned institution under the State Council, it supervises and manages the securities and futures markets in the country in a unified manner and maintains their order to ensure the lawful operation in accordance with laws, regulations and the authorization of the State Council.

5.4.1 Basic duties of the CSRC

Judging from the content of securities supervision, the CSRC's supervision of the securities market mainly includes four responsibilities: the regulation of the issuance and listing of securities, the supervision of the trading market, listed companies and securities business institutions.

5.4.1.1 Regulation of the issuance and listing of securities

At present, the approval system for the issuance of Chinese stocks, that is, the issuance of securities not only depends on the full disclosure of the actual conditions, but also meets certain substantial conditions suitable for issuance formulated by the securities regulatory authorities. Companies which are eligible for the issue can obtain the qualifications of issuance in the securities market to issue securities approved by the securities regulatory authority. The approval system is conducive to the healthy development of emerging markets, suitable for areas with imperfect securities market, investment service agencies of low morale and low business level, the lack of experience and business investors of low business experience and ability to judge the information.

The approval system means that regulators need to provide guidance to new issuers and establish a strict information disclosure system which meets the conditions of issuance. Therefore, China adopts a sponsor system whereby sponsors (brokers) recommend and coach securities issued by issuers and verify whether the information contained in the company's issuance documents is true, accurate and complete, to assist the issuer to establish a strict information disclosure system and assume the risk prevention responsibilities; to continue to assist the issuer in setting up a standardized corporate governance structure within the prescribed time after the listing of the company, supervise the company to abide by the listing rules, complete the promise in the prospectus, and at the same time take joint and several liabilities for the information disclosure of listed companies.

【Case】Registration System Reform

According to the *Decision on Several Major Issues Concerning the Comprehensively Deepening the Reform* of 2013, proposed on the third plenary session of the 18th CPC (Communist Party of China) central committee, one of the tasks of capital market reform is to push forward the reform of the stock issuance and registration system. *Opinions on Further Promoting the IPO System Reform* of the China Securities Regulatory Commission released on November 30th, 2013 marked the beginning of the transition from the approval system to the registration system.

In 1998, the *Securities Law* was promulgated and implemented. It was clearly announced that the stock issuance system will be governed by an approval system. In the case of the approval system, the following disadvantages exist: first, the value judgement of stocks made by the regulators instead of the investor is inaccurate. Judging from the regulatory logic, the issuer examination and approval department strictly examines the information submitted by the listed company during the IPO process. Its starting point is to stop the unqualified company from the stock market and select the outstanding company and recommend it to the market investors. However, market practice shows that bad companies haven't been kept out of the stock market after many years of implementation of the issuance approval system in China. On the contrary, the performance of many companies is deteriorating after the issuance of stocks. In other words, regulators cannot substitute investors to make the value judgement. Second, rent-seeking behavior is breeding, which distorts the formation mechanism of stock prices. A large number of junk stocks is seriously overvalued. Due to their high sensitivity to the number of new shares issued, it is inevitable to control the quantity and pace of IPO issuance in order to maintain these overvalued share prices. As a result, a large number of companies cannot finance through the stock market, while a large number of savings do not have the proper investment channels, making the stock market fail to play its due role of resource allocation. In short, these shortcomings seriously reduce the efficiency of capital markets.

The registration system makes it possible for the market participants to regroup their respective responsibilities and force the self-restraint to be strengthened. This will help perfect the investment and financing functions in the capital market, reduce the financing costs for enterprises, increase the convenience of financing and promote the development of the direct financing market.

The registration system is a securities issuance system as well as a basic rule of the securities market involving all participants in the market. Thus, the reform plan needs to be gradual and the introduction of policies is also very important. First, the registration system of new shares issuance is more important than the market-based approval system in the past. In fact, we can say it was a relationship adjustment between the government and the market. The core of the registration system is information disclosure. The issuer's disclosure of various kinds of information related to securities issuance in accordance with the law and the sponsor agencies and intermediaries also assume greater responsibilities. Investors also need to make value judgments at their own risk. Regulators also need to shift focus from the proactive regulation to the post-mortem supervision. Second, the purpose of the registration system is to give better play to the role of the market. However, the realization of the registration system must also be decided by the market. On the one hand, it should be guaranteed by a market-oriented, well-regulated market and better laws and regulations. On the other hand, intermediaries such as issuers and underwriters are required to equip with strong self-discipline capability and investors, mature investment concept, and the management, mature regulatory tools of marketization. However, judging from the current situation, China's capital market is still far from these standards. Third, the reform of the registration system requires legislation to be taken as the first step and a more honest operation of the market and a reasonable protection mechanism for investors should be formed through the legal constraints.

5.4.1.2 Regulation of the trading market

The regulation of the trading market includes the information disclosure system in stock exchange, the regulation of market manipulation behavior, the regulation of defrauding customer and supervision of insider trading behavior.

5.4.1.3 Regulation of listed companies

The supervision of listed companies is mainly reflected in the supervision of information disclosure. Due to the nature of information asymmetry in the securities market, which affects the market efficiency, information disclosure is particularly important. Information disclosure is the legal obligation of a listed company, which is conducive to restrain the securities issuer's behavior and promote its management; it is conducive to the reasonable formation of the issuance price and the transaction price of the securities market; it is good for safeguarding the legitimate rights and interests of investors; it is conducive to securities supervision and raising the efficiency of the stock market.

Information disclosure regulation requires the securities issuer to provide the actual or potential buyers with public financial information about the trading securities. Including pre-release disclosure and continuous information disclosure after the listing. For example, listed companies need to issue prospectuses and listing announcements, periodic reports and interim reports.

5.4.1.4 Regulation of securities institutions

The regulation of securities institutions includes the supervision of the entry of securities institutions, the approval of the operations of securities companies and the routine supervision of securities companies.

5.4.2 The opening-up of securities industry

Opening to the outside world is an important driving force for the development of China's capital market. Over the past 20 years, the capital market in China has grown from nothing to small and large, and the scale, efficiency, influence and transparency of the market have been continuously improved. During this process, CSRC actively and steadily promoted the opening up of the securities and futures industry and the capital market.

5.4.2.1 Promote further liberalization of the capital market

The QFII and RQFII system is a transitional arrangement that partially opens up the capital market under the condition that the capital account has not yet been completely liberalized. QFII refers to investment fund management institutions including insurance companies, securities companies, commercial banks and other asset management institutions that meet certain conditions and have been approved by the CSRC to invest in the securities market in China and have obtained the approval of the State Administration of Foreign Exchange. RQFII refers to an overseas legal person who meets the requirements of the CSRC and obtains the investment quota approved by the State Administration of Foreign Exchange and uses domestic RMB funds from overseas for domestic securities investment.

In order to speed up the introduction of QFII, in 2013, CSRC approved 45 QFIIs, after which the total number of QFIIs reached 251, of which 84% were intermediate and long-term institutions including asset management institutions, central banks and sovereign funds and pension funds. As of the end of 2013, QFII had a total investment of 49.801 billion U.S. dollars. In May, the QFII investment was USD 12.258 billion, with a total investment of RMB 422.2 billion, including RMB 379.9 billion of securities assets, accounting for 89.84% of the total assets. The stock market value accounts for about 1.5% of China's A-share market capitalization.

In order to further expand the RQFII pilot area, in 2013, the CSRC expanded the scope of its RQFII pilot program from Hong Kong, China, to Taiwan, London and Singapore. The restrictions on the allocation of assets and liabilities were removed and the type of product can be determined by the pilot institutions itself; the scope of RQFII investment were further clarified, the stock index futures, SME private placement bonds and other assets and products were increased. Requirements for application documents were simplified.

In addition, RQFII regulations were revised in 2013. The main contents of the amendment include: allowing domestic commercial banks, insurance subsidiaries in Hong Kong, financial institutions with registered places and principal places of business in Hong Kong to participate in pilot projects; removing restrictions on the allocation of assets and liabilities to the public, pilot institutions can decide on their own product types; further clarified the scope of RQFII investment, increase the stock index futures, SME private debt and other asset products; simplified application requirements.

In 2013, the CSRC newly approved 35 RQFII qualifications, bringing the total number of RQFIIs to 61. The newly approved RQFII quota reached RMB 90.5 billion. As of the end of 2013, the total investment amount of RQFII was RMB 157.5 billion with total assets of RMB 61.85 billion. Its market capitalization accounted for approximately 0.2% of that of China A-shares[*].

5.4.2.2 Supporting the introduction of domestic securities and futures business agencies

The promise in the Chinese mainland and Macao Closer Economic Partnership Arrangement was carried out in 2014 to further liberalize the shareholding ratio and business scope of Hong Kong-Macau financial institutions participating in mainland securities companies, fund management companies and securities investment advisory institutions.

Research can promote the securities companies, fund management companies to carry out foreign exchange business. Guotai Junan Securities and Harvest Fund have formally approved the foreign exchange settlement business qualifications.

---

[*] Source: CSRC

Securities and futures institutions are supported to set up overseas subsidiaries to carry out cross-border investment business.

5.5 The China Insurance Regulatory Commission

The insurance industry is an important part of the social and economic compensation system, providing security for people and having a great responsibility for social and economic stability. However, its liability nature poses a high operating risk which bulks extreme importance of insurance supervision. Second, the professionalism of the insurance industry requires special regulation. In the meantime, the development of China's insurance industry is lagging behind. The regulatory guarantee can ensure that it can be in line with international insurance standards and realize the regionalized and internationalized operation and development of the insurance industry. In summary, the supervision and management of the insurance industry is particularly necessary.

5.5.1 The CIRC's basic responsibilities

On November 18, 1998, the State Council approved the establishment of the China Insurance Regulatory Commission which is responsible for the insurance supervision and management functions. According to the content of insurance supervision, it can be divided into institutional supervision, business supervision, financial supervision and solvency supervision.

5.5.1.1 Institutional supervision

Institutional supervision generally includes the supervision of the access and exit to insurance market, as well as the insurance company's organizational form.

When opening an enterprise, an insurance company should not only have assets for business like general enterprises, but also must have reserves to meet the catastrophic or huge risks in the early days after its establishment, otherwise it will not be able to fulfill its contractual obligations. Therefore, it is not possible to run insurance without certain capital and reserves. In terms of requirements of capital or reserve, due to the different national conditions of each country, the requirements for the minimum statutory capital are also different according to different insurance laws.

In order to avoid bankruptcy of insurance companies that operate improperly and financially in crisis and safeguard the legitimate rights and interests of the insured, the government generally adopts the assisting policy and make use of various measures to help them to tide over the difficulties and continue their normal business. However, if an insurance company runs a business illegally or has made major mistakes which result in insolvency, the government acts as supervisor to suspend its operations or issues a liquidation order and appoints a liquidator to directly intervene in the liquidation process. The specific regulatory measures include rectification, takeover, dissolution and liquidation.

All countries have special restrictions on the form of insurance organization according to their national conditions. For example, limited liability companies and mutual companies are the two legal forms of insurance organizations in the United States. In the United Kingdom, in addition to the Limited Liability Company and Mutual Insurance Company, Lloyds is allowed to adopt a personal insurance organization. According to the relevant provisions of the *Insurance Law* and the *Company Law* of China, an insurance company shall take the form of a joint stock limited company and a wholly state-owned company.

5.5.1.2 Business supervision

Business supervision mainly includes the supervision of business scope, insurance clauses, premium rates and reinsurance. The supervision of business scope means that the government stipulates the types and scope of businesses that insurance companies can run through legal or administrative order. In addition to the unity of content and form of the policy, taking both theory and practice into account, simple and practicable operation, but more importantly, it is required in the terms of the insurance policy validation that the rights and obligations of both parties to the insurance contract shall be clearly stipulated. Regulation of premium rates varies from the nature of the insurance business. Even in the same nature of the insurance business, different countries also have different approaches. To sum up, the regulation of premium rates can be roughly divided into compulsory rates, regulatory rates, pre-approved rates, prior approval rates, post-approval rates and free competition rates. Insurance rate of insurance policies concerning the public interest in China, insurance under compulsory laws and life insurance under new development shall be submitted for examination and approval to the insurance supervision and administration department. The rates for other types of insurance shall be formulated by insurance companies and reported to the competent authority for the record. To supervise and manage the reinsurance business will help the insurance companies to disperse the risks in a timely manner and maintain stable operations, which will help to limit the outflow of premiums and protect the development of the national insurance industry. In the developing countries and regions, reinsurance programs companies or the carry-out of semi-official policy reinsurance business are generally government-sponsored.

5.5.1.3 Financial supervision

Financial supervision mainly focuses on the assets and liabilities of insurers, in which the withdrawal of insurance reserves and the utilization of funds have become the focus. Insurance reserve refers to a certain amount of funds deposited from the premium income or surplus by the insurer in accordance with the relevant government laws or business-specific needs. Government regulation of reserves is mainly reflected in the types and amount of withdrawals of reserves which varies by type of insurance. Generally speaking, deposit for property insurance business mainly includes unexpired statutory reserve, reserve for indemnity and special reserve. The reserve for personal insurance business mainly includes statutory reserve, unexpired reserve for premium and special reserve. The use of funds is an important source of income for insurance companies as well as an important mean of expanding and guaranteeing the solvency of insurance companies. The principles of investment, insurance, liquidity and profitability as well as the purpose of all countries in supervising and managing the use of funds by insurance companies, should be adhered to in applying insurance funds. However, due to the differences in the development of economic systems and financial markets in various countries, the control over the use of funds by insurance companies also has its own characteristics. The main content of general supervision and management is the extent and scope of fund utilization, the funds allocation and the proportionality limit.

5.5.1.4 The supervision on the solvency of an insurance company

As the core content of insurance regulation, solvency regulation includes a series of supervision ensuring insurance companies with solvency such as capital requirements, risk capital requirements, margin extraction, the establishment of an information index system, the establishment of insurance protection funds, and others.

The solvency of an insurance company generally refers to the insurance company's ability to compensate for the risks it incurs when compensating and paying are more than those of the normal years. The supervision and management of solvency is the primary objective as well as the core of the state supervision and management of the insurance market. The requirements on the standard of solvency of insurance companies in insurance laws of different countries have their own characteristics.

5.5.2 Foreign-funded insurance companies

Since its admission to the World Trade Organization in 2001, China's insurance market has seen profound changes in the past 12 years. A large number of foreign-funded insurance companies have entered China, which played a positive role in promoting enrichment of the main structure of China's insurance market and introduction of advanced management techniques and tools, products and services innovation. The sufficient solvency, business structure optimization, risk management awareness and strong compliance concepts are the advantages of the business development of foreign insurance companies.

5.5.2.1 Restrictions on foreign-funded insurance companies

First, limitations on the foreign life insurance companies operating forms.

It is explicitly stipulated in Article 3 of the "Detailed Rules for the Implementation of the Regulation of the People's Republic of China" on the Administration of Foreign-Funded Insurance Companies where foreign insurance companies and Chinese companies or enterprises form insurance companies engaging in the business of personal insurance within China in the form of equity joint ventures. The foreign stake in such a joint venture shall not exceed 50% of the total shares of the joint venture, with the exception of American International Assurance, the only foreign-owned life insurance company.

Second, limitations on the establishment of foreign-funded insurance asset management companies.

It is stipulated in the Article 8 of the 2011 revision of "Interim Provisions on the Administration of Insurance Assets Management Companies" revised by the CIRC that there shall be at least one shareholder or promoter to be the insurance company or insurance shareholding (group) company when establishing an insurance asset management company. It shall meet the following conditions: undertaking the insurance business for over five years. The net assets are no less than RMB 1 billion. The total assets are no less than RMB 10 billion, while the total assets of the insurance shareholding (group) company and the insurance company that have life insurance business shall be no less than RMB 15 billion. It is said in Article 9 that the total share of insurance assets management companies held by a domestic insurance company shall not be less than 75%. The "domestic insurance company" as mentioned in the preceding paragraph shall refers to the insurance company or insurance shareholding (group) company with legal person status, which is approved by the CIRC and registered according to law. The above paragraphs restrict the operating period and assets of insurance companies that establish insurance assets management companies. What's more, the regulation of "total share of insurance assets management companies held by a domestic insurance company shall not be less than 75%," which forces foreign insurance companies to manage their own assets with Chinese companies, only occupying a minority stake. The impact on foreign life insurance companies is particularly tremendous, even greater than their 50% stake restrictions. As the main business area of the life insurance industry, the limits set on the establishment conditions of insurance asset management companies hampers the utilization of rich overseas investment experience of foreign-funded life insurance companies and thus the profitability has been affected to a certain extent.

5.5.2.2 Further opening-up of insurance industry to abroad

The original purpose of the regulatory environment for foreign insurance companies is to protect the Chinese-funded insurance companies. However, with the further liberalization of China's insurance market and the gradual maturity of Chinese-funded insurance companies, these regulatory constraints are gradually liberalized. The State Council decided to revise the Paragraph 1 of Article 7 of the "Regulation of the People's Republic of China on the Administration of Foreign-Funded Insurance Companies" as follows: "The minimum registered capital of an equity joint venture insurance company or a wholly foreign-owned insurance company shall be RMB 200 million or an equivalent in freely convertible currencies, and must be paid-in monetary capital." The second paragraph was revised as follows: "The head office of a foreign insurance company shall grant not less than RMB 200 million or an equivalent in freely convertible currencies to a branch of the foreign insurance company as working capital". The revisions further relaxed access conditions for foreign insurers. The Regulation on Compulsory Auto Liability Insurance was revised by the State Council on April 30th, 2012. The open of the third-party mandatory insurance business for foreign-funded motor vehicles is in line with the trend of the opening insurance industry to the outside world.

5.6 Q&A

5.6.1 What is the original intention of Shanghai-Hong Kong Stock Connect?

Shanghai-Hong Kong Stock Connect is a major decision made by the Party Central Committee and the State Council in accordance with the strategic needs of the development of capital markets in Chinese mainland and Hong Kong. A major reform of initiatives to implement the decision of the third plenary session of the 18th CPC central committee and the several opinions of the State Council on further promoting the sound development of the capital market as well as a major policy innovation of capital market.

Shanghai-Hong Kong Stock Connect is the result of giving full play to and respecting market innovation. The idea is derived from the market and rooted in practice. It is the result of the keen grasp of capital market demand and joint innovation in both Shanghai and Hong Kong Stock Exchanges, reflecting their willingness to cooperate was strongly supported and responded positively by them. The actuality of the markets in both places were taken into full consideration in the system design of Shanghai-Hong Kong Stock Connect, which means that the current rules of the markets in the two places were not changed and the trading habits of the other party's markets are fully respected at the level of the subject-matter management of quoted shares, the quota control and the closed operation of funds implemented.

In China's capital projects fully convertible circumstances, it helps create a new, secure and orderly model of cross-border securities investment with convenient operation, controllable risk, which also facilitate the regulators of the two places to complete the cooperation mechanism of cross-border regulation and intensify cross-border law enforcement and investigation. All the effort was made to build a regulatory system adaptive to an open capital market system.

As a major breakthrough in the two-way opening up of China's capital market, Shanghai-Hong Kong Stock Connect has enriched the investment varieties in both places, optimized the market structure, expanded the breadth and depth of the market, conductive to consolidate the two financial centers in Shanghai and Hong Kong and enhance the overall strength of China's capital market. It not only provides convenience for overseas funds to invest in the A-share market but also provides opportunities for Chinese mainland investors to invest in the Hong Kong stock market, which is conducive to the joint prosperity and development of the capital markets in both places. Meanwhile, Shanghai-Hong Kong Stock Connect also sets up a new platform for capital market reform and financial reform of which, if used properly, will promote the overall deepening reform of the capital market and promote internationalization of the RMB for more flexibility of cross-border capital flows and higher convertibility of financial transactions. With the concerted efforts of all parties, Shanghai-Hong Kong Stock Connect can produce the "one plus one is greater than two" effect.

5.6.2 Thus far, the deposit insurance system in China's banking sector has not been established. The most intuitive sense in the market is that there is no obvious risk loss in bank deposits in the existing implicit and full guarantee system. What are the positive implications for China if regulators promote the deposit insurance system?

The establishment of deposit insurance system will make China's financial system more complete and have positive significance to the overall financial reform. First, the deposit insurance system can solve the issue of risk disposal, which is a precondition for the marketization of interest rates. Second, the deposit insurance system promotes the opening-up of the banking sector to the internal and external and enhances the confidence of private capital entry. Private banks are often small and medium-sized financial institutions which are naturally at a disadvantage in credit, scale and competition. Thus, the establishment of a deposit insurance system helps form an effective competitive environment to create favorable conditions for the survival and development of private banks. Third, the deposit insurance system kicked off the establishment of an exit mechanism for banking marketization that relies on the protection for bankruptcy of the troubled banks provided by deposit insurance system. Fourth, the deposit insurance system, together with the banking regulator and the Central Bank, forms the three pillars of the financial safety net. Deposit claims by deposit insurers can prevent runs on bank and contagion of crisis, reducing working pressure on regulators and pressures of the Central Bank for rescue. Coordination between them will make the Chinese financial safety net more complete and solid.

Chapter 6 China's Foreign Exchange Administration System

6.1 The Historical Development of China's Foreign Exchange Administration System

Before China's Reform and Opening-up, due to the shortage of foreign exchange resources, a highly-centralized planned economic system had been implemented. After 1978, however, aimed at narrowing the scope for mandatory plans and nurturing the direction of market mechanism, China began to carry out reforms toward its foreign exchange administration system and steadily and orderly transformed the highly centralized and unified foreign exchange administration system into a system suitable for the socialist market economy. In December 1996, RMB current account began to be convertible and a foreign exchange administration system suitable for socialist market system was preliminarily established. Ever since the foundation of the People's Republic of China, the foreign exchange administration system has gone through four stages, from planned economy, economic transformation, the preliminary establishment of socialist market economy system to the further improvement of socialist market economy system.

6.1.1 The highly centralized and unified foreign exchange administration system established under the planned economic system (1949-1978)

Foreign Exchange was under the centralized planned administration. From the time when the People's Republic of China was established to the time before the Reform and Opening-up, China has long been in shortage of foreign exchange. During that period, owing to relatively low level of productivity and relatively weak export capacity, there appeared a large funding gap of foreign exchange. As a result, the payment power appeared inadequate for organizing imported commodities or participating in international exchanges, let alone for investing overseas.

Under the circumstances, China began to implement the highly centralized planned administration of foreign exchange, monopoly control over receipts and disbursements in order to deal with the shortage of foreign exchange and ensure that the limited amount of foreign exchange funds was utilized properly. Authorized by the State Council of China, the People's Bank of China took the responsibility of foreign exchange administration and Bank of China was the one and only bank specialized in foreign trade and foreign exchange in China. All of the foreign exchange receipts must be turned over to the state, while all of the foreign exchange disbursements must be allocated according to the original plans. Meanwhile, foreign borrowings and foreign direct investment were also under control. As a result, there remained no external and internal debt at all in China during this period. Each year, the state worked out a new budget of foreign exchange receipts and disbursements, with "disbursements determined by receipts, while inflows determined by outflows". The balance of foreign exchange receipts and disbursements was maintained by mandatory plans and administrative means. Besides, the implementation of fixed exchange rate regime made RMB exchange rate just a tool for planning and accounting.

6.1.2 China's foreign exchange administration system during the economic transformation period (1979-1993)

From the beginning of the Reform and Opening-up in 1978 to 1993, in order to meet the needs of economic reform and development and opening-up, China stepped through the process of introducing market mechanism in the field of foreign exchange allocation. By the introducing the market allocation system on the basis of the existing planned receipts and disbursements system, a double-track system of planned allocation and market regulation came into being.

In 1979, the State Administration of Foreign Exchange was founded in China, of which the main responsibilities were to manage foreign exchange in a unified way and to carry out planned administration as well as inspection and supervision on foreign exchange receipts and disbursements. For exchange rate, the state implemented a dual exchange rate regime, i.e., the official exchange rate and foreign exchange swap market rate co-existed, which laid the foundation for the swap rate to gradually take effect.

The state implemented the foreign exchange retention system. In order to ensure that the limited amount of foreign exchange resources was utilized for economic construction, they were under the State's centralized administration and unified balance. Therefore, the resources were used with emphases, while a certain proportion of them were set aside for foreign exchange-earning enterprises in order to encourage such commercial behavior and to acquire the capital needed for importing goods. On this basis, China began to establish a tangible foreign exchange swap market. That is to say, enterprises could sell extra foreign exchange retention to the enterprises in need of them. From then on, the market mechanism was introduced in the field of foreign exchange allocation.

In November 1985, China's first foreign exchange swap center was founded in Shenzhen Special Economic Zone. By the end of 1993, a total of 121 foreign exchange swap centers had been founded in China, among which 18 were public swap markets. At that time, 80% of foreign exchange import payments or export proceeds were settled by the price of foreign exchange swap market, which reflects that the reform of foreign exchange system in China then met the need of economic reform and opening-up.

In order to meet the need of opening-up China's financial services to the outside world, the State loosened the restrictions on banks' access to foreign exchange business in a timely manner, and banks that were allowed to deal with foreign exchange settlement were expanded from Bank of China to other commercial banks such as Industrial and Commercial Bank of China and Agricultural Bank of China. With regard to the introduction of foreign investment, the State formulated and implemented policies that encouraged the use of foreign investment, relaxed the restrictions on the use of foreign investment, encouraged the introduction of foreign investment, and implemented a series of preferential policies such as tax exemption, low taxes and tax rebates for foreign-funded enterprises entering China according to the relevant policies. At the same time, domestic residents were allowed to hold foreign exchange by individuals and to open foreign exchange savings accounts at banks. Besides, the State also issued foreign exchange certificates. In terms of capital control, the export of capital was under restriction.

In general, during this period, China's foreign exchange administration system was in the process of transforming from a planned system to a system regulated by market. On the basis of the original planned receipts and disbursements system, the market mechanism emerged and developed continuously, which played a positive role in promoting foreign investments, encouraging earning foreign exchange through exports and supporting domestic economic construction.

6.1.3 The preliminary establishment of China's foreign exchange administration system under the conditions of socialist market economy (1994-2000)

The framework of foreign exchange administration system under the conditions of socialist market economy was preliminarily settled. During this period, China defended against the impact of the Asian Financial Crisis, while further promoting the convertibility of current account and preliminarily creating a framework of foreign exchange administration system suitable for the socialist market economy.

In order to meet the requirements of establishing a socialist market economy system in China, a significant reform of foreign exchange administration system was carried out in 1994. The main contents were: removing the turning over and retention of foreign exchange and implementing the system of settling and selling foreign exchange through banks; merging the exchange rate and implementing a single, managed floating exchange rate based on market supply and demand; establishing a unified and standardized inter-bank foreign exchange market throughout the country; further liberalizing the restrictions on RMB current account, which laid a foundation for the convertibility of RMB current account; continuing to reiterate the prohibition on the pricing, settlement and circulation of foreign currency within the territory, and stopping issuing foreign exchange certificate and gradually withdrawing it from circulation. In December 1996, China officially announced accepting the Article 8 of *Agreement of the International Monetary Fund*, which resulted in the complete convertibility of RMB current account, the removal of all restrictions on current international payment and transfer, and the preliminary establishment of market's foundational status in allocating foreign exchange resources. It is another significant milestone in the process of China's integration into the world economy, and is of symbolic significance through the history of the reform of the foreign exchange administration system in China. The outbreak of the Asian Financial Crisis in 1997 had a huge impact on the sustained and healthy development of China's economy and society and its financial stability. In order to prevent the spread of the crisis and maintain the sustained and healthy development of the national economy, China promised that RMB would not devalue. While maintaining the stability of RMB exchange rate, China earnestly fulfilled its obligations in current account convertibility and focused its administration on strengthening capital outflow control, successfully resisting the impact of the Asian Financial Crisis and being highly praised and affirmed by the international community.

In general, during this period, China preliminarily established a framework of foreign exchange administration system suitable for its national condition and adapted to the socialist market economy system. The market basis for the supply and demand of foreign exchange was continually expanding, which established the foundational status of market mechanism in allocating foreign exchange resources.

6.1.4 The further improvement of the foreign exchange administration system regulated mainly by market (2001 to present)

The foreign exchange administration system regulated mainly by market was further improved. During this period, following the new situation of accession to WTO and integration into economic globalization, China has streamlined administration and delegated power to lower levels, and enhanced the capability of performing duties to guide the reform of foreign exchange administration.

China joined the WTO at the end of 2001. Since then, China has quickened its pace in economic globalization and opened wider to the outside world. The balance of payments surplus continued to increase, overseas funds continued to inflow, and the situation of foreign exchange fundamentally changed. Meanwhile, China's domestic economic development was in good condition, with its comprehensive national strength further enhanced, its international influence continuously expanding, and the conditions for deepening the reform of the foreign exchange administration system gradually mature. On July 21st, 2005, China announced the reform of the formation mechanism of RMB exchange rate that transformed the single-pegged dollar foreign exchange regime into a managed floating exchange rate regime based on market supply and demand, adjusted with reference to a basket of currencies. The starting level of currency exchange was adjusted from 8.2765 RMB/USD to 8.11 RMB/USD. Besides, China continuously improved the construction of foreign exchange market, launched over-the-counter transactions and a series of risk-avoiding tools such as forwards, swaps and options between RMB and foreign currency, improved the bank-listed exchange rate and other basic institutional arrangements, and consolidated the micro foundation for the formation of exchange rate. Meanwhile, a series of supporting exchange rate administration policies were implemented, including increasing the convertibility of RMB capital account, realizing the convertibility of most direct investment account, launching the Qualified Domestic Institutional Investors (QDII) and the Qualified Foreign Institutional Investors (QFII), abolishing the preapproval of all cross-border guarantees, allowing multinational enterprises to conduct pilot centralized operation of foreign exchange funds within the group, expanding banks' forward foreign exchange settlement and sale business for their clients and initiating the swap between RMB and foreign currency, raising the guide limit of personal purchase of foreign exchange and simplifying the procedures and vouchers, adjusting the administration of bank-listed exchange rate, and reinforcing the campaign and training of foreign exchange policies, etc. All these measures set the stage for the enterprises and banks in the new era of the Reform and Opening-up to adapt to the fluctuation of market exchange rate.

Since 2009, based on the complexity and increasing scale of cross-border capital flows and the ever-increasing demand for the facilitation of market entities, China has accelerated its transformation in the idea and mode of foreign exchange administration, shifting the focus from examination and approval to monitoring analysis, from pre-regulation to post-administration, from behavior administration to subject administration, and from "positive list" to "negative list", and others. Based on the premise that the bottom line of risk is kept, China has facilitated the overseas trade and investment activities of market entities as much as possible. On June 19th, 2010, the reform of foreign exchange was restarted. In November 2012, in order to further deepening the reform of the foreign exchange administration for direct investment and simplify the procedures of administrative examination and approval, the State Administration of Foreign Exchange issued *Notice of the State Administration of Foreign Exchange on Further Improving and Adjusting Foreign Exchange Administration Policies for Direct Investment*, making a substantial adjustment to the foreign exchange administration policies for direct investment, further promoting the facilitation of investment and trade, and relaxing the foreign exchange control of capital account.

In general, during this period, the reform of foreign exchange administration system has been further deepened, the idea and mode of foreign exchange administration has been accelerated, and the role of the market in allocating foreign exchange resources has been continuously strengthened, which played an active role in promoting the rapid development of foreign trade, guiding the orderly and bidirectional capital flows, making full use of two markets and two kinds of resources, and serving the development of the real economy.

6.2 The Development Status of China's Foreign Exchange Administration System

With the economic development and the expansion of the opening-up to the outside world, the international balance of payments of China has undergone tremendous changes. From the early decades of New China to the time before the Reform and Opening-up, the international balance of payments of China was small, and the foreign exchange reserve remained at a relatively low level. In 1978, the foreign exchange reserve of China stood at only USD 167 million. After the Reform and Opening-up, it has greatly increased and its scale has been expanding, the total of which reached USD 3,843 billion in 2014. However, the growth of foreign exchange reserve has slowed in recent years. In 2014, excluding the impact of non-transactional value changes such as exchange rate and price, the international reserve asset of China increased by USD 117.8 billion, a year-on-year decrease of 73%. Among them, the net increase of foreign exchange reserve was USD 118.8 billion, a year-on-year decrease of 73%, while the net decrease of SDR and the reserve position in the International Monetary Fund was USD one billion.

Viewing from current account, in the past five years, the balance of current account was the largest in 2010, with RMB 1,604.3 billion, and was the smallest in 2011, with RMB 873.6 billion. Though it increased in 2014 compared with that of 2013, but it was still smaller than that of 2010. In 2014, the current account surplus reached USD 219.7 billion, increasing by 48% year-on-year, and was 2.1% of GDP, remaining within the internationally recognized reasonable level. In 2014, while China's current account revenue reached USD 2,799.2 billion, increasing by 5% year-on-year, its current account expenditure reached USD 2,579.5 billion, increasing by 3% year-on-year, and its current account surplus reached USD 219.7 billion, increasing by 48% year-on-year. Trade in goods continued to grow steadily. In 2014, according to the statistics of international balance of payments, while China's trade in goods surplus was USD 476 billion, increasing by 32% year-on-year, China's trade in services deficit was 192 billion USD, increasing by 54% year-on-year. While the income deficit narrowed sharply, the current transfer deficit expanded.

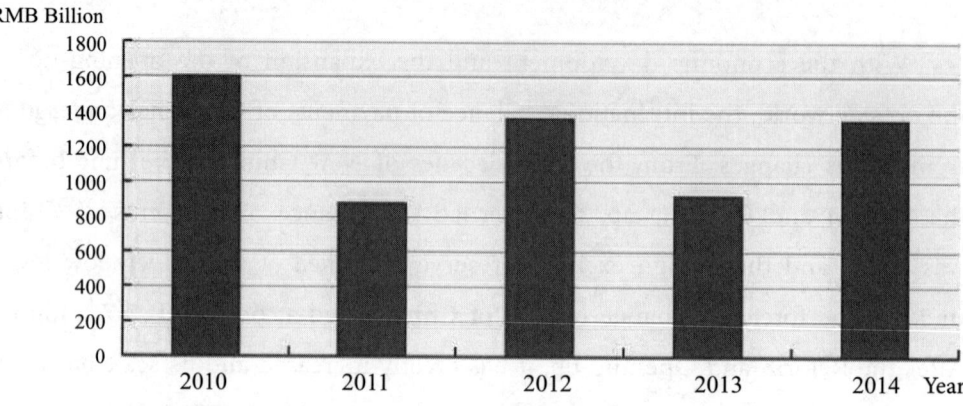

Source: The website of the State Administration of Foreign Exchange.

Figure 6–1 The Time Series Analysis of China's Balance of Current Account

Viewing from capital account, it remained in surplus from 2010 to 2013, reaching a maximum of RMB 35.2 billion in 2011, and then gradually decreasing year by year. In 2014, the capital account deficit reached RMB -0.2 billion.

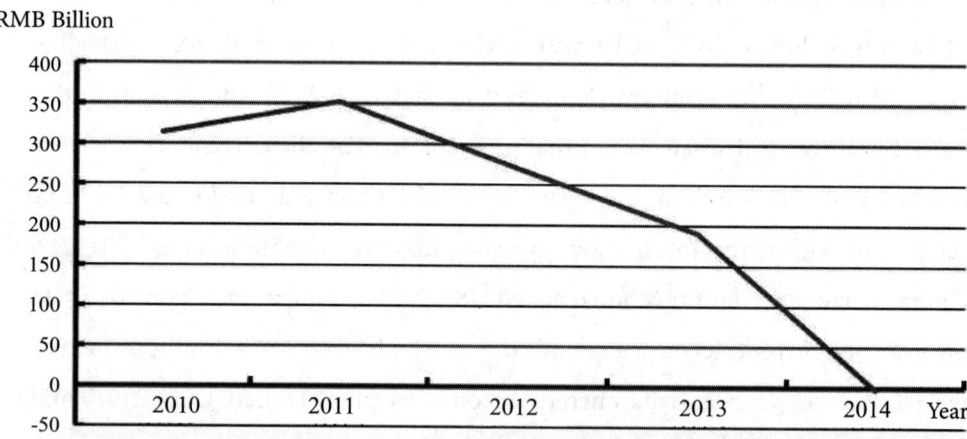

Source: The website of the State Administration of Foreign Exchange.

Figure 6–2 The Time Series Analysis of China's Balance of Capital Account

Chapter 6
China's Foreign Exchange Administration System

Faced with the new situation, taking promoting the balance of payments as its goal and preventing the shock caused by cross-border capital as its premise, China has actively carried out reforms and innovations of foreign exchange administration, taken the initiative to adapt itself to the new situation of the balance of payments and foreign exchange, and focused on significant reforms such as promoting the convertibility of RMB capital account. The main contents are: first, accelerating the convertibility of RMB capital account and actively promoting the development of foreign exchange market; second, continuing to promote the decentralization of foreign exchange administration so as to facilitate trade and investment; third, accelerating the construction of foreign debt and capital flow administration system under a macro and prudent administrative framework, and improving policy reserve and response plans; fourth, cracking down on illegal operations and criminal activities in the field of foreign exchange and maintaining tough stance on the anomalous cross-border capital inflows and outflows; fifth, promoting the innovative use of foreign exchange reserve and improving the operation and administration of foreign exchange reserve.

6.2.1 The foreign exchange administration of current account

The current account of RMB has been fully convertible already, i.e., China has no restrictions on the payment and transfer of regular international transactions, and no discriminatory monetary arrangement or multiple monetary system, the principle that all the laws and regulations conform to. This will help provide a more relaxed market environment, attract foreign trade and investment into China, and promote Chinese enterprises to the world.

In terms of foreign exchange administration of RMB current account, **the achievements of the foreign exchange administration reform of trade in goods are further consolidated.** The foreign exchange monitoring system for trade in goods is further improved, while the special monitor index increased, and the functions of system administration are further enriched. The business executive interviewing system is further implemented, while the administration of safety notice system is further improved, and the administration during and after event is further strengthened. **The foreign exchange reform of trade in services is further deepened.** The foreign exchange monitoring system for trade in services begins to run all over China. The system includes functions such as multi-level monitoring, early waring analysis and comprehensive analysis, and provides more abundant data information to help the background monitoring, early warning and subject management of foreign trade administration of trade in services. **The pilot payment agencies that deal with foreign exchange payment for cross-border e-commerce are further popularized.** Cross-border e-commerce and internet payment are further developed, and there have been altogether 22 pilot foreign exchange payment agencies for cross-border e-commerce. Fourth, personal use of foreign exchange becomes more convenient. **The personal foreign exchange settlement and sale business via e-bank is further developed.** Agricultural Bank of China, China Guangfa Bank and Ping An Bank are permitted to deal with foreign exchange settlement and sale business via e-bank. Until the end of 2014, more than half of the personal foreign exchange settlement and sale business had been via e-bank.

6.2.2 The foreign exchange administration of capital account

The basic convertibility of RMB capital account is further accelerated, and the degree of liberalization in using RMB increases, making it easier for domestic personal cross-border investment and overseas institutional investors to invest in China's capital market, which helps promote the internationalization of RMB.

In terms of foreign exchange administration of RMB capital account, **the reform of the key areas of capital account is further deepened.** The China (Shanghai) Pilot Free Trade Zone takes the initiative to carry out pilot reform of the administrative method of foreign exchange capital settlement and sale and deepens the reform of the foreign exchange administration of cross-border

M&A. **The reform of the foreign exchange administration of capital account is further promoted.** The quota of expenses for the early stage of overseas investment by domestic enterprises is raised through the relaxation of restrictions on the subject of overseas loans and terms of loans. The reform of the annual inspection of foreign-funded enterprises is implemented, with requirements of compulsory audit abolished, etc. **The administration of cross-border securities investment business is further simplified.** The administrative method of investment quota adjustment and the delayed fund remittance of RMB Qualified Foreign Institutional Investors (RQFII) are transformed from approval to record, so as to bring convenience to RQFII and promote the effective use of investment quota.

6.2.3 The operation and administration of foreign exchange reserve

The State Administration of Foreign Exchange is the regulatory agency for China's foreign exchange reserve. A vast majority of China's foreign exchange assets are operated and administrated by the State Administration of Foreign Exchange and the remaining small number of foreign exchange assets are managed by commercial banks such as Bank of Communications and Bank of China on its behalf.

At present, the operation and administration of China's foreign exchange reserve has been further improved. To be specific, first, the administrative mode of investment benchmark is more complete, the investment strategies and investment channels are more diversified, and the investment capabilities in various fields have been continuously improved, resulting in good operating earnings. Second, the application of foreign exchange reserve is more diversified, and the platform for foreign exchange reserve entrusted loans has been continuously improved, which plays a positive and important role in serving the real economy. Third, the risk management has been further strengthened, the logic, integrity and consistency of risk management have been continuously enhanced, and the multi-dimensional risk assessment system has been further improved. Fourth, the institutional administrative capabilities as well as the rational personnel management system have been continuously improved, and the talent is more specialized and meritocratic.

6.2.4 The basic establishment of foreign exchange administrative laws and regulations system in the field of financial derivatives

At present, China has preliminarily established the basic framework for foreign exchange administration, and revised, improved and promulgated a series of laws and regulations, including the *Regulation of the People's Republic of China on Foreign Exchange Administration*, *Trading Rules for RMB-Foreign Exchange Options in the National Inter-bank Foreign Exchange Market*, the *Foreign Exchange Administration of the Overseas Direct Investment of Domestic Institutions*, the *Detailed Confirmation Rules of Inter-bank Exchange Market Trading*, etc. Besides, China has put emphasis on guiding all aspects of the foreign exchange administration system from the perspective of law, which is more standardized than before. However, at present there are still some problems in the legal system of foreign exchange administration, such as the over complicated legal system, the low effectiveness of the legislative hierarchy, and the ineffectiveness of certain laws and regulations.

6.2.5 Reform of the administrative method of foreign exchange capital settlement and sale by foreign-funded enterprises

The reform of the foreign exchange administration system is further deepened, and the business operation as well as capital operation are more convenient for foreign-funded enterprises. The foreign invested capital of the invested enterprises shall be subject to the administration of settlement of foreign exchange, and the enterprise is free to choose the timing of the settlement of capital; the use of clear capital of the foreign invested enterprise and its foreign exchange settlement funds shall be in conformity with the relevant regulations on the foreign exchange administration and the negative inventory administration shall be implemented on the use of capital; the investment enterprises shall conduct domestic equity investment by using the proceeds from the settled foreign exchange; further regulate the payment administration of the settled funds, clarify the banks' obligations of authenticity audit in accordance with the three principles of the exhibition industry; clarify and simplify the administration of the settlement and utilization of funds in the foreign exchange accounts under other direct investments; strengthen the foreign exchange's incident and after-incident administration, and further intensify supervision and violation investigation afterwards.

6.2.6 The unified national inter-bank foreign exchange standard

At present, with the continuous development of electronic trading mode and Internet technology, China's foreign exchange market adapts to the information age today by using new trading methods. The establishment of Internet trading platform lays the foundation for the formation of a unified and standardized national inter-bank foreign exchange market. With the increasingly fierce market competition, banks keep on launching new financial products in order to expand their market shares, among which financial derivatives within the permitted scope of law are included. Meanwhile, trading method and trading mechanism are also under innovation, which has greatly enhanced the enthusiasm of market participants and helped diversify the market. In 2006, new systems were introduced into the national inter-bank foreign exchange market, such as inquiry, an international trading method, and market-maker system. Besides, the market also continuously attracts powerful banks to join the ranks of market markers, facilitates financial innovation, launches the financial derivatives that adapt to the development of the market and satisfy different types of clients, and enhances the price discovery function of the market. What's more, the national inter-bank foreign exchange market also attracts a large group of excellent talent with professional literacy, which lay a solid foundation for the further development of the market.

6.2.7 Regulations on the remittance of profits, dividends and bonuses by foreign-funded enterprises and enterprises issuing stocks abroad

6.2.7.1 All foreign investors of foreign-funded enterprises or enterprises issuing stocks abroad that remit the profits, dividends or bonuses due to the foreign side the current year must provide a designated bank (hereinafter referred to as "bank") with the following materials:

1) Tax payment certificate and tax return (enterprises that enjoy preferential treatment shall provide the tax exemption certificate issued by the local authority in charge of tax)

2) Audit report on the current year's profits, dividends and bonuses issued by accounting firms

3) Resolution of the board of directors on profits, dividends and bonuses distribution

4) Foreign exchange registration certificate of foreign-funded enterprises

5) Capital verification report provided by accounting firms

6) Other materials required by the administration of foreign exchange

6.2.7.2 When foreign-funded enterprises or enterprises issuing stocks abroad need to remit the profits, dividends or bonuses of the previous years abroad, apart from the materials mentioned above, accounting firms need to be entrusted to conduct an audit of the profits or the financial condition of the year when dividends and bonuses occur and issue an audit report to the bank.

6.2.7.3 The bank shall rigorously examine the authenticity of the above-mentioned materials. After verifying their correctness, the bank shall sign the words "the remittance of profits, dividends or bonuses is cleared" with the bank's seal on the foreign exchange registration certificate and the tax payment certificate. After going through the formalities for remittance, copies of the relevant documents mentioned in the first and second articles of the notice shall be kept.

6.2.7.4 The bank should report the remitted profits, dividends and bonuses of the previous month by foreign-funded enterprises or enterprises issuing stocks abroad to the local administration of foreign exchange in the form of statements within the first five working days of each month. When the amount of remittance is the equivalence of USD 100,000 or above, or if there are any questions, the administration of foreign exchange has the right to carry out spot checks on the authenticity of the remitted profits, and the sampling rate shall be no lower than 50% of what are reported by the bank. All banks failing to audit according to the regulations or enterprises having false profit remittance found in the spot checks shall be punished according to relevant laws and regulations.

6.2.7.5 All foreign-funded enterprises that fail to have their registered capital meet the amount stipulated in the contract shall not remit the profits or dividends of foreign exchange abroad. All registered capital that fails to meet the amount stipulated in the contract owing to specific circumstances shall report to the original approval department for approval. With the documents approved by the original approval department and the materials stipulated in the Notice, the enterprises can remit abroad the profits and dividends earned according to the proportion of actual registered capital.

6.2.7.6 When dealing with the formalities for the remittance of foreign exchange dividends or bonuses for enterprises issuing stocks abroad, the designated bank shall examine the situation of these enterprises repatriating the stock issuing abroad back to China according to this notice. For the enterprises issuing stocks abroad whose dividends and bonuses are real but who haven't repatriated the foreign exchange capital raised by issuing stocks abroad back to China, the designated bank shall deal with the formalities for the remittance of foreign exchange dividends or bonuses for them first, and then report the enterprise's situation to the administration of foreign exchange. The administration of foreign exchange shall punish the enterprises for remaining abroad the income earned by issuing stocks abroad without authorization based on the 39th article of the Regulation on Foreign Exchange Administration.

6.2.8 The rules and process of overseas personal agiotage business, a case study of Postal Savings Bank of China

6.2.8.1 Personal purchase of foreign exchange

Since there is no annual limit on the purchase of foreign exchange for individuals overseas, their legal RMB income of current account earned in China is valid for purchasing foreign exchange with valid identity document and relevant credentials of the amount of transaction (including tax vouchers). The credentials include: employment contract signed with a Chinese enterprise, details of income, tax vouchers, etc.

The Redemption of Overseas Personal Foreign Currency: Overseas individuals can redeem the unused RMB into foreign currency banknote. For the redemption of which the total on a given day is no less than the equivalence of USD 500 (including USD 500), and the redemption of which the total on a given day is no less than the equivalence of USD 1,000 (including USD 1,000) inside the territory while outside the customs before departure, clients can go through the procedures with their own valid identity document. For the redemption of which the total exceeds the above-mentioned ones, clients need to provide the original foreign exchange settlement memo (e.g. the original foreign exchange slip or the wild card's ATM withdrawal slip, etc.). The redemption of the original foreign exchange settlement memo is valid for 24 months from the date of redemption.

Handling procedures

1) Clients fill in the Application for Personal Purchase of Foreign Exchange. The application should be filled in accurately according to the requirement

2) Clients submit the finished application, valid identity document and RMB to the branch teller

3) The teller reviews clients' usage of the annual limit of foreign exchange purchase and the amount of purchased foreign exchange within the domestic annual total. Then, the purchase can be handled after the identity document is verified. If the amount of the foreign exchange purchase exceeds the annual total, clients also need to provide relevant credentials, and then go through the process after the teller's verification

4) Clients confirm the information of the foreign exchange purchased, and sign the relevant documents

5) The teller sends back clients' identity document, relevant credentials and the foreign currency gained from the purchase of foreign exchange

6.2.8.2 Personal settlement of foreign exchange

Annual total management is implemented on overseas personal settlement of foreign exchange, and the annual total is equivalent to USD 50,000 per person per year (including USD 50,000). The foreign exchange settlement of which the amount is within the personal annual total can be handled after the bank's verification of clients' valid identity document. For the foreign exchange settlement under current account of which the amount exceeds the annual total, relevant credentials need to be provided.

The following credentials need to be provided for the overseas foreign exchange settlement of which the amount exceeds the annual total:

1) Rent: The housing leasing contract, invoice or payment advice registered by the administrative department of housing

2) Living expenditure: Contract or invoice

3) Expenditure on healthcare and education: the payment certificate issued by domestic hospitals (schools)

4) Others: Relevant credentials and payment receipts

Handling procedures

1) Clients fill in the Application for Personal Settlement of Foreign Exchange. The application should be filled in accurately according to the requirement. When inward remittance of foreign exchange is directly settled, it is not necessary to fill in a separate Application for Personal Settlement of Foreign Exchange since the Application for Collection of Foreign Exchange includes the relevant information.

2) Clients submit the finished application, valid identity document and foreign currency to the branch teller.

3) The teller reviews clients' usage of the annual limit of foreign exchange settlement and the amount of settled foreign exchange within the domestic annual total. Then, the settlement can be handled after the identity document is verified. If the amount of the foreign exchange settlement exceeds the annual total, clients also need to provide relevant credentials, and then go through the process after the teller's verification.

4) Clients confirm the information of the foreign exchange settled, and sign the relevant documents.

5) The teller sends back clients' identity document, relevant credentials and the foreign currency gained from the settlement of foreign exchange.

6.2.8.3 Personal foreign currency exchange

1) Overview

Personal foreign currency exchange refers to the transaction in which personal clients can make conversions among freely convertible foreign currencies through our bank.

2) Features

Diversified currencies: seven currencies including USD, EUR, GBP, HKD, JPY, CAD and AUD Affordable charge: There is no additional charge for personal foreign currency exchangeSimple formalities: Customers can go through the formalities by holding valid identity document and proceeding to the branch or directly logging in to the e-bank.

3) Regulations on Limit

There is exchange limit on foreign currency banknote. For the exchange of which the total on a given day is no less than the equivalence of more than USD 5,000 (excluding USD 5,000), clients need to provide the Baggage Declaration Form for Inbound and Outbound visitors of the People's Republic of China signed by the Customs, or the foreign currency banknote and the foreign exchange purchase memo issued by their original deposit bank in order to go through the procedures.

While there is exchange limit on foreign currency account, there is no transaction limit on the personal foreign currency exchange of foreign currency current account. For the exchange of which the amount is the equivalence of more than USD 10,000 (excluding USD 10,000), clients need to go through the procedures with valid documents. For those who entrust an agent to go through the procedures, the agent's valid document shall be provided as well.

【Case】 The Regulation on Massive Inflows of Personal Foreign Exchange Funds

According to the statistics of recent years, personal channels are the main channels for the inflows and outflows of foreign exchange funds. Among the inflows of foreign exchange funds, there are not only real legal funds, such as remuneration for personal services for overseas workers, but also illegal abnormal funds. The main ways of exchanging RMB with these funds include borrowing other's identity documents, passports, or forging vouchers and receipts, the purpose of which is to convert foreign currencies into RMB and introduce them into Chinese stock market and real estate market in order to gain from the appreciation of RMB. The inflow of these funds shall cause an imbalance in China's international payments and have an impact on the sustained, healthy and steady economic development.

In response, China has innovated its administrative methods, established a sound regulatory system and effectively regulated the inflows of foreign exchange funds. Specific measures to be taken are: first, establish an administrative mode of personal annual total of foreign exchange settlement and sale and set an upper limit for the annual total of personal foreign exchange purchase and settlement. For those of which the annual total of personal foreign exchange purchase and settlement is within the upper limit, clients can directly go through the formalities at the bank with valid identity document. For those of which the annual total exceeds the upper limit, those under current account could be handled after clients' valid identity document and relevant credentials are examined by the bank, while those under capital account need necessary approval. This could benefit the regulation on large foreign exchange settlement and foreign exchange purchasing behavior. Second, establish a personal foreign exchange settlement and sale information system, record the detailed information of personal foreign exchange settlement and sale, and make accurate statistics and judgments so as to further improve the regulatory efficiency. The introduction of the above measures is conductive to the implementation of deal-by-deal monitoring and focused tracking on personal foreign exchange settlement and sale, and the effective regulation on personal foreign exchange settling and selling behavior so as to safeguard the sustained development of China's economy.

6.3 Q&A

6.3.1 What do you think about the issue of the proper scale of China's foreign exchange reserve?

It's not necessarily better for a country to maintain as large foreign exchange reserve as possible. China pursues neither the large scale of foreign exchange reserve, nor the long-term favorable balance of payments. Since "double surpluses" in balance of payments could bring an increase in foreign exchange reserve, the fact that China's current account and capital account have both remained in surplus for years reflects the long-term sustained and steady growth of China's economy, which results from the stage and features of China's current economic development.

The currently sufficient foreign exchange reserve is conducive to the stability of China's financial environment and the sustained and steady development of China's economy. As a major developing country, China still needs to maintain a certain amount of foreign exchange reserve even if measured by traditional indicator of moderate scale.

6.3.2 Why China reduced its holdings of US treasury bonds for six consecutive months?

Since the Fed pulled out of quantitative easing, USD has entered a period of appreciation. As a result, RMB weakened slightly against USD, which caused the balance of payments of China to decrease and tend to balance. The current trade surplus accounts for 2% of GDP, achieving a comparatively ideal state. Generally speaking, US debt will decrease as new flows into foreign exchange decreases. Besides, the demand for foreign exchange increases in China, among which outbound travel alone caused a USD 100 billion of deficit in 2014. Enterprises' foreign exchange spending for overseas investment is also increasing. They are willing to hold more USD and demand more USD assets.

China's reduction of US debt is closely connected to the growing number of enterprises investing overseas and individuals consuming overseas. This kind of change in the form of assets is what China hopes for. In the past, because of the unilateral appreciation of RMB currency value, the People's Bank of China had to hold a large amount of foreign exchange, but the goal of the People's Bank of China is to leave the foreign exchange with the people. Nowadays, there are good signs. RMB has appreciated as well as depreciated against USD, and RMB market exchange rate has tended to balance, which has then steered itself out of unfavorable situation of unilateral appreciation against USD. The fact that China had a large-scale foreign exchange reserve before requires the control over its growth rate, which is consistent with China's original intention. The appreciation of USD turns more people away from foreign exchange settlement, i.e., they are unwilling to convert the foreign exchange they hold into RMB, which decreases China's foreign exchange reserve. However, what should also be noted is that the situation of China's foreign trade is not so good, and the capacity of earning foreign exchange through export is not as strong as before. By contrast, since there are more channels for foreign exchange reserve abroad, capital outflow, overseas M&A and investment have all increased. In addition, the end of US debt's redemption period may cause China to reduce its US debt.

6.3.3 What will change in China's foreign exchange reserve investment in the future?

The growth of the scale of US debt and foreign exchange reserve held by China slows down and may not even increase any more. By contrast, overseas direct investment increases, and the acceleration of overseas M&A and investment will become a new trend soon. Since China becomes a net capital exporter with more capital outflows, the increment in foreign exchange reserve may decrease. China's reduction of US debt can be regarded as a redistribution of global assets, and the outflows of currency can be used for a wider variety of purposes, not just for purchasing bonds.

After the reform of RMB exchange rate formation mechanism, RMB becomes more internationalized, and market supply and demand are the decisive conditions for foreign exchange. Meanwhile, USD exchange rate is also market-oriented. The situation of China's foreign exchange market is the key condition that decides whether China will reduce its US debt. However, in the future, China will not keep reducing its US debt, but still hold a large amount of it. Viewing from the previous data, the amount of US debt held by China has dropped to No. 2, while Japan takes the place of No.1 instead, with USD 700 million slightly more than that of China.

It will take quite a long time for China to make adjustments. USD is the main reserve currency in the world today, while the situation of European debt is not as good as US debt. Though Europe is also implementing the quantitative easing policy, generally speaking, the economic situation in the U.S. is relatively better. US treasury bonds not only will bring risks but also represents national strength. However, what is certain is that China will usher in a New Normal with greater overseas investment and better use of foreign exchange assets.

Chapter 7 Emerging Internet Finance

7.1 Internet Finance: An Emerging Power of China's Financial Industry

The reform of China's financial industry is a global event, especially the liberalization of interest rates and exchange rates and the financial deregulation. Every major institutional change in the world's major economies is often accompanied by major financial innovations. China's financial reform comes at a time when the trend of Internet finance is on the rise. Under the impetus of the traditional financial sector and Internet finance, profound changes will take place in China's financial efficiency, transaction structure and even overall financial structure.

With the development of information and communication technologies and the Internet, the impact of Internet financial information on financial markets has become increasingly harder to ignore. The occurrence of a new event or the hot debate on a particular stock on the Internet can largely affect the behavior of financial practitioners and at the same time further influence the trend of changes in the stock market. On the other hand, in financial markets, the influencing factors of traditional financial markets also play a huge role.

In China, the development of internet finance is mainly caused by regulatory arbitrage. On the one hand, there are no capital requirements for Internet finance companies and they do not need to accept the regulation of the People's Bank of China, which is the essential reason. From a technical perspective, although

Internet finance has its own advantages, the compliance and risk management (risk control) issues should also be considered.

It is easy to see from the financial, fiscal and tax reform policies unceasingly enacted by the government that it is already the main theme to benefit and support the development of micro, small and medium enterprises, so the importance of these enterprises accounting for over 98% of the total number of Chinese enterprises for China's economic development is evident. However, compared with the traditional financial institutions and channels, internet finance, characterized by its light application, fragmentation and timely wealth management, is more likely to be favored by micro, small and medium enterprises and more in line with their development mode and rigid demand.

7.2 The Main Types of Internet Finance

7.2.1 Crowdfunding

Crowdfunding means raising money for the general public or the masses, which refers to the mode of raising project funds from netizens in the form of pre-ordering group purchase. The purpose of crowdfunding is to make use of the propagation characteristic of internet and SNS (Social Networking Services) so that start-ups, artists or individuals can show their creativity and projects to the public, get their attention and support, and then get the financial assistance in need. The operation modes of crowdfunding platforms are all much of a muchness: Individuals or teams in need of the funds submit the project plans to the crowdfunding platform, then, after relevant approval, they can create their own page on the platform's website to introduce the project to the public.

7.2.2 Peer-to-peer lending (P2P)

P2P means peer-to-peer lending. It refers to the match between the capital of debtors and creditors through a third party. Individuals who need to borrow money could find those who are capable and willing to lend money based on certain conditions. It will help creditors spread the risk by sharing a sum of loan with other creditors, and also help debtors to select attractive terms of interest rate among fully compared information.

There are two operation modes. The first is purely online, which is characterized by completely online capital lending activities free of offline approval. The measures these enterprises usually take to review the qualifications of debtors include video authentication, bank statements checking, identity authentication, and others. The second is a combination of online and offline procedures: after the debtor submits the loan application online; the platform reviews the debtor's creditability and repayment ability through the household survey conducted by the agent in the debtor's city.

7.2.3 Third-party payment

Third-party payment in a narrow sense refers to a kind of electronic payment mode in which non-bank institutions with certain strength and reputation guarantee use the means of signing with major banks through communication, computer and information security technologies to set up connections between users and bank payment and settlement system. According to the definition of non-financial institutions' payment services given by the People's Bank of China in the Administrative Measures for the Payment Services Provided by Non-financial Institutions in 2010, third-party payment in a broad sense refers to the services including internet payment, prepaid card, bank card acquiring and other payment services defined by the People's Bank of China. Third-party payment has not just limited to the original Internet payment, but become a more comprehensive payment tool with complete online and offline coverage and more various application scenarios.

7.2.4 Digital currency

Apart from the thriving third-party payment, P2P lending mode, small loan mode, crowdfunding financing, Yu'e Bao mode, etc., internet currency represented by Bitcoin has also begun to show its own fangs. The outbreak of the internet currency, represented by digital currencies such as Bitcoin, is in some ways more revolutionary than any other form of Internet finance. On August 19th, 2013, the German government officially recognized the legitimate "currency" status of Bitcoin which can be used for tax purposes and other legitimate purposes. Germany has also become the first country in the world to recognize Bitcoin. This means that Bitcoin began to be gradually justified, from the plaything of tech groupies, into a kind of currency accepted by the public. Perhaps, it can spawn a true internet financial empire.

Bitcoin is also trending in China, but it has plummeted as well. In any case, the internet gold seeking feast that once seemed very far away from us has slowly come into our sight, which allows people to see that the ultimate form of internet finance is internet currency. All internet finance just poses a challenge to the existing commercial banks and securities companies. When it develops into the form of internet currency in the future, it will pose a challenge to the Central Bank. Bitcoin may subvert the traditional finance and grow into the first global currency, and it may also collapse eventually. In any case, it is certain that Bitcoin will leave meaningful mark in the global society.

7.2.5 Big data finance

Big data finance means collecting massive unstructured data, making real-time analyses to provide Internet financial institutions with all-round customers' information, getting hold of customers' consuming habits and accurately predicting customers' behavior by analyzing and digging out customers' transaction and consumption information, so that financial institutions and financial service platforms will have a definite object in view in marketing and risk control.

Big-data-based financial service platform mainly refers to the financial services carried out by e-commerce enterprises that have massive data. The key to big data is the ability to quickly access useful information from a large amount of data or the ability to quickly liquidate from big data assets and use them. Therefore, the information processing of big data is often based on cloud computing.

Wind, Hundsun, Royal Flush and other financial information service providers have made frequent appearances since the bull market in China in 2014, giving the public an initial insight into the tremendous role big data plays in financial transactions.

7.2.6 Digitalized financial institutions

The so-called digitalized financial institutions refers to the banks, securities companies, insurance companies and other financial institutions that transform the traditional operating process by using information technology in order to achieve the complete digitalization of operations and management. Financial digitalization is one of the trends in the financial industry, while the digitalized financial institutions are the product of financial innovation.

From the perspective of financial industry as a whole, banks' digitalization construction has always been in the leading position in the industry. It not only has the world's leading financial information technology platform and has built a three-dimensional electronic banking service system consisting of self-service banking, telephone banking, mobile banking and online banking, but also has taken the lead in the industry with data centralization project, a great work of digitalization. In addition to the innovative financial services based on the Internet, a one-dragging-three financial e-commerce innovative service mode of "portal", "online banking, financial product supermarkets and e-commerce" has also been formed.

However, in recent years, the pure online banks represented by WeBank have also suddenly emerged and started to take a share in the field of the digitalized financial institutions.

7.2.7 Financial portal

Internet financial portal refers to the platform using internet to sell financial products and providing third-party services for the sale of financial products. Its core is the "searching price comparison" mode, i.e., the use of vertical price comparison among financial products through which products of various financial institutions are put on the platform for users to select the suitable ones by making comparisons among them.

The diversified and innovative development of Internet financial portals has led to the formation of third-party wealth management institutions that provide high-end wealth management and investment services and wealth management products, and also the formation of insurance portal websites that provide services of insurance product consultation, price comparison, purchase, etc. This mode does not have too many policy risks, because the platform neither is responsible for the actual sale of financial products, nor bears any undesirable risks, and at the same time funds do not completely go through the intermediate platform.

7.3 China's Representative Internet Financial Institutions

7.3.1 Ant financial services group

Ants Financial Services Group was officially established in October 2014, focusing on serving small and micro enterprises and ordinary consumers. The company has an affiliation with Alibaba, a company that is also listed in the United States.

Based on internet ideas and technology, Ant Financial Services is committed to creating an open ecosystem, working with financial institutions to jointly provide support for the finance of future society and realize the vision of "making credit equal to wealth".

Ant Financial Services Group's brands are Alipay, Zhima Credit, Ant Small

Loans, Yu'e Bao, Zhaocaibao, etc.

From 2003 when Alipay secured transactions launched in Taobao for the first time to 2014 when Ant Financial Services Group was officially established, it can be said that Ma Yun started from the field of e-commerce he was familiar with, and took a more indirect path of "encircling the cities with rural areas" to achieve his goal. Unwittingly, Ants Financial Services has become a financial holding group across many forms of finance.

7.3.2 JD finance

Yao Naisheng, Jingdong's vice president of JD Finance responsible for the financial strategy research and internal management of JD Finance, described the ambition of JD Finance as "interested in all financial licenses".

Independent in October 2013, the layout of JD Finance has been completed at an extremely rapid rate in less than two years, just showing its potential of becoming a financial titan. Currently, JD Finance has set up seven major business segments, which are supply chain finance, consumer finance, crowdfunding, wealth management, payment, insurance and securities, and successively launched investment and financing (Wangshangdai, Jingbaobei, Jingxiaodai) and crowdfunding services for businesses; for individual users, it launched IOU (JD IOU, JD Coin), crowdfunding (product crowdfunding, equity crowdfunding, light crowdfunding), wealth management, etc. In terms of licenses, JD has won multiple licenses, including payment, small loans, factoring, fund sales payment settlement, etc.

It can be said that in the development of financial forms, the pace of JD has surpassed Ants Financial Services in some areas. It is foreseeable that there will still be a fierce battle between the two leading Chinese e-commerce providers in the field of internet finance.

7.3.3 Lufax

Lufax, the full name of which is Shanghai Lujiazui International Financial

Asset Exchange Co., Ltd., is a member of Ping An Group, and also one of the largest network investment and financing platforms in China. It was incorporated in Shanghai in September 2011 with a registered capital of RMB 837 million and headquartered in Shanghai Lujiazui, an international financial center.

The network investment and financing platform owned by Lufax was formally launched in March 2012, and it is a platform created by Ping An Group of China. Combining the global financial development and internet technology innovation and based on a sound risk management and control system, Lufax provides SMEs and personal clients with professional and reliable investment and financing services and help their wealth appreciate. Till the end of January 2014, Lufax has owned over 5.7 million registered users.

Lufax is the only financial assets trading information service platform surviving the cleaning up towards trading venues carried out by the State Council.

Lufax's services include: research and development of financial products, portfolio design, consulting services, various transaction-related ancillary services for equity investment funds offered privately, financial and economic advisory services, market research and data analysis services, financial application software development, e-commerce, conference services, business consulting, financial consulting (not engaged in bookkeeping as an agency) and so on.

Lufax is currently the most reputable P2P platform in China. Backed by Ping An Group's strong reputation, it's expected to develop a good path in the field of Internet credit in China.

7.4   Q & A

7.4.1   Can foreigners open Alipay accounts?

Yes. They should proceed as follows:

1. Open the home page of Alipay and click "Sign up"

2. Click [Personal account], with the system's default region or nation of [Chinese Mainland], click the drop-down box to select the user area, enter the email address and verification code, and click [Next]

3. Fill in the phone number, enter the verification code received on the phone, and click [Next]

4. After receiving and filling in the validation code, click [OK]

5. Fill in the information (the information needed to fill in is different for users of different nationalities), and click [OK]

6. The register is completed. Users can shop online, but cannot recharge or check income details and the amount collected.